MARY OF NAZARETH

MICHAEL HESEMANN

Mary of Nazareth

History, Archaeology, Legends

~

TRANSLATED BY MICHAEL J. MILLER

IGNATIUS PRESS   SAN FRANCISCO

Original German edition:
Maria von Nazareth: Geschichte, Archäologie, Legenden
© 2011 by Sankt Ulrich Verlag, Augsburg, Germany

Cover: *The Advocata*, Rome
Photograph by Michael Hesemann
Used by permission

Cover designer: Riz Boncan Marsella

© 2016 by Ignatius Press, San Francisco
All rights reserved
ISBN 978-1-62164-090-5
Library of Congress Control Number 2015949859
Printed in the United States of America ∞

My Mother

Awake your strings, O my harp,
to praise the Virgin Mary!
Lift up your voice and sing
the wondrous story of the Virgin,
the Daughter of David,
who gave Life for the life of the world.

Ephrem the Syrian (d. 373)

Contents

About This Book

Writing a book about Mary is no small challenge for an author. Of course you can make it easy for yourself and degrade the most fascinating and likewise the most mysterious woman in history to a simpleminded farmer's daughter in the little village of Nazareth. Then you can report what archaeologists have found out about the living conditions of rural dwellers in Galilee, supplement it with the appropriate dose of romantic sociology, and there you have it: the picture of a slightly naïve but certainly deeply devout and probably quite uneducated village teenager, into whose dreamy routine the supernatural burst in, or at least an unintended pregnancy.

Of course it requires a lot of cosmetics to ensure that this picture holds up to comparison with the Mary of the Gospels. Ultimately she is depicted there as a descendant of the traditional Jewish line of the Davidic kings, thus as an impoverished noblewoman from a family with a great tradition. Furthermore, she has a relative who is married to a Temple priest, seems to have taken a rather unusual vow of chastity at an early age for a Jewish girl from the country, and has a surprisingly thorough knowledge of Sacred Scripture, as the *Magnificat* impressively demonstrates. Of course, if you attribute all that to the vivid imaginations of the evangelists, as people nowadays like to do, that makes things at least considerably simpler.

But anyone who belittles the Mother thereby downgrades the Son as well. Granted, it is true, and all ages have shown, that God "lifts up the lowly", as we hear from Mary's own lips in Luke's account (Lk 1:52, ICEL liturgical translation), yet that does not compel us to draw conclusions about the biography and social status of the virgin from Nazareth. Certainly, the Mother of God herself has often enough chosen simple rural children—from Bernadette Soubirous to the shepherd children of Fatima—to convey prophetic messages to her Church. Yet this task also requires especially pure, intellectually unencumbered "channels". Yet the greatest event in world history, the Incarnation of

God, was surely something else entirely! If even the biblical prophets had to be purified interiorly in order to see God, if only the high priest was allowed to appear before the Ark of the Covenant, then how distinguished did the young woman have to be whom God himself selected to be his dwelling place on earth for nine months, the new Ark of the Covenant, as it were?

So, as I was working on this book, again and again I heard ringing in my ears the words of the gifted British theologian John Henry Newman, whom Pope Benedict XVI beatified in September 2010 during his historical journey to England:

> It would not have sufficed, in order to bring out and impress on us the idea that God is man, had His Mother been an ordinary person. A mother without a home in the Church, without dignity, without gifts, would have been, as far as the defence of the Incarnation goes, no mother at all. She would not have remained in the memory, or the imagination of men. If she is to witness and remind the world that God became man, she must be on a high and eminent station for the purpose. She must be made to fill the mind, in order to suggest the lesson. When she once attracts our attention, then, and not till then, she begins to preach Jesus. "Why should she have such prerogatives," we ask, "unless He be God?"[1]

Every historical biography is based primarily on sources, preferably ones that are contemporary or nearly so. In Mary's case, these are the Gospels and the Acts of the Apostles, which were produced within the first two or three decades after her Dormition. Yet they provide us with only a limited amount of information, for of course in those documents Jesus and the apostles are in the foreground. The second group of sources is a good century younger and is considered *apocryphal* ("secret", not officially recognized by the Church). The fact that they are less ancient should not worry us, because, in dealing with the biographies of the Greek philosophers, we even take it for granted that they were written several centuries after their demise. Tacitus and Suetonius, authors of the first biographies about Caesar Augustus, both wrote in the early second century. Flavius Josephus, our chief source of information on Herod the Great, wrote more than a century af-

---

[1] John Henry Cardinal Newman, "The Glories of Mary for the Sake of Her Son", discourse 17 in *Discourses Addressed to Mixed Congregations* (London: Longman, Brown, Green, and Longmans, 1849), 350.

ter Herod's ascent to the throne. Since in antiquity many things were handed down orally at first and often were set down on parchment or papyrus much later, a certain interval in time is the rule rather than the exception. On the other hand, there was a tendency in the Christian milieu also to compose edifying literature full of imaginative embellishments. Yet even the most time-honored tradition, the most beautiful legend, can have a grain of historical truth, as reluctant as modern "demythologizers" may be to hear it. Therefore, it becomes a matter of removing the husk and getting to this true kernel, even though that is often a laborious process. In doing so, we ought to ask ourselves, first, whether one or another of these sources contains historically or archaeologically verifiable information, and, if so, to what extent. Could it at least have happened the way it is reported; does the scenario being described fit in the Judea at the time of the Second Temple? Scholars like to exaggerate the value of the Dead Sea Scrolls, but at least they provide us with an authentic, contemporary picture of Jewish religiosity at the turn of the first century A.D. and can be consulted in many questions for purposes of comparison. Most of the aforementioned apocryphal texts originated in a milieu where close relatives of Jesus and of the Mother of God were still influential, which makes them all the more interesting. When they are combined with the Gospels and the archaeological findings, the result really is, then, a consistent picture that fits into the time and the cultural setting of Mary, without calling into question the miraculous things that happened then—for we would have no right to do that. God's incursion into history can also explode everyday reality and even the laws of nature; this is one of the foundations of the Christian faith, and it must not be denied by hasty attempts at rationalization.

But before we examine these earliest sources thoroughly, we will first go on another search for clues. We will do no less than try to look Mary, the mysterious Woman, in the face and to understand with her help the era that brought us salvation.

One final word about this book: Naturally the path always leads by way of Mary to Jesus. But at one time in the production of it, this was reversed. Only when I was working on my book *Jesus von Nazareth: Archäologen auf den Spuren des Erlösers* [Jesus of Nazareth: archaeologists tracking down the Redeemer] (2009) did I become aware of the wealth of archaeological discoveries that have more to do with the Mother than with the Son. So as to avoid repeating myself unnecessarily (and thus boring my more faithful readers), I have mentioned only briefly here the themes and places that are central to my "archaeological biography of Jesus" or else have written about them from a different perspective, so that a clearer overall picture emerges. That may encourage readers of this book to let themselves be led in this respect as well to our Redeemer by the Mother of God:

> *Et Jesum, benedictum fructum ventris tui,*
> *nobis post hoc exsilium ostende.*

(from the *Salve Regina*, my favorite Marian hymn)

Rome, November 1, 2010
Sixtieth Anniversary of the Proclamation of the
Dogma of the bodily Assumption of Mary into Heaven

Michael Hesemann

Advocata Nostra

"Peter visits the Advocate", read the headline in the German-language *Vatican-Magazin* in June 2010, getting straight to the point. For in a year when dark clouds were brewing over old Europe and the Church was running into especially strong head winds, Benedict XVI called on the *Advocata* and asked her for her protection.

The *Advocata* is, of course, not a female Roman lawyer, or maybe she is, in a manner of speaking. At any rate, for at least 1,500 years, whole generations of Romans have entrusted themselves to her intercession. From a purely external perspective, we are talking about a very ancient image on a cracked, partially worm-eaten piece of wood. But even a first glance tells you that she is more than that. Once you have looked into the almond-shaped eyes of this woman's face, you will never forget them; they stay with you for the rest of your life. For these eyes penetrate deep into the viewer's heart, as though they were about to guess his most secret thoughts, his fears and hopes, and to read his soul like a book. The profound compassion expressed in her gaze allows her to become an understanding intercessor, more than any female lawyer. She is our mother, as she was His Mother. The Mother of God and the Mother of mankind. Mary.

That was how she looked into the heart of Benedict XVI, too, when he entrusted his concerns to her. He is, after all, the head of the Universal Church now [2010]. Thank God, she is the *Mother* of the Church; not just since Pope Paul VI conferred the title of *Mater Ecclesiae* on her immediately after the Second Vatican Council, but as early as that Pentecost Sunday in the year 30, the birthday of the Church.

Of course we do not know what the pope asked the *Advocata* for in their silent conversation, as he spent time praying before her on June 24, 2010; he gave us no glimpse of it in any of his addresses. Generally speaking, as papal protocol goes, it was an almost intimate meeting, to which none of the press or even the members of Roman Curia were admitted. Only Monsignor Georg Gänswein, his faithful secretary, accompanied Benedict XVI; also present were a Vatican photographer—who kept a respectful distance—and the nuns of the Dominican Order, who for eight centuries have been custodians of this most mysterious of all Marian images, which for exactly seventy-nine years [as of this writing] has been in the Convent of Our Lady of the Rosary on Monte Mario, high over the roofs of Rome.

So, on that sun-drenched birthday of Saint John the Baptist, I, too, failed in my attempt to come anywhere near this convent, because they had barricaded such a large area. My colleague, the journalist Paul Badde, who ingeniously hunts down lost images and divine countenances, had no luck, either, although he truly would have deserved to be present; after all, he was the one who snatched the *Advocata* from oblivion. Instead, we met on that same evening in his pleasantly cool apartment right next to the Vatican, and then I asked him to tell me the story of his discovery.

It began in Jerusalem, where the former editor of the *Frankfurter Allgemeine Zeitung* started his new job as Israel correspondent for the daily newspaper *Die Welt*, during the Holy Year 2000, no less. One day, as he was strolling through the Armenian quarter of the Old City, he found himself in a back yard that turned out to belong to the episcopal see of the Syrian Christians. Saint Mark's Church, into which a wooden door at the other end of the yard led, is regarded by Syrians as the oldest church in the world; at least its claim competes with that of the Cenacle, the room on Mount Zion where the Last Supper was celebrated. If you talk to them nicely, they might take you into the oldest part of their premises, the underground "upper room". Then they tell you that the Last Supper and the Pentecost event actually took place there, although there is good reason to doubt that. On the other hand, it is plausible that it is a place mentioned in the Acts of the Apostles: "the house of Mary, the mother of John whose other name was Mark, where many were gathered together" (Acts 12:12), when the primitive Church suffered the first great persecution under Herod Agrippa in A.D. 41. The fact that it served only as an alternative safe house, moreover, is likewise clear from Luke's account: "James and the brothers" were not there; they were probably "holding the fort" on Mount Zion, which was too dangerous for the fugitive Peter, because they were perhaps already looking for him there.

Nevertheless, the Syrians claim to be the heirs of the primitive Christian community. As proof of this, they point to their liturgy, which is still celebrated in Aramaic, the language of Jesus, and which, according to tradition, goes back to that very same James, the "brother of the Lord". Or to the episcopal see, the *kathedra* of Saint James, which they preserve in their church. But especially to what they regard as the oldest Marian image in the world, a dark icon on deerskin, which the Syrian archpriest proudly presented to Paul Badde as well: "Saint Luke painted it with his own hand, when he met the Blessed Virgin here."

Badde furrowed his brow. He was fascinated by the venerable old image of Mary. "Oh, a Lucan icon?" he asked skeptically. As someone who had studied history, he knew that there are quite a few of them. The most venerable icons in the Christian world, for instance, the *Lucan image of Freising* or the *Salus Populi Romani* ("Protectress of the Roman People") icon in the papal Basilica of Saint Mary Major in Rome, Our Lady of Czestochowa at the national shrine of the Polish people, the cave painting in Mellieha on the island of Malta, the *Panagia* icon of the Kykkos monastery on Cyprus, and the *Portaitissa* Madonna on Mount Athos are all supposed to have been painted by the prolific physician and evangelist; you can rest assured, however, that almost all of them can be dated to the early Middle Ages.

But then at the Abbey of the Dormition in Jerusalem, Badde met a Polish monk by the name of Bernhard Maria and told him about the treasure at the church of the Syrians. The Benedictine, too, dismissed it with a wave of his hand. He himself was a painter of icons; his family in Poland had the unique privilege of being allowed to produce copies of Our Lady of Czestochowa. He knew of twelve purported Lucan icons in all. Only one of them, he assured the journalist, had any chance of being authentic. But for centuries now, it was to be found no longer in Jerusalem but, rather, in Rome: somewhere in a convent on Monte Mario.

Not until fate, Providence, and the editor-in-chief of *Die Welt* called him away from Jerusalem and appointed him the new Rome correspondent was Badde able to investigate that tip. But as he was gradually getting settled in along the Tiber and making his initial, often high-ranking contacts in ecclesiastical circles, again and again he met with shrugs whenever he asked about the purportedly most ancient Marian image in Christendom. Almost everyone sent him to Santa Maria Maggiore, others to Santa Maria del Popolo, Santa Maria Antiqua, Santa Maria

Nova, to the "Altar of Heaven" of Santa Maria Aracoeli, or to the Pantheon; in Rome there are supposed to be seven Lucan images in all. A very learned lady even referred to the Marian shrine in Avellino, which possesses a very ancient, highly respected Marian image from Constantinople. In the Basilian monastery in Grottaferrata, a similar miraculous icon is venerated. None of these icons, however, convinced the skeptical journalist of its alleged production by the evangelist Luke.

So he had almost forgotten the tip from the monk in Jerusalem and filed the rumor away when, in December 2005, he received a card from a good friend in Aachen that read: "For Christmas I am sending you this very beautiful icon (from the Convent of Our Lady of the Rosary on Monte Mario)." On it the woman whom he had presumed to be missing finally looked at him with her deep, soulful eyes that would never again let him go!

Again Badde felt a tremendous desire to stand at last opposite the most beautiful and oldest of all the icons of our Lady. But first he had to find the convent, which proved to be not that simple at all. Neither a tourist guide nor his pastor nor any taxi driver knew about it. So he had a bus leave him and his wife, Ellen, off somewhere along the *Via Trionfale* on Monte Mario, at the place where, according to tradition, Constantine the Great saw the Cross of Christ in the heavens and heard a voice that commanded him: *In hoc signo vinces!* "In this sign you will conquer!" The emperor had the sign of the cross painted on the shields of his soldiers when, on the following day, October 27, 312, he marched toward Rome, only to run up against the army of his opponent, Maxentius, at the Milvian Bridge. By an arrangement of fate or of Providence, he was in fact victorious—and he became the first ruler of Rome to favor the Christians, the "thirteenth apostle" (as they call him in the Eastern Churches, although he put off being baptized until he was on his deathbed) and the founding father of Christian Europe.

But Badde had no such vision to show him the way, nor could a Carmelite nun whom he encountered offer him any help. No one on Monte Mario, it seemed, had ever heard of the convent of Our Lady of the Rosary, much less about the fact that the oldest Marian icon in the city and perhaps of the whole world (*urbi et orbi!*) was supposed to be there. He was about to give up, but they could not find a taxi, either. "Let's go back", his wife said. Five minutes later, out of a combination of feminine intuition and final despair, they discovered a plaque overgrown with vines at the roadside, right next to the grille of a closed gate. It led to a neglected yard, beyond which a rather undistinguished Baroque church loomed alongside ruined walls and steps. Now all they had to do was find an open door or at least a doorbell. Not until they reached the other side of the property did the Baddes find one, but the door was locked. So the journalist rang. "Ave Maria", a faint little voice announced through the intercom, only to dampen Badde's enthusiasm a moment later. "No, you cannot go into the church now. This house is cloistered, and the community is dedicated to perpetual prayer." But tomorrow morning early, punctually at 7:30, he was welcome to come to Mass. At seven o'clock, an iron door in one of the side walls is open, and through it he could come into the church.

In the cool radiance of the morning sun, with weary limbs, Paul and Ellen Badde walked through the cloister gate the following day. A narrow corridor, perhaps fifty-five yards long, led from there to the porch of the hidden house of prayer on the slope of Monte Mario. They walked up a few steps and through the main entrance into the interior of the church, where just a few worshippers had taken their seats on a couple of narrow benches. As they entered, they were greeted by a far-off, delicate song, as though in an angelic tongue, that resounded from a wide grille on the left side of the sanctuary. And then the couple noticed that they were being observed. Through a heavy iron grill right beside them, two warm, brown eyes were looking over at them, like those of a mother watching her children. It was, they thought, the Madonna for which they had been looking. She seemed to look a little sad, so far away from the people, encrusted with gold and jewels, rosaries and other ornaments, which the pious pilgrims and her faithful devotees had left behind with her.

"One moment, please", whispered a soft little voice behind the image, as Badde and his wife rather shyly drew closer to it. Had the words not been so trite, they might have thought that our Lady herself had spoken to them. But this faint whisper also announced a revelation; as two little windows opened, the whole frame revolved and the real *Advocata* appeared. The ornamented image was only the back side, a copy of the true image, on which the only decoration was a layer of gold leaf on her hands, a cross on her breast and another cross on her forehead. Those eyes, Badde sensed immediately, were looking even deeper into his heart:

The panel is about one yard wide, one and a half yards tall.[1] Hairline cracks run through her skin, which is the color of a cornfield, and the coral-red lips, interrupted by many little restored islands. The rest was probably unsalvageable. Only this countenance was preserved in incomparable splendor amid all the deterioration and decomposition, infinitely tender. Like the round full moon of a mother's face in front of the squinting gaze of every newborn when she bends over him for the first time. She does not look sad. Her hands are overlaid with gold and point toward the right, as though to a way.

Overwhelmed, he noted his impressions that same day.

It was not long before the journalist had made an initial survey at least of the more recent history of the *Advocata* in the libraries and archives of Rome. As early as the ninth century, it was in the possession of the nuns of the Benedictine Order, who venerated it in their monastery, Santa Maria in Tempulo, in the Trastevere district. It was regarded as a miraculous image and attracted so many of the faithful that Pope Sergius III (904–911) had it transferred to the Lateran Basilica, the parish church of the popes, who at that time still used to reside in the southern part of Rome. The Benedictine nuns were so dismayed by the loss of their icon that they prayed through an entire night for its return. The next morning, or so the legend says, angels carried the icon back to its ancestral place.

Then, in the early thirteenth century, the sisters learned of the salutary activity of Saint Dominic and decided to join his religious community. But in order to do that, it was necessary to move to the nearby Dominican convent of San Sisto. The nuns were worried, wondering whether their beloved Madonna likewise wished to move or whether she would return again to her ancestral home in the old convent. Finally they decided to give it a try and to let the icon decide for itself. So Saint Dominic personally brought the *Advocata* to the new convent on February 28, 1221, followed by a procession of two cardinals and numerous friars and sisters of his Order. After that, days, weeks, and even years went by without the icon moving again from the spot; it is "still here today", the convent chronicler noted several decades later with a sigh of relief.

She patiently put up with a second move in 1575 to the newly

---

[1] In fact it measures twenty-eight by seventeen inches.

founded convent of Santi Domenico e Sisto on the Quirinal and, also, with a third on August 14, 1931, this time to Monte Mario. Along the way, the nuns, together with their most precious treasure, were received in audience and blessed by Pope Pius XI in the Vatican. Since then, the Convent of Our Lady of the Rosary has been the home of the *Advocata*, and she is venerated there along with many priceless relics of the Order, from the breviary of Saint Dominic to the hand of Saint Catherine of Siena. Pope John Paul II, a great devotee of Mary, paid her a visit in November 1986, and just recently Pope Benedict did the same.

"But when was the *Advocata* produced?" Badde asked, and none of the experts knew the answer. Nor did an investigation that took place in 1960 as part of the restoration work bring to light any clear solution to the riddle. Art historians agreed about only one thing: she must be very old and might have originated between the second and the fifth century. That means that she would be perhaps the oldest Marian icon in the Christian world!

The painting technique used is evidence of this. The *Advocata* is a work of *encaustic* painting (from the Greek word meaning "burned in"), a method whereby pigments suspended in a mixture of molten wax and mastic (an aromatic resin) are applied to the undercoat while still hot. The ancient Egyptians had developed this method, which flourished in the age of the Roman Caesars, until the special formula for it was forgotten in the sixth century. Only a handful of encaustic icons has been preserved to our day, for example in Saint Catherine's Monastery on the Sinai Peninsula; most of them were destroyed by iconoclasts in the eighth century during the Byzantine controversy over religious images.

Another indication of her advanced age is the fact that the icon depicts Mary worshipping and without her Child: in the Eastern Church, this motif was called *Hagiosoritissa*, "Intercessor", which is translated into Latin as *Advocata*. It must have originated from the time before the Council of Ephesus in 431, when bishops from all over the world convened to define the first Marian dogma. From then on, the Blessed Virgin was venerated as the *Theotokos*, literally, the "God-bearing One", which previously had still been far from self-evident. Nestorius, the powerful patriarch of the imperial city of Constantinople, had even vehemently opposed this Marian title in the years leading up to the council; at Ephesus, he was declared a heretic, and soon afterward he was deposed and sent into exile. Once this article of the faith that had been declared as binding, however, artists were then commissioned to propagate it by means of iconography as well. Whereas previously Mary could be found with her Child on her arm or her lap only in depictions of the birth of Jesus or of the adoration by the magi from the East (for instance, in the paintings in the Roman catacombs), now this motif became generally accepted. Henceforth, it was theologically un-desirable to show Mary without Jesus. In the process, the hitherto pre-ferred *Hagiosoritissa* motif was modified only slightly, of course. They simply turned the right hand around and made her hold the Infant, while the left hand, formerly uplifted in a gesture of adoration, now pointed to the Child Jesus. This new type of icon was called *Hodegetria*, "She who Shows the Way".

It is obvious that Saint Luke could never have painted a portrait of the Madonna and Child, even though he described the night in Bethlehem with such a wealth of detail. We do not even know whether he ever met Mary; according to the Acts of the Apostles, he did not become Saint Paul's traveling companion until the year 50, although it is quite possible that he professed Christ earlier than that in his hometown of Antioch. Nevertheless, it is certain that he was brought up in the Greek culture and therefore certainly had a creative relationship with the vi-sual arts, which were unknown in Judaism. It is conceivable, therefore, that there was an artist in his circle who was able to paint a portrait of Mary, if he himself did not do so. It is certain, too, that Luke stayed from 57 to 59 in Jerusalem and there "did research" for his Gospel, which probably was written around the year 62. Yet the oldest version of the legend of the Lucan images, handed down to us by the monk Epiphanius from the Kallistratos Monastery in Constantinople, claims to have more detailed knowledge. According to this account, the first picture of our Lady came into being miraculously in Lydda while Mary was still living. The biblical town of Lod (also called Lud in modern times) is located on the Plain of Sharon, right on the ancient via Maris, or, for visitors to Israel today, south of Ben Gurion Airport. The Acts of the Apostles reports the activity of Saint Peter in Lydda, where he healed the paralyzed man Aeneas (Acts 9:32–35), which led to a mass conversion. That must have been around the year 37 and, therefore, still during Mary's lifetime. And here the legend comes in: For as Peter and John set out from Jerusalem in order to dedicate the first church for the Jewish and pagan Christians of Lydda, they invited Mary to come with them. The Mother of God was reluctant to make the long journey to the coast on foot—a good thirty-one miles—but she promised them nevertheless: "Go in peace, I will be with you." When the apostles arrived in Lydda, they saw her image imprinted miraculously on a pillar. The legend goes on to say that Luke later copied that original picture. Epiphanius was not the only one acquainted with the story; it was also confirmed by three patriarchs who wrote in 833 to the Emperor Theophilus to protest against the prohibition of religious images. The first description of Mary, reconstructed from much older sources, dates back to this period also, again recorded by Epiphanius of Constantinople:

> Mary . . . was of middle stature, but some say that she was of more than middle height. . . . Her complexion was of the color of ripe wheat, and her hair was auburn (or reddish). Her eyes were bright and keen, and light brown in color, and the pupils thereof were of an olive-green tint. Her eyebrows were arched (or semicircular) and deep black. Her nose was long, her lips were red and full, and overflowing with the sweetness of her words. Her face was not round, but somewhat oblong (that is, oval). Her hand was long and her fingers were long.

It was as if he had described the *Advocata*. Was it a coincidence, as Badde soon found out, that the Madonna of Monte Mario is called by the Russian Orthodox not only *Rimskaya* ("The Roman Madonna", a name that later on was used instead for copies of the *Salus Populi Romani*), but also *Lyddskaya* ("The Lyddan Madonna")? Did Saint Luke really paint it then, sometime between the years 37 and 59, as a copy of the miraculous image in Lydda, originally intended for his mother church in Antioch, as the legend goes on to claim?

We do not know. Eusebius of Caesarea, author of the first Church history (around 315), does mention images of Jesus and of the apostles Peter and Paul, which were produced during their lifetimes, but not a Lucan image of our Lady. Later, around the year 400, after a rather long sojourn in Rome, Saint Augustine wrote: "Nothing is known about the appearance of the Virgin" (*De Trinitate*). That is surprising, because a fourth-century graffito by a pilgrim is evidence of the fact that even then an *eikos*, or a "likeness", of Mary, originally from the house of the Holy Family, was venerated in the Jewish-Christian synagogue of Nazareth. But only in the year 438 did the pious Empress Eudokia

"discover" during her pilgrimage to the Holy Land the miraculous Lucan image and send it to her sister-in-law Pulcheria in Constantinople. The latter immediately had a special church built, on the *Hodegeres*
(commander-in-chief) Road in the Blachernae district, in which to
venerate the icon; this shrine incidentally stood as godparent when the
icon was christened *Hodegetria*, "She who Shows the Way". At least
that is what the Byzantine historian Theodorus "the Lector" reported
a hundred years later. When two noblemen from Constantinople managed around the year 450 to obtain the *maphorion*, the purplish-blue,
cape-like mantle of our Lady, in the Holy Land, there was great joy;
the precious relic resembled the mantle that Mary wore on the Lucan
icon. Not until 730, during the iconoclasm controversy, did the Marian image allegedly disappear from Constantinople. Was the *Advocata*
brought to Rome at that time?

That is possible, but not likely. For as early as 592, the nuns of
Monte Mario believe, Pope Gregory the Great carried the *Advocata* in
a solemn procession through the streets of Rome, which at the time
was plague-stricken. His prayers of petition were answered when the
Archangel Michael appeared over the Mausoleum of Hadrian, which
today is called Castel Sant'Angelo. Perhaps he, the first Benedictine
pope, entrusted the precious icon afterward to the perpetual veneration
of the Benedictine nuns.

Well when did she come to Rome? Maybe as early as 439, when
Valentinian III needed a heavenly intercessor more urgently than any
other emperor ever did. This was during the age of migration, and Rome
was threatened by the Vandals. Did his cousin Theodosius, who sat on
the throne in Constantinople, entrust the precious Marian image to
him? What is certain is that Valentinian commissioned a large-format
icon at that time and had it installed in Domitian Hall at the foot of
his palace on the Palatine, which thereby became the Church of Santa
Maria Antiqua. This Madonna, now with her Child, is likewise an encaustic painting, but it was clearly executed by an artist of the Roman
school; the parallels to the paintings in the catacombs are too striking. Her face with its big, owlish, all-penetrating eyes resembles that
of the *Advocata*, which may have served as a model; only the position
of the right hand was altered, which now holds the Christ Child. As
Santa Maria Antiqua in the ninth century became dilapidated, this icon
was transferred to the new church of Santa Maria Nova right behind

the Arch of Titus, on which the Temple treasures from Jerusalem are depicted. Since the fifteenth century, this church has also been called Santa Francesca Romana, after a Roman saint whose remains were laid to rest here. Of the original icon, which was painted on a canvas, only the faces of the Mother and Child are preserved. In the seventh century, they were cut out and glued onto a wood panel, which Pope Sergius I had an artist cover with a protective sheet of pure silver.

The icon of our Lady in Santa Maria in Ara Coeli on the Capitoline Hill is quite certainly a copy of the *Advocata*. The thirty-two-by-twenty-inch Marian image was restored between 2002 and 2007 and scientifically studied at the same time. Radiocarbon dating indicates that the wood goes back to the seventh century.

Yet little more can be said about the *Advocata* than that she probably came to Rome even before the sixth century, probably as early as 439. Consequently, it could very well have originated from the time of Saint Luke. The technique with which it is painted, encaustic, flourished in the first century in Egypt. Evidence of this are the eight hundred mummy portraits that were found in the Faiyum Oasis on the left bank of the Nile, the most recent of them from the third century, the oldest from the late first century before Christ. Paul Badde could not help thinking of them as he was studying the countenance of the *Advocata*, for, as chance or Providence would have it, he had already dealt with them intensively on one occasion. "The Radiant Ones of the Enlightenment: Images from the Desert Sands", he had called them in a report that he wrote in 1988 for the *Frankfurter Allgemeine Zeitung*. A friend had put a book about these images on his writing table: images that immediately moved him. Faces that looked at him with an odd familiarity, as though they had all gathered in order to lead him to his great assignment. "A path to reality leads by way of images", he read at the same time in a memoir by Elias Canetti. This quotation, which perhaps became his lifelong motto, was a revelation and had a great effect on him. As he read it, he accepted his vocation to track down lost images, seized by the "stirring fire of a first love", as he wrote at the time. So he flew immediately afterward to Vienna, to meet Frau Hilde Zaloscer, the widely acclaimed art historian, who at great expense and sacrifice had composed the book about the images of the dead from Faiyum.

Paul Badde went through this book once again as he was trying to classify the *Advocata* chronologically, and in doing so he made an unsettling discovery. For the older the mummy portraits were, the more they resembled the Marian icon, which soon convinced him completely that it must have originated in the first century. Yet there was one small but subtle difference that perhaps only a specialist would notice: although the painting technique of the Madonna is ancient Egyptian, the style of painting is unequivocally Syrian. This is suggested already by the general distortion toward roundness, a characteristic of the mosaics in Antioch and Palmyra. The artist, therefore, must have been a Syrian who had learned the encaustic technique and the art of portraiture from the Egyptians, which at least theoretically would fit and perhaps clarifies how the tradition came to be—for Luke, too, was a Syrian. It is quite possible, therefore, that the artist in fact was from his circle of acquaintances or at least from the Christian community in his native city.

Does the *Advocata*, then, as the original model for all Marian icons, go back to an authentic, contemporary portrait of the Mother of God? That can probably never be settled definitively. But in any case, she speaks to our hearts, and it is a miracle that she has reappeared. "An image needs *its own* experience in order to awaken", as Badde likes to quote from the Canetti biography: "This explains the fact that images slumber for generations, because no one is able to look at them with the experience that wakes them."

I visited the Convent of Our Lady of the Rosary[2] when I began research for this book. It has long since been renovated, with the help of German donations, and even before the papal visit it shone with new splendor. Again and again I returned, looked deep into the eyes of the *Advocata*, and asked her to accompany me on my search. Nothing seemed to me more fitting than to intone the *Salve Regina* under her gaze. It is my favorite Marian hymn, precisely because it has supported me even in sorrowful moments of my life and, moreover, sounds as though it had been written face-to-face with this, the most beautiful of all icons:

Eia, ergo, advocata nostra, illos tuos misericordes oculos ad nos converte. Et Jesum, benedictum fructum ventris tui, nobis post hoc exsilium ostende. O clemens, O pia, O dulcis Virgo Maria.

---

[2] Its address is: Via Cadlolo Alberto 51, 00136 Rome; a visit is possible only during Mass on weekdays at 7:30 A.M., Sundays at 11:00 A.M.

Turn then, most gracious advocate, thine eyes of mercy towards us.
And after this, our exile, show unto us the blessed fruit of thy womb,
Jesus. O clement, O loving, O sweet Virgin Mary.

The *Salve Regina* was composed at the time of the First Crusade; the
last line was added by Saint Bernard of Clairvaux, the great devotee
of Mary and the spiritual father of the Order of the Temple (that is,
the Knights Templar). In those days, people flocked by the tens of
thousands to the Holy Land in order to pray at the spots where the
Annunciation, the Nativity, and the Passion of Jesus took place—and
Mary, too, was always with them and led them to her Son.

Hers are the footsteps in which I follow here; the story that this
book tells is hers.

She is the woman most often portrayed in history and also the one
most praised in song, with honorary titles of absolutely cosmic dimensions. Yet all these millions of images, all these thousands of songs
and invocations, can be traced back to only one original model. Moreover, they are concentrated in one word, through which Mary became
unique in world history and salvation history and which therefore jus-
tifies all this veneration: *Fiat*: "Let it be done to me!" Through this
one word, she made the Incarnation of the Son of God possible and,
consequently, our redemption. It caused the Virgin from Nazareth,
who was not yet even thirteen years old, to become the Queen of the
Universe.

But who was this most fascinating of all women? The attempt to
describe her brings a writer to the limits of what is possible, since
she long ago became a superhuman, indeed, transcendental figure, an
icon of herself. In order to comprehend what really happened then in
Nazareth, we must return to her home and her time and consult archaeological findings and the contemporary sources, which endow the
icon with flesh and blood. Only here, at the intersection of everyday
life and miracles, history and salvation event, do we encounter the historical Mary; only in this way can we get some inkling of what really
happened, when a single word sufficed, so that God might become
man and we all might become children of this blessed Virgin.

～

2

The Fullness of Time

Anyone who wants to comprehend the time in which the turning point of salvation history occurred should begin his search in Rome, at the place where 124 steps lead to heaven. At the end of the flight looms the mighty brick façade of a church that perhaps even today could be described as the heart of the Eternal City. It stands, according to the legend, over an *ara coeli*, an "altar of heaven", which Caesar Augustus constructed when a prophetess announced to him the impending birth of Christ.

Today it appears somewhat constricted amid the monuments from later eras. On the left, it is crowded by the snobbish, snow-white national monument that testifies to the unification of Italy under King Victor Emmanuel II and also to the colossally bad taste of the period. The Romans ridicule this "altar of the fatherland" by calling it the "typewriter". On the right extends the much more tasteful Palace of the Senators, designed by Michelangelo, Rome's city hall, flanked by two more palaces that today house the Capitoline Museums. From the rear of the palace, the visitor has the finest view of the Forum Romanum, the political center of ancient Rome.

The hill on which these monuments stand was, so to speak, the Acropolis, the holy mountain, and Golgotha [Place of the Skull] of the Eternal City. For it owes its name to the mythical Etruscan King Olus (or Aulus), who was buried there three thousand years ago and whose skull the first Romans once preserved: *caput Oli* = Capitol. On its northeastern knoll stood at that time the Arx, the fortress and refuge of the original Romans, and on the southwestern knoll, they built their highest shrine, a temple to the gods Jupiter, Juno, and Minerva, who since then have also been called the "Capitoline Triad". At the time of the Caesars, the shrine was the sacral center of the empire, whereas the Arx was the residence of the Oracle. This was the location of the

Auguraculum, the place of the augurs, or oracular priests, who on their airy height studied the flight of birds. Beside it stood the temple of the goddess of fate, Juno Moneta (from the Latin *monere*: "to admonish, warn"), right next to the mint of Rome where coins were stamped, which gave money its Latin name, *moneta*. Her sacred geese became famous when their honking betrayed the Gauls one night in the year 387 B.C. just as they were creeping over the rock in order to attack the city and the fortress under cover of darkness. Mysterious things took place within the temple itself, also. As Cicero relates, a voice in its Holy of Holies warned the Romans of an earthquake, so that they were able to take safety measures in time. After the conquest of Carthage, another temple to the *Virgo caelestis* ("heavenly virgin") Tanit was added, and, after the conquest of Egypt, a shrine to Isis as well, who held the boy Horus in her arms. No wonder they quickly Christianized the holy mountain and dedicated a newly constructed church to the Virgin Mary, whose miraculous icon, as we said, goes back to the seventh century, according to the latest findings, and is unmistakably a copy of the *Advocata*. Although at first the church was called Santa Maria in Capitolio, in the twelfth century it received a new name: Santa Maria in Aracoeli, "Saint Mary of the Altar of Heaven". The explanation for this is provided by the book *Mirabilia Urbis Romae* (Marvels of the City of Rome), written around 1130, which records a legend about the Roman Emperor Augustus Caesar. One day, we read there, he learned that the senate intended to grant him divine honors. Consequently, he asked one of the great prophetesses of ancient Rome, the Tiburtine Sibyl, for advice as to how he should act in this regard. After three days, the wise woman appeared to him in his bedchamber and prophesied a "sign of justice": the earth would be bathed in sweat, but from heaven the king of the epoch would descend. Even before the emperor was able to reflect on the meaning of these words, the seeress pointed toward heaven. There, in a radiant light, appeared Mary with the Child Jesus and descended upon an altar: *Haec est Ara Coeli*, "This is the altar of heaven." "This Child, O Emperor, is greater than thou art, and therefore thou shalt worship him", the sibyl admonished him. As a result, the emperor dedicated the altar to him.

What sounds at first like a pious fantasy by all means has a kernel of truth. For there was in fact an old, Sibylline prophecy that speaks about the virginal birth of a child that would redeem the world and usher in a new epoch. Augustus was convinced that this prophecy referred to his time—and he had a new *saeculum* proclaimed, while he himself was revered throughout the empire as a redeemer, peacemaker, and "son of the divine" (*divi filius*). It is true also that he had an altar constructed; only the *ara pacis Augustae*, the "altar of the Augustan peace", stood, not on the Capitol, but rather on the edge of the Field of Mars that bordered it to the north; since then, it has been relocated, and it can still be seen today on the bank of the Tiber. The legend is also correct in saying that the emperor consistently refused to be divinized.

Actually "Augustan messianism" is one of the most fascinating chapters in Roman history, for it demonstrates how universally redemption was expected in the decades before the birth of Jesus. "Rain down, O heaven, the Just One", cried the people in anxious nights not only in the kingdom of Judea but also throughout the ancient world, which was about to be "globalized". The great ancient historian Dietmar Kienast of Düsseldorf speaks in his standard reference work *Augustus, Prinzeps und Monarch* about an "intensified yearning of wide sectors of the population for redemption not only in Rome but also in Italy and the provinces. . . . After a century of civil wars, they hoped for and awaited a savior and redeemer, who was to bring peace and happiness to a world tormented by violence and killing."

No less than the brilliant Roman orator and politician Cicero first praised the young Octavius as this providentially appointed savior of Rome. He could have spared himself the trouble, though, since the ambitious young man had felt himself called to higher things ever since an astrologer genuflected before him upon learning his date of birth. Various other omens confirmed him in his awareness of having a mission, and so he regarded his destiny as fulfilled when his murdered great-uncle and patron Gaius Julius Caesar adopted him posthumously by his last will and testament and designated him his principal heir. An aureole in the form of a colorful rainbow surrounding the sun on the day of his entrance into Rome appeared to him to be a heavenly ratification. But what impressed him and the citizens of Rome even more was the fact that for the exact duration of the seven days of games that were organized in honor of the deceased, a comet appeared in the northeastern sky. Astronomers have been able to verify the *Caesar Comet*, or C/−43 K1, as it is called in the scientific literature; moreover, there is evidence of it also in the protocols of ancient Chinese celestial observations. "The people believed that this star heralded the reception of Caesar's soul among the immortal gods", the Roman author Pliny wrote a century later; but Augustus was "joyfully convinced that the star had arisen for him and that he would rise with it—indeed, if we wish to tell the truth, for the salvation of the world". From then on, he was quite officially regarded as *Filius Divi*, as the "Son of the Divine" (Caesar), which in the Greek-speaking East quickly became *huios theou*, "Son of God". "We swear by Caesar (Augustus), God, descended of a god", read the formula of an oath dated 30 B.C. that was found on a papyrus discovered in the Egyptian city of Oxyrhynchus. From then on, Octavius put a star over the head of each statue of Caesar that he set up, and he commemorated the *sidus Julii* on his coins, also. The Roman *haruspex* (soothsayer who inspected entrails of animals) Vulcatius went even farther with his interpretation. In his view, the star announced the beginning of the tenth *saeculum*, the new Golden Age, in which peace would finally reign on earth. First, however, it was necessary to impose a new order on the world.

After settling scores with Caesar's assassins and subduing his rival Mark Antony, Octavian ended a whole century of Roman civil wars and internecine political conflicts. As a symbol that peace prevailed throughout the empire, on January 12, 29 B.C., the gates of the temple of Janus on the Forum Romanum were closed—for only the third time since the legendary foundation of the city in 753 B.C. Two years later, the city solemnly awarded him the title of *Princeps* ("Prince") and the name *Augustus* ("the Majestic"), which marks not only the climax of his forty-year reign but also the beginning of a new, golden age in Roman history. As the historian Velleius Paterculus summarized the effects of the reign of Augustus: "The fields again were cultivated, the sacred places were honored, the people enjoyed peace and quiet and were secure in the ownership of their property."

Three centuries after Alexander the Great, whose rule was to last only a short time, in the first century before Christ, the first world empire worthy of that name came into being. Under Augustus, the *Imperium Romanum* extended from the Atlantic to the Euphrates River, from the North Sea to the interior of Africa. In this gigantic territorial power, which spanned forty-four nations of our day, only two official languages were spoken: the administrative language, Latin, and the cultural language, Greek; today there are twenty-seven national languages in all on that same territory. The first project that the Romans undertook after conquering a new province was to build an infrastructure. An excellent network of roads with inns at intervals of a day's ride (every twenty-two to twenty-five miles) connected the most remote corner of the empire with the capital city of Rome. Within its boundaries, every freeman could travel unhindered: a great opportunity for commerce, but also for new ideas. Apart from occasional uprisings, mostly in young provinces, peace and security prevailed within the confines of the empire—and continued to do so for the next four centuries. If any historical point in time was optimal for the Incarnation of the Son of God, this time of peace beginning with Augustus was it; never again in the next two thousand years, indeed, not until the dawn of the modern age of communication after World War II were initial conditions so favorable for the spread of the gospel.

The *Roman Martyrology*, which is read aloud every year on Christmas Eve, places the Incarnation of the Son of God at the center of history when it says (in the version approved by Pope Benedict XIV):

> In the five thousand one hundred and ninety-ninth year of the creation of the world from the time when God in the beginning created the heavens and the earth; the two thousand nine hundred and fifty-seventh year after the flood; the two thousand and fifteenth year from the birth of Abraham; the one thousand five hundred and tenth year from Moses and the going forth of the people of Israel from Egypt; the one thousand and thirty-second year from David's being anointed king; in the sixty-fifth week [of years] according to the prophecy of Daniel; in the one hundred and ninety-fourth Olympiad; the seven hundred and fifty-second year from the foundation of the city of Rome; the forty-second year of the reign of Octavian Augustus; the whole world being at peace, in the sixth age of the world, Jesus Christ the eternal God and Son of the eternal Father, desir[ed] to sanctify the world by his most merciful coming.

The very same thing, though, had been foretold, probably also in the *Sibylline Books*, a collection of prophecies of the great seeresses of antiquity. The Romans considered them to be state oracles. After they were destroyed in A.D. 405, there were numerous more or less fantastic attempts in the Middle Ages to reconstruct their contents. Much more interesting, though, is a quotation from the original books that the Roman poet Virgil rather inconspicuously wove into his *Bucolia*, which is actually a collection of poems about shepherds dating from around 40 B.C. The *Fourth Eclogue* thereof heralds nothing less than the beginning of a new golden age with a divine boy who is born of a virgin! Alluding to a prophecy of the Sibyl of Cumae, the most important seeress in Italy, it reads:

> Now the last age by Cumae's Sibyl sung
> Has come and gone, and the majestic roll
> Of circling centuries begins anew:
> The Virgin comes, returns old Saturn's reign,
> With a new breed of men sent down from heaven.
> Only do thou, at the boy's birth in whom
> The iron shall cease, the golden age arise.

The text is puzzling; the only thing certain is that it does not refer to Octavian. The emperor's mother was quite definitely not a virgin; moreover, the passage goes on to mention the tenure of the consul Pollio as the approximate time of the birth of this boy who "shall receive the life of the gods" and be considered one of them; Pollio was consul in the year 40 B.C. So it is much more likely that Virgil himself did not know who the divine boy of the prophecy was; he was sure that time would reveal it. For Constantine the Great, the emperor who died as a baptized Christian, the matter was clear. When he assembled the bishops of the empire for a council in Nicaea in the year 325, he stated categorically that the boy "sent down from heaven" could only have been Christ, who, as everyone knew, was born of a Virgin during the reign of Augustus. Soon afterward (around 400), the Church Father Augustine adopted this interpretation and even declared Virgil to be the "prophet of the Messiah", who proclaimed the Incarnation of the Son of God to the Gentiles. After the fifth century, this gave rise, initially among Byzantine authors, to the legend about the appearance of a seeress (first Pythia, in later versions the Tiburtine Sibyl) to Augustus, from whom he learned that a Jewish boy, the "Firstborn Son of God", would rule after him. It goes on to say that he then set up an altar for this child on the Capitol. Even today in Santa Maria in Aracoeli, especially in the days leading up to Christmas, the *Bambino Gesu*, the Roman Christ Child, is fervently honored.

The emperor took this prophecy as well as the other omens seriously; this is demonstrated by the fact that in the year 17 B.C. he had the onset of the new age celebrated officially—the tenth *saeculum*, which the Romans viewed as the "end time of the world" (according to Kienast). Previously Augustus had commissioned Virgil to compose the *Aeneid* almost as a Roman Book of Exodus. It offered a mythical-historical

justification of the redemptive mission of the Romans as an "elect people" of the gods, who allegedly were led out of the "holy city" of Troy
to the Tiber, in order to rule the world from there forever: a message
that was central to the Secular Celebrations, in which Augustus was
declared to be the direct descendant of the Trojan Aeneas.

Although the Altar of Heaven on the Capitoline Hill is only a pretty
legend, the historical model for it is located not that far away—today
precisely nine-tenths of a mile as the crow flies. There, on the bank of
the Tiber, the Ara Pacis Augustae, the "Altar of the Augustan Peace",
was restored in 1938, after Italian archaeologists had unearthed the
last fragments of it under the foundation of the Palazzo Fiano-Almagia
along the Via del Corso—exactly 1094 yards north of the Capitol.
Even before the construction of the palace in the early sixteenth century, its sumptuously decorated marble slabs had been recovered and
incorporated into various collections. Until then, the place where it
had stood had been consigned to oblivion for a whole millennium—
a fact that probably explains why the Christian legend was compelled
to situate it on the Capitol.

Its splendid bas-relief ornamentation depicts Augustus as a high
priest, placating the pagan gods and invoking their peace. Decorative
plants symbolize the fruitfulness of the new age; the figures on the
frieze, the prosperity and order in the empire as well as the promise
of the tenth age of the world, the peaceful coexistence of all creatures,
in the center of which a veiled woman carries two children in her
arms. This in particular, the most beautiful and best-known relief image of the altar, poses the most riddles for art historians. The woman is
variously identified as the earth-goddess Tellus, the *Venus genitrix* (the
mythical ancestress of the Julian emperors), or Ceres, the goddess of
the harvest and fertility; however, it might just as well be the virgin
from Virgil's *Fourth Eclogue*. It is quite possible that this image gave
rise to the legend about a Marian apparition to Augustus; at any rate,
it quite obviously inspired Raffaello Santi (1483–1520), who between
1504 and 1510 painted a whole series of Madonnas seated with the
Child Jesus and the little John the Baptist on her lap or at her feet.
From then on, the motif was copied by countless artists of the Renais-
sance and Baroque periods, since its message was unambiguous: with
Jesus, Mary, and John, the herald and forerunner of Christ (and of the
"priestly Messiah" of the Essene tradition), God's true reign of peace
had begun, which lasted longer than the "Golden Age" of Augustus.

Yet the altar, which was dedicated by Augustus in 9 B.C., was only part of a gigantic building complex—the most impressive monument that had been set up to propagate the cosmic dimensions of his rule. At its southern end stood the Pantheon, the largest domed construction of antiquity, which Marcus Agrippa had already built in 27–25 B.C. (the Emperor Hadrian had it rebuilt after a fire in the year 110). Here at first the family gods and ancestors of Augustus and of the Julian emperors were honored, among them a statue of the divinized Caesar. Only when Agrippa tried to set up a statue of Augustus there too did the emperor intervene, as the Roman chronicler Cassius Dio reports. They had to find for it some place outside the temple, in the *pronaos* (court or vestibule), so as to avoid an apotheosis during his lifetime. (This, too, is reminiscent of the Aracoeli legend!)

To the north, the complex was bounded by the Mausoleum Augusti, the round, concentrically arranged tomb of the emperor; to the south, exactly midway between the two southern corners of the campus, by the Ara Pacis. In front of it loomed the Solarium Augusti, which at first glance looked like a gigantic sundial dedicated to Sol, the sun god. An obelisk shipped especially from Heliopolis in Egypt served as the pointer, which stood in the middle of a cobblestone pavement criss-crossed by a network of lines. The shadow that it cast indicated the time and the season, but that was not all: the equinox line ran through the middle of the Ara Pacis, and the winter solstice line, too, was connected with it by two points, so as to indicate two dates according to the position of the sun: September 23, the birthday of Augustus, and December 23, the day when he was begotten. He took the latter date so seriously that he had Aries the Ram and not Virgo the Virgin stamped on coins as his astrological sign. Thus the Solarium became like a gigantic horoscope of the emperor, with the dates of his birth and begetting stylized as the cosmic vertices of a new era of peace. Augustus had no idea how close he came to the dates that were soon celebrated by the Christians as the birthdays of Jesus (December 25) and of his Virgin Mother (September 8). "Whereas finally the birthday of the Divine One signifies for the whole world the beginning of his good tidings (*evangelia!*), let us begin a new age with the date of his birth and henceforth observe his birthday as the beginning of the year," we read in a calendar inscription from the year 9 B.C., which was found in Priene in Asia Minor: "Providence, which reigns over all living things, filled this man with such gifts for the salvation of mankind that he is

sent to us and to coming generations as the savior (*soter!*). He will put
an end to all war and make everything magnificent."

As striking as the parallels between Augustan Messianism and the
Christian hope for salvation are, they, too, only reflect the basic mood
of this historical period. For in the Eastern part of the empire, in one
of Rome's vassal states, a ruler was doing everything possible to be
regarded as the messiah of his people. His name was Herod; posterity
would give him the title "the Great" but also would condemn him as
one of the biggest scoundrels in history.

The Jewish expectation of the Messiah, most textbooks say, originated in the period immediately after the fall of the Kingdom of Judah in
586 B.C. At that time, during the Babylonian Captivity, there was a glim-
mer of hope for a liberator, who would found a new Israel and rebuild
the temple that had been destroyed by Nebuchadnezzar. Of course, he
would be a descendant of the House of David, of the divinely elected
dynasty of Jewish kings; his title *Mashiach* = "the Anointed" already indicated this. "The Anointed One of God" was a title that King David
bore. Yet Israel's destiny in salvation history goes much farther back. It
began four thousand years ago, when Abraham followed God's call and
traveled to the new land that the Lord showed him. It lay exactly midway between the highly developed civilizations of Sumeria and Egypt
and, thus, at the intersection between Asia and Africa, moreover, on
the Eastern shore of the Mediterranean, which, so to speak, divides the
three continents of the ancient world from each another and connects
them with one another. There stood Jericho, the oldest city in the
world, first settled thirteen thousand years ago, in a fertile oasis, at the
point where the Jordan flows into the Dead Sea, at the deepest point
on earth. "By you all the families of the earth shall bless themselves"
(Gen 12:3), God had promised Abraham, and at least geopolitically all
that had made a great deal of sense. For this was not only the crossroads
of the old trade and caravan routes that went all over the world and led
to the Far East; this place was literally "the navel of the world". For
the medieval cartographers were not altogether wrong when they depicted Europe, Asia, and Africa as three petals emerging from an ovary,
Jerusalem. There, on Mount Moriah, Abraham had almost sacrificed
his son; there, two thousand years later, God would sacrifice his only
begotten Son Jesus on Mount Golgotha, where, according to an ancient
tradition that is difficult to date, Adam's skull was buried. Abraham's

grandson Jacob became the patriarch of the twelve tribes of Israel, one of which, Judah, was blessed with the prophecy: "The scepter shall not depart from Judah, nor the ruler's staff from between his feet, until he comes to whom it belongs; and to him shall be the obedience of the peoples" (First Book of Moses, Gen 49:10). Either fate or Providence led the sons of Jacob, the great-grandsons of the Sumerian Abraham, first to Egypt, into the heart of the second world power of that time, and then, freed from slavery, back into the Holy Land. At that time, as Moses and the Israelites were already encamped on the eastern bank of the Jordan across from Jericho, one of the most mysterious figures of the Old Testament appeared on the scene: Balaam, the son of Beor, a renowned seer, or oracular priest, who actually lived "on the bank of the Euphrates" in the ancient Babylonian Empire of that time. Balak, the king of Moab (modern Jordan), had summoned him for a princely sum, so that he might put a curse on the intruders. Three times Balaam tried to curse the Israelites after offering animal sacrifices, and three times he failed, for God placed words of blessing on his lips instead. Then, however, before he was driven away in disgrace, he uttered a prophecy that was to be fulfilled only many centuries later:

> "I see him, but not now; I behold him, but not near: a star shall come forth out of Jacob, and a scepter shall rise out of Israel. . . . By Jacob shall dominion be exercised." (Fourth Book of Moses, Num 24:17–19)

The Jews applied this prophecy initially to King David and, only then, to the future Messiah, and in fact, if read in its entirety, it is at first glance too bloodthirsty to refer to Jesus. Yet in 1967, during excavations in Succoth and Jordan, archaeologists found an Aramaic inscription that was dated back to the ninth century B.C. and contains another prophecy "of Balaam, son of Beor"; this fact proves that the pagan seer was still renowned centuries later. From his day on, at any rate, the Jews believed that a star would herald the coming of the Messiah. To Moses, also, it was revealed by God that a new, greater prophet would come, who could proclaim the new Torah in God's name:

> "The LORD your God will raise up for you a prophet like me from among you, from your brethren—him you shall heed—just as you desired of the LORD your God at Horeb on the day of the assembly." (Fifth Book of Moses, Deut 18:15–16)

King David (circa 1000 B.C.) sang in his Psalms about a prince of peace
who was to come, who would be both "the Anointed One of God"
and also the "Man of Sorrows" of Psalm 22, betrayed and abandoned,
with his hands and feet bored through, yet ultimately full of confidence
that in the end he would conquer death.

Then the four major prophets (Isaiah, Jeremiah, Ezekiel, and Daniel),
who lived between 740 and 550 B.C., took up again the vision of the
Messiah, the future prophet and prince of peace. To Jeremiah, the Lord
announced a new covenant, "not like the covenant which I made with
their fathers" (Jer 31:32), when he raises up "for David a righteous
Branch" (Jer 23:5). "I will set up over them one shepherd, my servant
David, and he shall feed them", God revealed to the prophet Ezekiel
(34:23). In the form of a "good shepherd", the Almighty himself would
care for his sheep and provide for justice and righteousness: "A new
heart I will give you, and a new spirit I will put within you . . . and
the nations will know that I am the LORD" (Ezek 36:26, 23).

Most specific is the vision of Isaiah, the first of the major prophets.
He foretold to Israel not only God's judgment in the form of the Babylonian Captivity but also the dawning of the Messianic kingdom:

> There shall come forth a shoot from the stump of Jesse, and a branch
> (Hebrew; *nezer!*) shall grow out of his roots. And the Spirit of the
> LORD shall rest upon him, the spirit of wisdom and understanding,
> the spirit of counsel and might, the spirit of knowledge and the fear
> of the LORD. And his delight shall be in the fear of the LORD. He shall
> not judge by what his eyes see, or decide by what his ears hear; but
> with righteousness he shall judge the poor, and decide with equity
> for the meek of the earth; and he shall strike the earth with the rod
> of his mouth, and with the breath of his lips he shall slay the wicked.
> Righteousness shall be the belt of his waist, and faithfulness the belt
> of his loins. (Is 11:1–5)

There are many similar passages in Isaiah that talk about the LORD's
"Anointed" on whom "the Spirit of the LORD God" shall rest and who
would be sent "to bring good tidings to the afflicted" (Is 61:1). But
also passages in which the Messiah is described as a suffering "Servant
of God", as the "Man of Sorrows": "Surely he has borne our griefs
and carried our sorrows . . . he was wounded for our transgressions,
he was bruised for our iniquities; upon him was the chastisement that
made us whole, and with his stripes we are healed." Finally, he would

rise from the dead, for "when he makes himself an offering for sin, . . . the will of the LORD shall prosper in his hand" (Is 53:4−5, 10).

Only Daniel, though, had a specific chronology. In a vision of four beasts that rose out of the sea (a lion, a bear, a leopard, and a horned creature), he foresaw four world empires that would rise up by then (namely, Babylon, Persia, Greece, and Rome). In another vision, he learned that this would occur within seventy "weeks of years", in other words, seventy times seven equals 490 years, beginning with the "going forth of the word to restore and build Jerusalem". After a total of sixty-nine weeks of years, "an anointed one shall be cut off, and shall have nothing" (that is, no just sentence, according to some versions of the Bible). This will serve "to put an end to sin, and to atone for iniquity, to bring in everlasting righteousness, to seal both vision and prophet, and to anoint a most holy place." But then will come also the time of the destruction "of the city and the sanctuary" (Dan 9:24−26), which will be destroyed in the course of another week of years, a seven-year war.

Of course, immediately after their release from the Babylonian Captivity by an edict of the Persian King Cyrus in 539 B.C., the Jews puzzled over this prophetic chronology—if it was already known at all in those days. Some skeptical exegetes regard the Book of Daniel as a so-called "pseudo-epigraph", a text from the second century B.C. that was attributed to Daniel. But that is not supported by the tradition recorded by the Jewish historian Flavius Josephus. He writes that when Alexander the Great invaded Jerusalem in 332 B.C., the Jewish elders showed him the prophecy of Daniel that the Persian Empire would be replaced by that of the Greeks. At any rate, it is certain that the Dead Sea Scrolls testify to the fact that the Jewish people took these prophetic counting games more and more seriously, the closer they seemed to come to the predicted point in time.

This was done first and foremost by the Essenes. They considered themselves the elite of Israel in the end times, and they withdrew to the desert in order to prepare for the coming of the Messiah. Their history began at a point in time when the country was fighting at first for its freedom, was victorious, and then a new dynasty ascended to the throne of David.

The only successful Jewish uprising in history broke out when the pagan king defiled the reconstructed Temple. As a result of the conquest of the Persian Empire by Alexander the Great, the Near East had

come for the first time under European influence, in this case Greek
influence, which was to shape it for a thousand years. After the death
of the Macedonian ruler, his empire was divided among his generals;
Judea was allotted at first to the territory of Ptolemy, who resided in
Alexandria. About a hundred years later, it was conquered by the descendants of General Seleucus, who had inherited Syria; they extended
their empire as far as the border of Egypt. This, too, is described in
the Book of Daniel, when it says the "King of the North" (Syria)
waged war against the "King of the South" (Egypt) (Dan 11:11) and
in doing so occupied "the glorious land" (Israel). The Hellenophile
Jew Menelaus offered the Seleucid King Antiochus IV (175–163 B.C.)
a large sum of money if he would appoint him as high priest of the
Temple in Jerusalem. The king accepted the offer, but the Jews refused
to accept the newly rich upstart as their spiritual leader. Antiochus IV,
in turn, who adorned himself with the epithet "Epiphanes" ("the [di-
vine] one who appears"), took that as outright rebellion. He had his
troops march against Jerusalem, where they demolished the city walls
and confiscated the Temple treasury. In order to humiliate the insolent
Jews completely, in 167 B.C. he dedicated the Temple of Yahweh to
Zeus, the father of the gods, and had a pig sacrificed to him on the
altar of holocausts in front of the Holy of Holies.

Yet with this blasphemous provocation with an "unclean" animal,
he had gone too far. The Jews were indignant about the "desolating
sin" committed against their sanctuary (as described in Daniel 8:13
NAB) and revolted. The leader of the uprising was the elderly priest
Mattathias, of the house of Hasamoneus, followed by his sons, first
and foremost Judas, who as a warrior took the name *Maccabee*, "the
Hammer". The Maccabees, together with a whole underground army
of strict-believing Jews, conducted guerilla warfare against the occupying Seleucid forces, dealing them a series of hard hammer blows. It was
to their advantage that King Antiochus happened to be on a campaign
against the Parthians in the eastern territories of his empire. So, through
a clever strategy of attrition, they succeeded in routing several units
of the occupying troops, until finally they captured Jerusalem. Then,
when the king died, all resistance collapsed. On the twenty-fifth day
of the month Chislev in the year 164 B.C., they were able to rededicate
the Temple, an event that is still commemorated today by the Jews in
their feast of Hanukkah. That occurred exactly 1,335 days after the

desecration of the Temple, exactly as Daniel is said to have foretold it (Dan 12:12).

For another twenty-two years, the Maccabees kept fighting, and they played the next three successors of Antiochus so skillfully against each other that Judea finally won national autonomy in 142 B.C. The head of the clan at the time, Simon, thereupon declared himself the "leader of the civil government" and high priest. His sons were even supposed to wear the royal crown and bequeath the office of high priest to their descendants. But for many conservative Jews, that went too far. In any case, it was a clear offense against the tradition that the high priest must be a descendant of Zadok, the first high priest in the Temple of Solomon. The king, moreover, could only be a descendant of David, to whose line the crown of Israel had been promised by God himself. As much as the faithful welcomed the uprising of the Maccabees and the restoration of the Jewish kingdom, the founding of a new dynasty was just too much for them to accept. At around this time, three groups formed in Judaism, and they were to set the tone in the next two centuries. The establishment was made up of the opportunistic *Sadducees* ("the righteous"), who came to an agreement with whoever happened to be in power and fostered a very pragmatic sort of Judaism. Its basic components were Temple worship and the Mosaic laws, which they followed strictly. In opposition to them were the *Pharisees* ("those set apart"), who strove to sanctify their daily routine and lived strictly according to the precepts concerning food and ritual purity found in their *Halakha*—for them, a second, "oral Torah", which, alongside the "written Torah" of Moses, regulated all departments of everyday life. Their name indicates that they kept away from anything that could result in ritual impurity. Together with the Sadducees, they too sat in the *Sanhedrin*, the "Supreme Council", but they were an often troublesome opposition party. They were dead set against combining the kingship with high priesthood and demanded that the Hasmoneans decide on one of the two offices. The result was a veritable civil war, which was put down bloodily by the ambitious Alexander Jannaeus; after six years, he ended up officially crucifying eight hundred Pharisees, an event that spread sheer horror throughout the land. The king justified the combination of the two offices by having his coins stamped with a star, the sign of the Messiah. The message was unambiguous: Even if he himself was not the promised savior, nevertheless, with him the messianic age had dawned. In fact, he exploited the support of the Ptolemaic Kingdom and the weakness of the Seleucid Empire so skillfully that he reestablished Israel almost with the boundaries of the Kingdom of Solomon. The prophecy of Balaam, it seemed, had come to pass in him.

A third group did not take part in the uprising but in protest left Jerusalem and at times the country, too. Their leader, whom they called only the "Teacher of Righteousness", was a descendant of Zadok, the first high priest, and was probably also their candidate for the supreme office. But now they followed him first to Damascus, where they formed their *jahad* ("alliance"), then to the northwest shore of the Dead Sea. There, where according to tradition Joshua camped after the capture of Jericho, in order to plan the conquest of the Promised Land, they went on to plan a "second annexation of the land", which would be a spiritual one, the purification and the sanctification of Israel. They tried to determine from the sacred writings when the time for that would be ripe. They were convinced that the Scriptures contained the key to the future. Thus, the Essenes, as they were called—which is probably derived from *Chassidim*, "the pious ones", in Aramaic: *Chassayya*—gained the reputation of being prophets. In the writings of Flavius Josephus, our most important source about the Judaism of this period, we read, for example, about one "Judah, the Essene", who could very well have been the "Teacher of Righteousness"; he is said to have taught his disciples to foretell the future. Sometime before 1947, when the Bedouins stumbled upon the hiding place of the extensive collection of Essene scrolls in the caves above the Khirbet Qumran ("Qumran Ruins") on the northwest shore of the Dead Sea, this observation of Josephus, too, was corroborated. Thus, we read in one of these texts, a commentary on the Old Testament Book of the Prophet Habakkuk (*Pesher Habakkuk*) that God "made keen the insight" of the Teacher of Righteousness, "so that he was able to explain all the mysteries in the words of his servants, the prophets". Consequently, he saw the events of his day in an eschatological context, almost as a prelude to the end times. The *Pesher* describes at length an historical event that we find in the writings of Josephus, also. In his first term as high priest, at the Feast of Booths (Hebrew: Sukkoth), Alexander Jannaeus deliberately refrained from celebrating the traditional water sacrifice, which was rejected by the Sadducees also, because it was not found in the Torah. When he poured the water on his feet instead, a shout of indignation went through the crowd; while they threw *etrogs* at him (a citrus fruit that was part of the rituals for the Feast of *Sukkoth*), he ordered his soldiers to attack. Six thousand Jews fell victim to their swords, which probably precipitated the aforementioned uprising of the Pharisees. The "Teacher of Righteousness" also wrote about the "sacrilegious priest" who "desecrated the sanctuary". He berated the Sadducees as "seekers of flattery", but he could not ally himself with the Pharisees, either; they would follow a "man of lies", it was said. In the first place, he was convinced, only the Messiah could save the country now. In order to be worthy of him, the community withdrew into the desert and lived a life of purity, continence, poverty, and prayer. At the same time, they tried to determine from the books of the prophets when the time would be ripe. One key, for example, was provided by the Book of Daniel with its rather specific reference to the sixty-nine weeks of years until the murder of the Anointed One; it was not difficult to calculate that he would be born sometime before the sixty-fifth week of years. In contrast, it was more difficult to explain the date from which the years were supposed to be reckoned, more precisely: whether Daniel meant the Edict of Cyrus in 539 B.C. as the starting point (whereby the Messiah would have to appear in the first century B.C.) or the Decree of Artaxerxes, which is referred to in Nehemiah 1:1, issued "in the twentieth year" of his reign, that is, in 446 B.C.; in that case, the Messiah was to be expected about a century later. (In the Habakkuk commentary, the "Teacher of Righteousness" complains: "That means that the Last Days will be long, much longer than the prophets foretold; for God's revelations are truly full of riddles.") Furthermore, the Essenes expected not only one Messiah but two at the same time: a high priest during the end times from the House of Aaron and a royal Messiah from the House of David, who would be anointed and installed in office by the Aaronic high priest.

The next few decades were marked by disputes about succession to the throne of the Hasmoneans and the ongoing rivalry between the religious parties of Israel. Finally, the sons of Alexander Jannaeus, Aristobulus and Hyrcanus, committed the fatal mistake of asking the Roman General Pompey, of all people, to settle their differences. He exploited the situation so as to bring the entire kingdom under his control. In short order, he set the weak, Rome-fearing Hyrcanus on the throne, marched into the country, and advanced against Jerusalem. In 63 B.C., after a three-month siege, he stormed the Temple, where

Aristobulus and his adherents had taken shelter. A bloodbath resulted, twelve thousand Jews were killed, and the Hasmoneans captured. But the Jews were even more shocked by the fact that Pompey penetrated into the Holy of Holies within the Temple. In doing so, he committed what was in their eyes a sacrilege that cried out to heaven; certainly no pagan, but only the high priest was allowed to set foot in God's earthly dwelling place.

What began amid such signs and wonders had to end badly. Judea had lost its autonomy and from then on was bound to pay tribute to the Romans. Hyrcanus was no longer allowed to call himself king, but was now the high priest and *ethnarch* (leader of the people), while his Idumaean prefect Antipater continued to rule his kingdom on behalf of Rome. The latter used his new position of power adroitly to build up a dynasty of his own. He divided the country into five provinces and installed his sons Phasael and Herod as governors. Of course, traditional Jews were displeased by the increase in power held by the converts, who were descendants of the Idumaeans, the Old Testament Edomites, ancient enemies of Israel. Finally, in 43 B.C., Antipater fell victim to a conspiracy and was poisoned at a banquet in Jerusalem. Consequently, Herod saw that his opportunity had arrived; in order to legitimize his claim to his father's position, he married the Hasmonean princess Mariamne. Yet he had not reckoned with Antigonus, son of Aristobulus, who in fact had allied himself with the Parthians, Rome's archenemy, in order to free the Jewish kingdom from the hands of his uncle and the Romans. Reinforced by a Persian army, in 40 B.C. he conquered Jerusalem in a surprise attack, killed Hyrcanus and Phasael, and set the crown on his own head. Only Herod managed to flee by night in the fog. Together with his retinue, his bodyguards, his wife, Mariamne, and his mother, Cyprus, he settled in the fortress of Masada, before traveling on alone to Egypt. From there he went to Rome, where he addressed the senate and offered to win back the rebellious vassal state, if they would reward him with the royal crown. The triumvirate reigning at the time (Octavian, Mark Antony, and Lepidus) and the senate agreed to the deal and sent him back to Judea at the head of an army. For two years he waged war against Antigonus, then in 37 B.C. he captured Jerusalem and had his opponent executed.

The next thirty-three years of his reign made him appear at first to be the Jewish version of Augustus. Whereas it was proverbially said of the Roman ruler that he transformed a city of bricks into a city of marble, you have to give Herod credit for leaving to his successors a provincial kingdom that was like an oriental fairyland. In order to finance his gigantic building projects, he not only squeezed the last ounce of taxes out of his subjects but also proved to be extremely clever in marketing raw materials. At the Dead Sea, he had bitumen extracted from pits, which was indispensable in making caulk, the sealant for wooden boats; the market for it then was booming because the Romans were expanding their fleets of warships and commercial vessels. Later he leased from the Roman Senate half of the Cypriot copper mines as well, while he had tin imported from Britain; in this way, he dominated the production of and trade in bronze.

Thus Judea under Herod became the Dubai of antiquity. A whole network of monumental edifices was supposed to show his subjects and the world that he was more than an illegitimate puppet-king sponsored by Rome. He wanted to go down in history as the greatest of all Jewish kings and to overshadow even Solomon in his splendor.

At first he erected a ring of fortresses, which was supposed to secure his power, among them the Herodium, his palace stronghold east of Bethlehem, which is still impressive today. Then he founded two cities, Caesarea and Sebaste, both named after Augustus (*Sebastos* in Greek), as a symbol of his loyalty to Rome. Caesarea was his gateway to the world, the first manmade harbor in antiquity, and one of the largest on the Mediterranean, with breakwaters that reached three-tenths of a mile into the sea. Over its moorings, on an artificial platform, loomed the Temple of Augustus and Roma, 164 feet tall, which dominated the skyline of the city. At the same time, the king built a second altar of Augustan messianism to his protector, a snow-white temple on the upper course of the Jordan, south of Paneas, modern Banias (which his son Philip would later rename Caesarea Philippi). Herod's masterpiece, however, was Jerusalem, his capital. He protected it not only through the expansion of the Jerusalem fortress, which he named Antonia after Mark Antony, but above all through a second city wall, which could withstand any siege. He endowed it with a theater and a chariot racecourse, which brought a bit of Greco-Roman culture to the Holy City. On the western hill of Jerusalem, he built his own residence, the most opulent palace of his day, which contemporary authors described in superlatives. "Its splendid furnishings defied description and eclipsed anything that had existed previously", Flavius Josephus noted with amazement. Looming over it was a protective fortress with three skyscraping watchtowers, which tell a lot about the paranoid king's need for security.

Most importantly, however, he gave Jerusalem a new Temple, one of the largest and most glorious sanctuaries of the ancient world, whereby he not only vied with King Solomon but also won the competition easily. Unfortunately, we have only very sketchy descriptions of the edifice that had been built over the ruins of the Temple of Solomon for those who returned from the Babylonian Captivity. We know its height and width precisely (89 × 30 feet) and know that over three courses of cut stones there was one course of timber (Ezra 6:3–4). Yet it probably was not all that impressive; although the Persian king had placed all the materials at his disposal, the work was completed under pressure of a deadline. Moreover, there were repeated interruptions, as the Book of Ezra reports, until the reconstruction was finally finished at Passover of the year 515 B.C. Consequently, its inadequacies soon became part of a national platform, and after the desecration of the Temple by Antiochus IV, an eschatological certitude as well. The "Second Temple", as the orthodox Jews in particular sensed, could and should be only a provisional arrangement, for it had been built on the orders of a king and not at God's bidding. They would have to wait until the Messiah came and built the Third Temple, which would eclipse even the work of Solomon.

For Herod, therefore, the rebuilding of the Temple was not only a matter of prestige; above all, there was political calculation behind it. It was, so to speak, his courtship to win the hearts of his people. He knew that he would thereby encourage the Jews and reconcile those who had watched with ever increasing mistrust his program of Romanizing Judea through the construction of chariot racecourses, theaters, fortresses, and gorgeous palaces. This was not just a question of surpassing Solomon and going down in history as the most glorious king of the Jews; there was more to it than that. Secretly Herod hoped to be "recognized" by his people as the Messiah. That alone would cover over the blemish of his dubious ancestry.

For this man who uniquely changed the image of ancient Judea was not a "genuine" Jew, as every one of his subjects knew. His father, as was mentioned, was originally from Idumea, the biblical Edom, a region in the South that was first annexed by the Hasmonean kings; thereupon its inhabitants were forcibly converted to Judaism. His mother, Cyprus, was even a pagan Nabatean from the city of Petra, perched on a crag in present-day Jordan. Consequently, he was of course even less predestined for the throne of David than the hated Hasmoneans, who could at least claim to be Jews from a line of Aaronic priests. But ironically, as fate would have it, Herod had one ally, at least at the beginning of his reign, whom we would least expect to side with him: the Essenes.

This implausible alliance, which can be explained most accurately by the old proverb "The enemy of my enemy is my friend", (an Arabic saying that was therefore probably familiar to Herod also), went back to the school days of the king. At that time, Flavius Josephus reports, he met an Essene by the name of Menahem. He was "endowed by God with the gift of foretelling the future" and told the youth that one day he would become King of the Jews. Apparently still modest at that time, Antipater's son demurred, saying that he was, after all, only a commoner. Yet Menahem insisted that his prophecy was correct: "You will in fact become king and have a fortunate reign", he declared to the young Herod. He should just keep in mind always that all good fortune can change, and he should therefore always treat his subjects with clemency. But since he, Menahem, knew how contrary to Herod's character that was, the latter would "indeed win eternal fame but forget piety and justice". For this reason, God would punish him at the end of his life.

Naturally the youth quickly put the second, admonitory part of the prophecy out of his mind. He remembered the first part, though, for the rest of his life. Thus, when he had in fact become king, he summoned Menahem in order to ask him how long his reign would last. But the Essene did not answer. "Will it be ten years, twenty?" the king asked. "Yes." "Thirty years?" "Yes." "How many more years?" Again the Essene remained silent. But the certainty that he would rule for more than thirty years was enough for Herod to confer extensive privileges on the community. So he granted to the Essenes a whole district of the city on the southern slope of Mount Zion (see chapter 11). There he had a gate in the city wall opened up for them, because their strict precepts concerning ritual purity forbade them to take the path through the city. Outside the gate, he installed a special *mikveh*, a bath for ceremonial purification, like the one that the Jews otherwise used before entering the Temple. The Essenes were even involved in planning the new Temple, to the great displeasure of the Sadducees, who were still a dominant force, and it appears certain that extensive concessions were made to them also in matters of the Temple worship.

The fact that the Essenes accepted this offer was not just the result of Herod's generosity. In the year 31 B.C., all of Judea was shaken by a severe earthquake, during which the monastery in Qumran was destroyed, as the excavations show. It is obvious that this was interpreted by the sect as a divine omen, since the Essenes looked for signs of the Messiah's coming in all the events of their day. Thus it is clear, at least to the archaeologists who unearthed Qumran, that the monastery was in fact abandoned for the next three decades, and all evidence indicates that the Essenes then moved to Jerusalem.

Of course they, too, realized that Herod was not the Messiah. Yet they were probably convinced that God was using him as an instrument to prepare the way on which the Anointed would appear. More than ever, they trusted their reckonings, whereby the "time of fulfillment", the New Covenant of God, was near, almost within reach. On the other hand, they, too, were uncertain how the rebuilding of the Temple should be interpreted. Had they misunderstood the prophecies? Would the Messiah appear only after the Third Temple was already standing? Or was Herod planning merely an embellishment of the Second Temple, while the construction of the third was reserved, after all, to the Messiah?

The Jews still debate this question today, and for good reason the time of Herod and of Roman rule in Israel is designated as the "Second Temple Period". Today in Jerusalem the rabbis dispute, as of yore, whether the construction of the Third Temple should finally be undertaken—after first removing the Muslim Dome of the Rock, of course! —or whether that suicide mission had better be left to the Messiah. But, however we may assess the events in Herod's time, one fact remains: "In the eighteenth year of his reign", in 20–19 B.C., as Josephus writes, when the king spoke to the people and announced his plan to build the Temple, there was also a promise of the birth of the human temple that God himself had chosen for his Incarnation. It was the year in which Mary of Nazareth was begotten.

~

3

The Gospel of Mary

It is practically impossible to compose a historical biography of Mary if we take the Gospels alone as our source. What they reveal to us about the Virgin of Nazareth fills precisely one chapter of a book (and not a particularly extensive one at that). In order to supplement this rather sketchy picture, we must refer to the traditions of the early Christians, which are generally known as the Apocrypha. The term, derived from the Greek word *apokryphos* (hidden), applies to all early Christian and Jewish writings that for a wide variety of reasons did not make it into the canon of the Bible. Some, because they are blatant forgeries; others, because they advocate erroneous doctrines; and still others, because their contents had no relevance to salvation history, at least in the opinion of the Church Fathers. The last-mentioned reason applies to a mysterious book that originated sometime around the mid-second century in a Jewish Christian milieu (although that, too, is disputed). Its original title was "Origin (or Birth) of Mary—Revelation of James", whereas today (since the sixteenth century) it is known by the name of the *Proto-Gospel of James*. For, indeed, it describes the events that preceded the Incarnation of the Son of God, the *Good News*.

There is ample proof for the antiquity of this scripture: the oldest extant manuscript (the *Bodmer Papyrus 5*) probably dates back to the third century. But long before this papyrus was discovered in Egypt, the work was very popular and widespread, especially in the Eastern Church; thus we know of manuscripts with translations into Syriac, Armenian, Georgian, Ethiopian, Coptic, Arabic, and Old Slavonic, as well as Latin, of course. Although a purported Decree of Pope Gelasius (492–496) rejected it along with a whole series of other apocryphal works and even put it under interdict, it decisively influenced iconography not only in the East but also in the Latin Church's sphere of influence. This is not surprising, for since a study by the great Church

historian Ernst von Dobschütz we know that the *Gelasianum* itself is a
pseudepigraphon, that is, a document that is falsely attributed to a well-
known author. It does quote from a decision by Pope Damasus I from
the year 382, but it originated in its present form much later in the
sixth century in Southern Gaul and is therefore by no means binding
for a Catholic. This is the only way to explain the fact that devotion
to the parents of Mary, Saint Joachim and Saint Anne, is based solely
on the *Proto-Gospel* and that a whole series of ecclesiastical feast days
(for example, the Feast of the Presentation of Mary in the Temple on
November 21) ultimately go back to this text.

Actually, though, the *Proto-Gospel* contains so many details that can
be verified historically and archaeologically—which we will examine
in detail—that we must assume that it has an authentic tradition at its
core. The fact that this tradition was originally oral is suggested already
by the characteristic spoken style of the text, especially the remarkably
frequent use of the Greek *kai* ("and"), which was regarded as a mon-
strosity in a literary text. We find it 440 times in the approximately
4,300 Greek words of the *Proto-Gospel*. Only in the Gospel of Mark do
we run into anywhere near as many *kai*-conjunctions, yet here, too,
at least in the opinion of the Church Fathers, we are dealing with the
written record of an oral tradition. Mark, who worked in Rome as
Saint Peter's translator, supposedly set down on paper the latter's stories about Jesus in a sensible chronology at the request of the Romans.
(That, in any case, was the conviction of Bishop Papias of Hierapolis
in the early second century, who was a disciple of John the apostle and
evangelist.)

It is obvious who handed down this oral tradition: it can only have
been the family of Jesus. In fact, there is evidence of *relatives of the Lord*
at least in Nazareth well into the third century, when one of them,
Konon (or Conon), suffered martyrdom precisely on account of this
lineage during the persecution of the Christians by Decius in the year
250. In Jerusalem, the Lord's relatives (in Greek, *desposynoi*) presided
over the ancient Christian community until the early second century.

Right after Peter was arrested by Herod Agrippa in the year 42 and
then miraculously escaped from prison, he appointed a certain James
as the first bishop of Jerusalem, who is described in the Christian and
Jewish literature as "James the Just, the brother of Jesus". Determining
his identity is one of the most difficult riddles of the New Testament.
For the word "brother" is not entirely clear, either in the Greek of the

Acts of the Apostles and the Letters of Paul or in Aramaic, the vernacular at the time of Jesus. Both the Greek *adelphos* and the Aramaic
ah (or the Hebrew *ach*) can mean "blood brother", "stepbrother", or
"cousin"; there was no separate word in Aramaic for "cousin". Who
was this James, then?

At least we can say with certainty that he was not a second son of
Mary. We find the best proof of the fact that Mary had no other children in the Gospel of John. In one of its most moving scenes, when
only "his mother" and "the disciple whom he loved" were standing
beneath the Cross, Jesus entrusted the widow (her husband, Joseph,
appears for the last time in the Gospel of Luke when Jesus was twelve;
at the time of his public ministry, Mary was clearly single) to the care
and protection of John: " 'Woman, behold, your son!' . . . 'Behold,
your mother!' And from that hour the disciple took her to his own
home" (Jn 19:26–27). If Mary had had a second son, it would have
been an outright affront to release him at that moment from his duties
as a son.

The second possibility, which is favored by Catholic exegetes, is that
he was a cousin of Jesus. As proof of this thesis, they cite Mark 15:40,
which speaks about that other Mary, the "sister" (namely, cousin or
sister-in-law) of the Mother of God, "the mother of James the younger
and of Joses". These two sons are also mentioned in another passage
in Mark, when the inhabitants of Nazareth reacted in such a hostile
way to Jesus' appearance and described him as the "brother of James
and Joses and Judas and Simon" and of several sisters as well (Mk
6:3). Mark 16:1 also, when it names the women who went to Jesus'
tomb on Sunday morning, speaks again about this Mary, the "mother
of James". Matthew (27:56) and Luke (24:10) also mention her. By
the epithet "the lesser" or "the younger", the evangelists distinguish
him from the other James, "the greater" (or "the older"), the son of
Zebedee and Salome, the brother of the evangelist John, who as one of
the "sons of thunder" belonged to the circle of Jesus' closest followers. In the lists of the apostles (Mt 10:3; Mk 3:18; Lk 6:15; and Acts
1:13), one James is described as "son of Alphaeus", who actually must
have been a brother of the tax collector Levi-Matthew, who, according
to Mark 2:14, was likewise a "son of Alphaeus". But he really could
not be identical to the "brother of the Lord", whose mother, Mary,
is described in John 19:25 as "the wife of Clopas", who is probably
identical to the Cleopas whom Luke (24:18) identifies as one of the

two disciples at Emmaus (the other disciple at Emmaus was his son Simon, or Symeon, whom the Nazarenes likewise numbered among the
"brothers of Jesus"). Accordingly, there were various solutions to this
problem offered by the Church Fathers. Some considered Alphaeus and
Cleopas to be one and the same person; others thought that "Mary the
wife of Clopas" was the widow of Alphaeus, whom Cleopas (perhaps
a relative) later married. But maybe Alphaeus and Cleopas lived at the
same time and each had a wife named Mary—one of them (Mary of
Alphaeus) would then be the mother of James and Joses, and the other
(Mary of Cleopas) the mother of Simon/Symeon and Judas. Cleopas
at any rate was, according to tradition, a brother of Saint Joseph, the
foster father of Jesus. That is why the Council of Trent (1545–1563)
declared it binding, at least on the Western Church, that James the
Lesser and "James the Just", the first bishop of Jerusalem, were identical.

But the Eastern Orthodox Churches have disputed this since the time
of Eusebius of Caesarea and Epiphanias of Salamis (fourth century).
In their view, as Eusebius writes in his *Ecclesiastical History*, "James is
called the brother of the Lord, because he too was said to be a son of
Joseph." Besides other traditions, both authors are said to have relied
on the *Proto-Gospel*, where it says that the foster father of Jesus was a
widower, who brought several sons with him from his first marriage.
But it does not follow directly from this that James was one of those
sons and thus a stepbrother of Jesus, because the text does not mention
their names.

The only thing certain, therefore, is that "James the Just" was a close
relative of Jesus, maybe a stepbrother, maybe a cousin. Probably it took
the Easter event to convince him that Jesus was the Messiah. It is certain
that he had a special encounter with the Risen Lord, as Paul notes in the
First Letter to the Corinthians (15:7). When the man who later would
become the apostle to the Gentiles visited Jerusalem in A.D. 37 after
his stay in Damascus, he met James for the first time. At the council
of the apostles in the year 48, he not only was considered one of the
three "pillars" of the early Church (after Peter and John); he clearly
had firm control of the original Christian community in Jerusalem.
Thus he was the one who dictated the formula for the compromise
that ultimately led to the first schism but initially brought about the
coexistence of Jewish and Gentile Christians: "Therefore my judgment is that we should not trouble those of the Gentiles who turn

to God, but should write to them to abstain from the pollutions of [meat sacrificed to] idols and from unchastity and from what is strangled and from blood" (Acts 15:19–20). The Letter to the Galatians, which refers to the events immediately after the Council, testifies to how strictly the Church of Jerusalem otherwise observed the precepts of Judaism under his leadership.

Another author who wrote about him was Hegesippus, who was born around the year 100 in Jerusalem:

> This [James] was holy from his mother's womb. He drank no wine or intoxicating liquor, nor did he eat flesh; no razor came upon his head; he did not anoint himself with oil or make use of the bath. He alone was permitted to enter the holy place: for he did not wear any woolen garment, but fine linen only. He alone was wont to go into the Temple: and he used to be found kneeling on his knees, begging forgiveness for the people, so that the skin of his knees became horny like that of a camel's, by reason of his constantly bending the knee in adoration to God and begging forgiveness for the people. Therefore, in consequence of his preeminent justice, he was called *the Just*.

He must have been an impressive man, whose asceticism is reminiscent of the way of life of the Essenes, and Hegesippus emphasizes that many Jews found their way to the Christian faith through him. This enraged the Sadducees, who took advantage of the power vacuum after the death of the governor, Festus, and before the arrival of his successor, Albinus, from Rome in the year 62 to get rid of him. So the high priest Ananus brought "the brother of Jesus, who was called Christ, whose name was James" to trial before the Sanhedrin, accused him of transgressing the law, and sentenced him to death by stoning. "But [those who] were the most uneasy at the breach of the laws, they disliked what was done", the Jewish historian Flavius Josephus goes on to report in his *Jewish Antiquities*. Hegesippus, the Jewish Christian, however, depicts the circumstances of his death differently.

According to the latter author, what made the Sadducees and the Pharisees uneasy was the expectation of Christ's Second Coming. Therefore they asked James to speak to the people from the pinnacle of the Temple at the Passover and to "restrain the people: for they are gone astray in their opinions about Jesus, as if he were the Christ." James accepted their invitation, positioned himself on the Temple walls, where everyone could see and hear him, and professed his faith: "He himself sitteth in heaven, at the right hand of the Great Power, and shall come on the clouds of heaven", while the people rejoiced and shouted, "Hosanna to the son of David!" This infuriated the Sadducees and the Pharisees so much that they threw James down from the pinnacle of the Temple and stoned him. With his last ounce of strength, "the Just Man" prayed for his enemies, quoting the words of Jesus: "I beseech you, Lord God our Father, forgive them, for they know not what they do." Then a fuller struck him with the staff that he used to wring out garments. James was buried right near the Temple, in one of the priests' tombs in the Kidron Valley, which still exist today.

Seven years later, when the Jewish uprising was crushed and the city and the Temple were burned down by the Romans, many Jews saw it as a punishment from God—not for the crucifixion of Jesus precisely forty years previously, but for the stoning of his "brother". According to Eusebius (the passage is preserved only in his writings), Flavius Josephus allegedly explained: "These things happened to the Jews as retribution for James the Just, who was a brother of Jesus who was called Christ, for the Jews killed him despite his great righteousness."

After the martyrdom of James, according to Eusebius' account,

> Those of the apostles and disciples of the Lord who were still alive gathered from everywhere with those who were, humanly speaking, relatives of the Lord, for many of them were still alive. They all discussed together who ought to succeed James, and all unanimously decided that Symeon, son of the Clopas mentioned in the Gospels, was worthy of the bishop's throne in Jerusalem. It is said that he was a first cousin of the Savior, for Hegesippus relates that Clopas was the brother of Joseph.

Thus, one of the two disciples at Emmaus became the second bishop of Jerusalem. His first task was to evacuate the early Christian community. After all, Symeon sensed that the period of which Jesus had spoken in his prophecy had begun. He probably relied on the very same prediction of the destruction of the city and of the Temple (for instance, Mt 24) that historical-critical exegetes today cite as "proof" that the Gospels must have been written in the years after the event and, therefore, later than A.D. 70. The fact that Jesus relied on the prophet Daniel (in Mt 24:15) in formulating his prophecy is quickly forgotten. Daniel predicted, at the end of the seventy weeks of years, the death of an anointed one without judicial sentence, which in the view of many Jewish Christians fit James better than Jesus, who had been legally sentenced by Pilate. And afterward, exactly one week of years later, would come the time of "the prince who . . . shall destroy the city and the sanctuary" (Dan 9:24–26). Before that, however, Jesus advised, "let those who are in Judea flee to the mountains" (Mt 24:16), and Symeon complied: he led the early Christian community out of Jerusalem to Pella in modern Jordan, where they survived the seven-year Jewish War unscathed. Only after the uprising had been put down and the troops of Titus had returned to Rome did they settle again on Mount Zion. Symeon continued to be their bishop, until he suffered martyrdom in the year 107. Hegesippus reports that a "heretic" denounced him to Emperor Trajan, who feared a second Jewish uprising and had all the members of the Davidic royal family hunted down. This fact proves, incidentally, not only that the Romans knew that the Jews expected their Messiah to come "from the house of David"; they were also aware that the family of Jesus belonged to this dynasty. And so the aged bishop—according to Hegesippus, he had reached the biblical age of one hundred twenty years—was put on trial by the proconsul Atticus, tortured, and finally crucified. But even that did not yet destroy the Jesus dynasty. Speaking about the reign of Trajan (98–117), "Hegesippus reports this as follows: 'Still surviving of the Lord's family were the grandsons of Jude, who was said to be his brother according to the flesh.'" Then, in 132, the second Jewish rebellion broke out, led by Simon Ben Koziba. The learned Rabbi Akiba declared him to be Messiah of Israel, and henceforth he called himself Simon Bar Kochba, the "Son of the Star", an allusion to the prophecy of Balaam. His first successful campaigns seemed to prove him right, until the Roman Emperor Hadrian put a bloody end to the revolt. Some 580,000 Jews lost their lives, and entire cities and towns of the country were destroyed. Over the ruins of Jerusalem the emperor had a new city built, Aelia, which was dedicated to the Capitoline gods. From then on, Jews were forbidden under pain of death to settle there. Although the Christians had not taken part in the uprising and Simon had even persecuted them violently, they, too, were among the mourners. Over their holy places, over Golgotha and the empty tomb, and also over the grotto in Bethlehem where Jesus was born, pagan places of worship were built. Since the ban on Jerusalem applied to them, too, the relatives of the Lord moved at that time back to Nazareth and the neighboring Kochaba (either Kakab, nine miles

north of Nazareth, or Kokab el Hawa, southwest of Mount Tabor),
as Julius Africanus (170–240), a Palestinian Christian, was still able
to report. Eusebius emphasizes that as late as the fourth century they
still possessed written tables of ancestors, by which the genealogies of
Jesus in the Gospels of Matthew and Luke were corroborated. Even in
the sixth century, a pilgrim from Piacenza in northern Italy reported,
one met women in Nazareth who claimed to be related to the Mother
of God.

It is therefore quite possible that a family tradition, which was connected with the name of James and perhaps went back to him directly,
was preserved until the second century and only then, during the second exodus of the Jewish Christians from Jerusalem, was set down
in writing. Some exegetes think that this happened in Egypt, which
had always generously welcomed Jewish refugees. Probably this took
place as a response to the Ebionites, a group of Jewish Christians who
did accept Jesus as the Messiah but disputed Mary's virginity. So no
doubt the main purpose of the *Proto-Gospel* was at any cost to dispel
doubts about Mary's immaculate purity. In doing so, the author may
have exaggerated and/or idealized the facts now and then, and what
he reports is certainly to be taken with a grain of salt. But to reject the
account because of these easily detectable exaggerations would be rash.
The document is too thoroughly imbued with Jewish local color; it
depicts the customs and usages of the Second Temple Period (many of
which we have been able to understand and classify historically only
since the discovery of the Dead Sea Scrolls) to be completely *legendary*
(which is almost a euphemism for *fictional*).

First of all, we owe to the *Proto-Gospel* a detailed account about
Mary's birth. According to it, her father Joachim was an "extremely
wealthy" cattle dealer, about whom a specific entry in the "history
books of the Twelve Tribes of Israel" clearly existed in the Jewish
Temple registers. He was known for his generosity and for the fact
that he always offered a double sacrifice. But there was one flaw in his
happiness: his marriage with his wife, Anne, had remained childless.
For a Jew, that was something shameful, a direct offense against God's
original commandment: "be fruitful and multiply" (Gen 1:28).

One day, specifically during the Jewish Feast of Booths *Sukkoth*,
which in the year 20 B.C. lasted from October 2 to 9,[1] there was an

---

[1] The Jewish holydays on any given year can easily be calculated with the help of com-
puter programs that can also be found on the Internet.

unpleasant incident in which an overzealous priest (in some versions he is called Reuben) reprimanded Joachim: "You are not allowed to offer your gifts first, because you have begotten no descendants in Israel." Now there was no rule among the Mosaic laws denying childless men the right to make the first sacrifice; but very probably there was a tradition of discrimination against barren men and women that went back to the time of the Book of Genesis. The most famous example, of course, was Abraham, who was already one hundred years old when his ninety-year-old wife, Sarah, finally bore him a son; out of sheer joy, the boy received the name Isaac ("laughter"). In any case, Joachim was deeply troubled as he returned to his house in Jerusalem; and since he could not stop thinking about the example of Abraham, he made a decision. He went out into the desert, built himself a hut, and fasted for forty days and nights, while begging God to give him a descendant at last.

The great Benedictine archaeologist Bargil Pixner (1921–2002), who was convinced all his life that the *Proto-Gospel* "goes back to traditions of Jesus' family", made an interesting observation in this regard. For although the text does not say where Joachim went in order to pray and fast, the tradition is very specific. A Georgian lectionary, which probably originated in the fifth century, mentions the grottos of Koziba in the Wadi Qelt in the Judean desert as the place of his penance. In 480, a monastery was built there with a Marian shrine, which the patriarch of Jerusalem, Elijah, dedicated in the year 501. It is worth visiting, even though it is not very easily accessible. At least on the road from Jerusalem to Jericho (Main Road 1) there is a sign marking the exit. From there you drive on the curving desert road to a narrow gate; the rest of the distance, a good six-tenths of a mile downhill, has to be covered on foot. The Wadi Qelt is a narrow stream that has cut its way deep into the rocks of the Judean desert and created a green oasis in the middle of the wilderness. So the visitor is greeted at first by a shady grove of olive trees and cypresses, the chirping of birds, and the rushing of the stream, which flows from here into the deepest valley on earth. Upon seeing this wildly romantic, craggy landscape, anyone who knows his Bible has to think of Psalm 23, which David may have composed when he walked along this path and which Joachim, too, might have prayed here:

The LORD is my shepherd, I shall not want;
he makes me lie down in green pastures.

He leads me beside still waters. . . .
Even though I walk through the valley of the shadow of death,
I fear no evil;
for you are with me.

On the other side of the stream, which the visitor can cross by means
of a little bridge, the Greek Orthodox Monastery of Saint George of
Koziba fits snugly against the rock like a swallow's nest. It is named
after a saintly monk, George of Cyprus, who lived there, and not after
the knight from Lydda (Lod) who killed the dragon. Over the course
of the centuries, the monastery was destroyed several times and then
rebuilt, the last time between 1878 and 1901. Since the Byzantine era,
when the Mother of God appeared to a noblewoman and invited her
to pray there, women have also been allowed to set foot in this holy
refuge. From the inside, courtyard steps lead down to its oldest sanctuary, the grotto church. Here, so the story goes, the prophet Elijah
hid, and the Lord sent a raven to feed him. But that is a rather recent
tradition about the place; if we are to believe the Book of Kings, the
prophet's cave was located instead on the bank of "the brook Cherith,
that is east of the Jordan" (1 Kings 17:3), the Wadi el-Kharrar in modern Jordan, the same "Bethany beyond the Jordan" where Saint John
was baptizing. Therefore, the modern attribution is probably based on
a simple misunderstanding, a confusion of the prophet with Patriarch
Elijah of Jerusalem (494–516), who in fact was buried in Koziba. The
cave was holy for him, however, because the birth of Mary was announced to Joachim there.

What makes this tradition plausible is not only the convenient location of the caves along the Roman road from Jerusalem to Jericho,
with which Joachim was certainly well acquainted, but also another circumstance altogether that Pixner pointed out. For Koziba was clearly
already a cave monastery of the Essene community.

The Benedictine archaeologist knew this from the most mysterious
of all the Dead Sea Scrolls, the so-called "copper scroll". It was discovered on March 20, 1952, in one of the caves of Qumran—not by
the Bedouins, but by a professional team of archaeologists. For several
days, collaborators from the École Biblique in Jerusalem and from the
Albright Institute, headed by the Dominican archaeologist Father de
Vaux, had been searching a five-mile stretch of the slope on the western shore of the Dead Sea for additional caves and traces of settlements

when they came upon ancient pottery fragments in a sort of gully. Upon closer inspection, it proved to be an entrance blocked by rubble. After they had rolled aside all the larger boulders, they were able to climb into a small grotto, what was left of a cavern that had once been larger but had caved in. Over the next few days, they teased from it not only fourteen fragments of ancient Essene texts, which had been written with ink on thin pieces of tanned goatskin and sheepskin, but also two copper scrolls. That in itself was already a sensational archaeological find, for they were the only ones of their kind. But why had they utilized this unusual material?

Since the metal proved to be brittle and badly oxidized, the only possible way of opening the scrolls was to saw them apart, bit by bit. This difficult operation was undertaken in 1955–1956 by Professor H. W. Baker at the University of Manchester in England. Afterward, the twenty-three resulting segments did not go to Jerusalem but, rather, to the Jordanian capital, Amman, since Qumran at that time was located on Jordanian soil. A Polish priest, Father J. T. Milik, was commissioned to translate and publish them. In the process, it became clear that it was not two different scrolls, but only one that had broken apart in the middle. The text on it was fundamentally different from anything that had been discovered before in Qumran and its environs. For it was not about biblical prophecies or apocryphal or canonical Scriptures or the rules of the community; instead, it was about the worldliest thing of all: a treasure of gold and silver. Apparently, as the Romans advanced in A.D. 66, all of the possessions of the Essene community were hastily hidden in sixty-four spots between Jerusalem and the Jordan. The copper scroll, which they hoped would last longer than parchment, neatly lists each one of these hiding places.

All of this was so specific that one researcher, John Allegro, was bitten by the prospecting bug. The moment he obtained an advance copy of the published text of the copper scroll, he started a search for gold using high-tech methods. But after five months he gave up; even when the description of the hiding places could still be understood by twentieth-century readers, it led to no discoveries. The Roman torturers of old were too skilled to leave the captured Essenes with their deepest secrets untold. More serious researchers, however, recognized the true value of the list of Essene treasures: It not only tells us how rich the community must have been, because everyone who entered it (as with a Christian monastic order) signed over his property to it;

most importantly, it provides us with a unique list of topographical
facts and ancient Jewish place names for the settlements of the Essenes
at the time of Jesus.

So Father Pixner gathered that the caves of Koziba were another place
inhabited by the Essenes. "At the source of the spring of Koziba", after all, was their thirty-fifth hiding place ("eighty talents of silver coins
and two talents of gold coins were buried there"). "Might this also
point to connections between Mary's parents and the Essenes?" the
Benedictine archaeologist asked logically.

One might still regard this as a fluke if it were not for a second
coincidence. For another hiding place, the fifty-eighth, was located at
the Bethesda Pool at the Sheep Gate in the northeastern part of ancient
Jerusalem; there is said to have been an Essene residence right next to
it. Moreover, it could very well be the house that was venerated in
early Christian times as the house where Mary was born.

This house is very easy for anyone visiting Jerusalem to find. The
northeast gate of Jerusalem, which leads to the Mount of Olives and
the Garden of Gethsemane, is also called *Stephen's Gate*, because since
the time of the Crusades it has been believed that the first martyr of
the Church, Saint Stephen, was stoned there. This place name, however, is rather recent; among the Byzantines, the *North* Gate (today the
Damascus Gate) was still called *Stephen's Gate*, not only because the
church over the holy deacon's tomb was located there but also because
it was the Sanhedrin's official place of execution—an old quarry whose
cliffs still loom behind a bus terminal. Jews today call the Northeast
Gate *Lion's Gate*, whereas Arabs have kept its old Byzantine name, *Bab
Sitti Maryam*, "Lady Mary's Gate". If you walk through this Marian
gate to get to the Via Dolorosa, then immediately to the right you see
a white limestone house, built in 1908, the entrance flanked by four
columns, with a black wooden door ornamented with artistic metal
fittings. A sign declares in Greek that this house belongs to the Greek
Orthodox Patriarchate and is revered as "Saint Anne's House". But
since most pilgrims cannot read Greek, clever monks have written the
really important thing in black paint over the entrance: BIRTH PLACE—
VIRGIN MARY! The visitor enters here and immediately descends a narrow staircase until he arrives at a cave in the rock, or, rather, a stone
cellar. It was customary in the Holy Land to carve entire rooms out of
the soft stone, even when houses were built over them, for only the
rock offered coolness in the hot summers. It is understandable that a

woman would withdraw to such a place in order to bring a child into the world. Then too, in Judaism, a woman was considered "unclean" for forty days after the birth of a son and for eighty days after the birth of a daughter. For that same interval, everything she touched and everyone who came into contact with her was likewise unclean; for that reason alone, a woman who gave birth retreated to a part of the house that was used less. Probably it will never be determined whether all this happened here or on the adjoining property, on which the stone cellar continues. The latter belongs to the Catholics, or, more precisely, to the French Dominicans. Over their part of the cellar, at least, stands a building with a wealth of tradition: what is today Saint Anne's Church was once the oldest Marian church in Jerusalem, built even before the Council of Ephesus.

As early as 420, a Byzantine church stood here; remnants of its mosaic floor are still preserved. Since it is decorated with crosses, it must date back to the time before Emperor Theodosius II, who in 427 forbade that motif for floor mosaics; to him it seemed impious to tread on the holy cross. Another Theodosius, the author of a pilgrim's guidebook to Jerusalem written around the year 520, declared explicitly: "Beside the Sheep's Pool is Lady Mary's Church." During the Persian invasion in 614, it was heavily damaged but by no means destroyed; a report that was drawn up in 808 for Charlemagne mentions five priests and twenty-five nuns who still lived there. It stood until the Fatimid Caliph al-Hakim, a fanatical Muslim, had it razed in 1009. When the Crusaders liberated Jerusalem, one of their first acts was to rebuild this church, which they now named after Saint Anne, the mother of Mary. Its dome was fifty-nine feet high—an architectural masterpiece in its day. The neighboring Benedictine monastery was soon so famous that queens and princesses traveled to it in order to do penance or to renounce the world forever. This changed abruptly when Sultan Saladin conquered Jerusalem in 1187; he ordered Saint Anne's Church to be made into a *madrasah*—a school where the Qur'an is taught. Consequently, it was inaccessible to Christians for centuries. Not until the Turkish period did the Franciscans negotiate terms (involving significant bribes) that allowed them, at least on the feast of the Nativity of Mary (September 8), to go down into the crypt and to offer the Sacrifice of the Mass there. Yet they were forbidden to set foot in the upper church. They had to make their way into the cave through a deep side window on the south side—the entrance that the Greek Orthodox Church uses today. Only in 1856, when the French stood by the Turks in the Crimean War, did Sultan Abdul-Medjid give the property to Emperor Napoleon III. Since then it has been the property of the French government, which the Dominicans are allowed to use. They not only restored the medieval church but also conducted extensive archaeological excavations on the tract of land in front of it. In doing so, they found, among other things, the ancient Bethesda Pool, the place where Jesus healed a lame man. (I describe in detail the circumstances and the spectacular results of the excavation in my book *Jesus von Nazareth: Archäologen auf den Spuren des Erlösers* [Jesus of Nazareth: archaeologists tracking down the Redeemer].) A visit to this place is a must for every pilgrim to Jerusalem and not only because the church is famous for its good acoustics and choral singing sounds especially moving there. When you go down a set of stairs from the right side of the nave, you arrive in the large, sixteen-by-twenty-three-foot crypt, which was built within the original stone cellar. Its altar is adorned with a marvelous icon of the Nativity of Mary.

Yet is it possible that two such important Christian holy places, Bethesda and the grotto of Mary's Nativity, should be so close to each other? Could Jesus in fact have worked his greatest miracle right beside his grandparents' house? Or was it all just a makeshift solution to an unsolvable riddle; did they just choose at random a place in which to build a memorial because everyone had long since forgotten where Mary really once lived with her parents?

The key to solving this riddle is the old name of the Bethesda Pool, which the pilgrim's guidebook by Theodosius called "Sheep Pool"! For the complex was not called *Beteshdatajin*, "House of the Twin Basins", until the third century B.C., when the high priest Simon had a second, southern pool installed beside the northern pool that dated back to the time of King Solomon. During the construction of the Herodian Temple, the pool was transformed into one gigantic *mikveh*, a bath for ritual purification, whereby the northern pool regularly provided the southern pool with fresh water through a system of underground conduits. The name *Sheep's Pool*, in contrast, recalled the fact that the *hanuth*, the market for sacrificial animals, was located here, at the northern edge of the Temple Mount. That was always the case; in the time before the Babylonian Captivity, as we gather from the Book of Nehemiah (3:1), the northeast gate of Jerusalem was still called the *Sheep Gate*. Until that time, and well into the early first century

A.D., sheep were sold there, which were later sacrificed on the altar of holocausts. Only in A.D. 28, with the completion of the "royal hall", a gigantic three-aisled basilica begun by Herod on the southern edge of the Temple Mount, was the sale of sacrificial animals transferred to that place. Everyone knows how Jesus reacted to that: with a whip he drove out the merchants together with the moneychangers (Jn 2:13–16). In the opinion of many traditionally minded Jews also, cattle and sheep had no business on the Temple Mount, since they defiled the House of God with their excrement. Commerce had therefore become more important than the cleanliness of the sanctuary; to Jesus, that was an outrage, which he vehemently denounced.

In his grandfather Joachim's day, however, things were different; then sheep and cattle were sold at the *Sheep Pool*. Is it not likely that he, a wealthy cattle dealer and owner of large herds of sheep, lived in the immediate vicinity of the cattle market, precisely where tradition situated the house in which Mary was born? After his death, he may have bequeathed it to the Essene Order, which would explain the mention in the copper scroll. Indeed, Essene hiding places in the northeastern part of the Temple city were rather unusual. After all, Herod had donated to the community the district in the southwest, on Mount Zion, where twelve of their treasure troves were located.

Further details are provided, not by the *Proto-Gospel*, but by a continuation of it that was handed down after the fourth or fifth century, the Jewish-Christian *Gospel of Pseudo-Matthew* (so called because it was falsely attributed to the evangelist). According to this document, Joachim was "of the tribe of Judah", while his wife, Anne, was "the daughter of Achar" and, indeed, of the house of David. This genealogical information was contradicted, however, by the usually well-informed Patriarch Eutychius of Alexandria (tenth century), who relied on older sources when he declared: "(Mary's) father was Joachim, the son of Binthir of the sons of David, the royal line, and her mother was Anne of the daughters of Aaron of the tribe of Levi, the priestly line." This is plausible, if only because Luke in the third Gospel explicitly classified a Levite family among Mary's "kin" (Lk 1:36), namely, Zechariah and Elizabeth, the parents of John the Baptist. Saint Paul, too, emphasized in the Letter to the Romans (composed around 57) that Jesus "was descended from David according to the flesh" (Rom 1:3), which can only mean through Mary and not because Joseph had adopted him. The Church Father Ignatius of Antioch (d. 117) confirmed that Jesus "was conceived in Mary's womb, according to God's plan of salvation, of the seed of David". Justin Martyr (d. 165), who was originally from Palestine, after all, emphasized that the Virgin "was lineally descended from David, Jacob, Isaac, and Abraham". The fact that the Essenes maintained regular contacts with the descendants of the Davidic and Aaronic lines is not surprising: after all, they expected that very soon—following the chronology of the prophet Daniel—these families would give birth to the two expected Messiah figures, the Messiah-priest from the House of Aaron and the Messiah-king from the House of David. The fact that Joachim of the Davidic line was said to be a wealthy cattle dealer should not surprise us, either; his distant ancestor Jesse, the father of the biblical king, owned large flocks of sheep, which he pastured on his meadows near Bethlehem. There is no reason why this land should not have remained in the possession of the family even after the Babylonian Captivity.

Not until the reign of the Hasmoneans was the greater part of the family forced to resettle in Galilee. This land west of Lake Gennesaret, which during the Persian era had been only sparsely populated, was conquered by King Aristobulus I by 103 B.C. and was Judaized by his successor, Alexander Jannaeus. The Jewish civil war, the brutally suppressed uprising of the Pharisees, was followed by an equally merciless hunt for potential agitators and pretenders to the throne. The Essenes had taken up residence in Damascus; members of the Davidic line had gone to Galilee, partly in protest and partly for safety's sake; perhaps they were even resettled forcibly by the Hasmoneans, in order to keep them under control far from Jerusalem. There they settled down on a lofty, fertile plateau, which offered a good view of the adjacent plain of Jezreel (so that the possible approach of the king's henchmen could be detected early). Because of its position, the town was called Nazar (from the Hebrew word "to watch"), a name that has a double meaning in written Hebrew. For *nzr = nazar* could also be read *nzr = nezer*, a word from the prophecy of the prophet Isaiah: "There shall come forth a shoot (Hebrew: *nezer!*) from the stump of Jesse, and a branch shall grow out of his roots" (Is 11:1). Thus the name *Nazar*, or Nazareth, also meant "Shootsville", which the Davidic settlers of course liked to refer to their lineage. And yet they struggled with their exile, with their life in a village in the rural north, so far from Jerusalem and the Temple, so far from Bethlehem, too, where, as they knew, the fate of their dynasty would be fulfilled and the Messiah would be born. It was a small town, maybe fifty stone houses, most of them built in front of or over caves that were carved out of the soft limestone, so that they provided warmth in the winter and cooled in the summer. Agriculture was central; there were extensive olive groves and vineyards, but crafts also, and a synagogue that was the heart of religious life: in it the male children of the families of Nazareth learned to read the Torah and other sacred writings. While the houses seemed poor and unadorned, perhaps because the townspeople resolved to be mindful of their exile, the tombs testified to the fact that they had not forgotten who they were. The rock tombs of Nazareth that were found on the property of the monastery of the Sisters of Nazareth are the most impressive necropolis in all Galilee. The largest of them, closed with a mighty boulder, resembled the tombs of the high-ranking nobility of Jerusalem and was worthy of the offspring of a dynasty.

After the hated Hasmoneans were driven out, we may assume that some men of the Davidic line ventured to return to Bethlehem; not all of them, of course, because flourishing Galilee still offered its inhabitants better opportunities. We may suppose, however, that Joachim moved to Bethlehem first, at the latest around 37 B.C., when King Herod ascended the throne, and that his life later revolved around Jerusalem, the terminal for sacrificial animals. Tradition maintains that his wife, Anne, was from Sepphoris, a major Jewish city only four miles distant from Nazareth. Aristobulus I had founded it in 103 B.C. and had given to this city perched on a hill, which was somehow reminiscent of a bird's nest, its picturesque name, *zipori*, which means in Hebrew "like a little bird". The Romans destroyed it in 4 B.C. to the last stone, but Herod Antipas rebuilt it shortly thereafter more splendidly than ever to be his capital and the "adornment of Galilee". However, during the reign of the Hasmoneans, it was already the most important city of the north. In the year 570, a pilgrim from Piacenza in northern Italy reported that he had visited the house in Sepphoris where Saint Anne was born; the Crusaders built there, on the western slope of the city hill, a three-aisled basilica. The Franciscans were able to obtain and uncover its ruins in 1870. In the process, they came across a mosaic floor inscribed with a dedication in Aramaic, which allows us to conclude that a Jewish-Christian synagogue once stood there. It recalls Joseph of Tiberias, son of Tanhum, a rich Jewish convert (before his baptism, his name was Judah), who received permission from Emperor Constantine the Great to build churches in Galilee. Epiphanias, a Greek monk

who recorded the story about him, explicitly mentioned Sepphoris as
one of his foundations. This proves how old the tradition about Saint
Anne's birthplace is; it must have been handed down by the *relatives of
the Lord* and in the Jewish-Christian milieu of Galilee, for there is no
talk about Sepphoris in the *Proto-Gospel* or in any other early Christian
source. Today the Saint Anne's Sisters run an orphanage on the site.

To return to the *Proto-Gospel*: Joachim fasted for forty days and
nights in Koziba, while his wife remained in Jerusalem, where she
lamented her loneliness and, even more, her childlessness. Then, however, prompted by a remark from her servant, she took new courage.
She set aside her mourning apparel, put on her bridal clothes, and went
into the garden of the house to sit down under a laurel tree. As she
squabbled there with God once again, an angel appeared to her and
said: "Anne, Anne, the Lord has heard your prayer. You will conceive
a child and give birth, and your offspring will be spoken of throughout the entire world." Thrilled by the good news, the Jewess took an
oath: "As the Lord God lives, whether my child is a boy or a girl, I
will offer it as a gift to the Lord my God." Then an angel appeared
to Joachim, too: "Go down from here; for see, your wife, Anne, will
conceive a child." The word "down" indicates that he was staying in
the caves of Koziba, in a cliff high over the stream. For otherwise, it
would have to read "go up to Jerusalem", since the city of the Temple
was in the mountains, several hundred yards higher than the Judean
desert. While still on the way to Jerusalem, he ordered his shepherds to
select for him twelve spotless lambs as a sacrifice for the Lord, twelve
calves as a gift to the priests, and a hundred male goats as a gift to the
people. And so the fourth chapter of the apocryphal work ends with
a scene that rather clearly favors the hypothesis of a house in front
of the Sheep Gate: "And behold, Joachim came with his flocks and
Anne stood beside the gate and saw him coming." He would not have
been allowed to drive a herd through Jerusalem, for the animals' dung
would have defiled the Holy City. Tradition says, of course, that his
wife waited for him, not at the door of the house, but at the *Golden
Gate*, the eastern gate of the Temple, through which it was said that
the Messiah would make his entrance one day. (In order to prevent
that, it was walled up by the Muslims in the seventh century.) The
Proto-Gospel, in contrast, says that Joachim waited until the next day to
go to the Temple and to offer his sacrifices. He now had every reason
to trust that God had taken his sins away and had heard his pleading.

That must have been in late November in the year 20 B.C. A few weeks and nine months later, according to tradition on September 8, Anne brought her long-awaited child into the world.[2] If the traditional date is correct, then it is in fact significant. For in 19 B.C., the eighth of September corresponded to the Jewish New Year, the first of Tishri in the year 3743. On that day, Rosh Hashanah was celebrated, which the Jews believed was the anniversary of the creation of the world, and, at the same time, Adam's birthday, the day on which one looks back at the past with remorse and asks God for a good fresh start—what day would be more meaningful as the birthday of the first new human being, Mary?

"My soul is exalted today", her mother, Anne, exclaimed as the midwife told her that it was a girl. Eighty days later—in Judaism a woman had to wait that long after giving birth to be ritually clean again—she gave her daughter a name: Miryam (in Greek: Mariam, Latinized: Maria).

At first glance, the name for the newborn girl was not particularly original. A glance at the Gospels gives us an idea of how popular it was in the years leading up to the Christian era: three Marys stood at the foot of the Cross. But there is another, more representative way to determine the frequency of first names at the time of Jesus, namely, by the ossuary inscriptions from Jerusalem. Ossuaries are stone chests for the purpose of a second interment. When a person died, his corpse was first wrapped in cloths and laid on the burial bench of a rock tomb. When his flesh had decayed, the bones were placed in a stone box that often bore an inscription with the name of the deceased. To save space, such boxes were then stored in narrow tunnels that were chiseled into the side walls of the tomb at ground level. A 1994 catalogue of the Israeli Antiquities Authority lists exactly 895 ossuaries; eighty of them contained the bones of Jewish women. One out of every four (that is, twenty of them) were named Miryam or Mariam. Martha (eleven times) and Salome (eight times) followed as the distant second and third most common names. Yet the meaning of Mary's name is disputed. In Hebrew, it might be composed of the elements *mir/mar* = "bitter" and *jam* = "sea" and thus would mean something like "bitter

---

[2] In some manuscripts of the *Proto-Gospel*, it is said that Mary was born "in the seventh month". But that is not conclusive proof that hers was a premature birth. It is more likely that this is a reference to the Latin name of the month of her birth, September, which etymologically means "seventh month".

sea". The affinity with the Latin *mare* = "sea" led the name Mary to be interpreted as "star of the sea". Moreover, the name contains the Hebrew root *r-y-m*, which means approximately "the one given (by God)", which in light of the circumstances of her birth would have been rather fitting. The verb stem *m-r-y* again signifies "to be fruitful". An interpretation of *Miryam* as "the exalted one" as a participle of the Hebrew verb "to lift up" is of course just as possible as the derivation from Aramaic in which *maryiam* is a form of the verb "to be wise/thoughtful" and *Mara* means "Lady, Mistress".

Of course, it is uncertain whether the name originally came from Hebrew or Aramaic in the first place. In any case, the earliest bearer of the name recorded in the Old Testament was Miriam, the prophetically gifted older sister of Moses and Aaron, who after the crossing of the Red Sea intoned the women's song of rejoicing (Ex 15:20–21). In Egyptian *mri* ("beloved") was a common prefix for women's names, usually followed by the name of a deity, for instance *Merit-Amun* = "Beloved by (the god) Amun" or *Merit-Ra* = "The Beloved of the (sun god) Ra". A combination of the Egyptian *mer*, "to love", with the Hebrew Divine Name *Yahweh*, abbreviated *Yam* (since it was forbidden to pronounce the Divine Name in its entirety), would also form the name *Meri-Yam* and mean "The Beloved (Woman) of God".

At that point in time, no one could have had any idea how well this name captured her entire being.

~

4

The Ark of the Covenant

The last day of the Feast of Booths, 21 Tishri 3742, according to the Jewish calendar (or October 8, 20 B.C., according to the Gregorian calendar), was selected by King Herod for an announcement of historical importance. It was the culmination of his efforts to lead Israel, after the days of the unpopular Hasmoneans, to unprecedented greatness and in so doing to surpass David and Solomon, the kings who were loved by God and the people. On this solemn feast day, Herod announced nothing less than the construction of the Third Temple—even though he did all he could to give the impression that he intended only to renovate the Second Temple. And that was sly, because it helped to safeguard him against the charge of arrogance. After all, every believing Jew knew that the construction of the Third Temple would mark the beginning of the Messianic age.

"I wish to show you now in just a few words that the work I presently intend to undertake is to be for the glory of God as well as for your renown", the king explained, although he did not forget to highlight his previous achievements: "Since I am now, by God's will, your governor and have had peace a long time and have gained great riches and large revenues, and, what is most important, since I have friendly relations with and am well regarded by the Romans, who, if I may so say, are the rulers of the whole world, I will endeavor to complete what our ancestors could not carry out, because they were under foreign rule, and thereby return pious thanks to God for the many blessings he has bestowed on me during my reign." But to his own amazement, Herod did not meet with a unanimously joyful response. Many Jews doubted that the king was acting with divine authority, and for that reason alone they considered his plan unfeasible. And what if the financial resources ran out? Would an unfinished building then stand on the Temple Mount, and would they be deprived of their sanctuary? Not until Herod promised to obtain all the necessary materials first before the old Temple was torn down and also guaranteed that the Jewish precepts would be followed to the letter, in their strictest form, did he succeed in silencing the skeptics. Did he mean by that the Essene precepts, as recorded in the *Temple Scroll* from Qumran? In fact, the many parallels between the *Temple Scroll* and what actually occurred then in Jerusalem suggests that he allowed the Essenes to cooperate at least in the Temple construction project and that the community from then on received special privileges in the Temple. Three years previously, he had already appointed Simon Bar Boethus (23–5 B.C.) high priest, whose family had fled from the Hasmoneans to Alexandria in Egypt. His sister married Herod, probably in order to strengthen the connection to the royal house. Simon could have been a compromise candidate who was acceptable to the Essenes also.

The Temple that Herod built became the most magnificent religious construction of his time. But he began his work only after he had acquired a thousand wagons to cart the stones, selected ten thousand experienced foremen, bought new vestments for a thousand priests, and had some of them trained in the art of stone-masonry and others in carpentry, so that no unworthy laborer had to set foot on the holiest ground. At first he had the new foundations laid and, later, the Temple platform enlarged also—from 656 by 656 feet, or almost ten acres, to 1,590 feet long by 1,030 feet wide with an area of more than 37.6 acres. This corresponded to the Jewish unit of area of 144 *dunam*, in which is hidden the square of twelve, the number of the tribes of Israel. Thus Herod created in only eight years the largest temple platform in the ancient world; the Acropolis in Athens, with an area of scarcely seven acres, paled in comparison.

Next, on these new foundations the Temple itself was built out of tremendous blocks of white marble, each of which was around 36 × 13 × 16 feet in size. The Temple was 174 feet tall and 144 feet long, whereby the central nave towered visibly over the two side sections. Its entrance was framed by golden grapevines and flanked by four mighty columns. "Now the outward face of the Temple in its front wanted nothing that was likely to surprise either men's minds or their eyes," Flavius Josephus gushed, "for it was covered all over with heavy plates of gold and, at the first rising of the sun, reflected back a very fiery splendor and made those who forced themselves to look upon it to turn their eyes away, just as they would have done at the sun's own rays. But this Temple appeared to strangers, when they were coming to it at a distance, like a mountain covered with snow; for as to those parts of it that were not gilt, they were exceeding white." This earned for it a name that outlasted millennia and finally became a Marian title: "House of Gold". For all its magnificence could not obscure the tragic fact about post-Babylonian Jewish Temple worship: the Holy of Holies, situated at the very end of the tripartite Temple building and always hidden from the eyes of the people, except for the high priest, by a thick, splendidly embroidered curtain, was empty. The Ark of the Covenant, whose entrance into the Temple is described so extensively in the Book of Kings, had disappeared sometime between the tenth and the seventh century B.C. Maybe, as the Ethiopians believed, Solomon's son Menelik had stolen it; maybe, as the Second Book of Maccabees maintains (2:1–7), the prophet Jeremiah hid it on Mount Nebo, or maybe it was still lying somewhere in the depths of the Temple Mount. But what was a Jewish Temple without the Ark of the Covenant? How could the high priest enter into the presence of God in the Holy of Holies on the Day of Atonement (Yom Kippur) if his mercy seat on earth no longer existed? Was the Temple worship centered on an empty Holy of Holies not ultimately a farce? Every believing Jew of the first century B.C. would have felt that this question was blasphemous. And truly, God entered Jerusalem again, when the "Second" (or Third) Temple in Jerusalem shone with new splendor. But that did not occur in the empty Holy of Holies but, rather, in a new Temple that came about at the same time in an even purer, more spotless way: Mary became the true "House of Gold", the new "Ark of the Covenant".

Mary's childhood is very closely intertwined with the building of the "Second" Temple. Not only was her father, Joachim, staying in Koziba, of all places, and her mother, Anne, near despair when King Herod announced his new construction plan. Since her parents' house was located by the Pool of Bethesda, Mary also grew up almost in the shadow of the Temple. The hammering of the stonemasons and the creaking of the winches was the background noise of her early years. The basis for her father's wealth was the sacrificial cult, which for another ninety years was to remain the central element of Temple worship—although in the year 30, God's Victim made any further living sacrifice as superfluous as the ram that Abraham found made the human sacrifice of his only son, Isaac. Yet if we are to believe the *Proto-Gospel*, there was another much closer connection between Mary and the Temple: as a little girl, she was entrusted by her parents to Yahweh's sanctuary—and remained there until she "came of age" according to the Jewish Law (that is to say, reached sexual maturity).

But this claim of the *Proto-Gospel* was vehemently disputed, indeed, was taken as an indication that the whole thing was an ahistorical fabrication that originated very late in a pagan environment. For "temple virgins", they thought, existed in pagan religions, but certainly not in a religious patriarchy like Judaism. Yet since the discovery of the Dead Sea Scrolls, experts have had to change their thinking in this regard, too. Thus, two of the leading Israeli Qumran researchers, David Flusser and S. Safrai, admitted as early as 1977 that such an institution very probably existed in the Herodian Temple. Not until 2004 did the American historian of religion Timothy Horner from Johns Hopkins University draw astonishing parallels between the *Proto-Gospel* and the tradition of the Jewish *Mishnah*. His study, *Jewish Aspects of the Proto-Gospel of James*, at any rate, confirms that "it makes use of Jewish images, originated in a Jewish environment, and addressed a public that tried to understand Christianity from a Jewish perspective."

Mary, so "James" reports, was already able to walk a few steps at the age of six months; credible parents have assured me that this is not altogether extraordinary (the times vary between six and eighteen months). Her mother, however, feared that she might defile herself; "she made a sanctuary in her bedroom and did not allow anything impure or unclean into it." When Mary was one year old, Joachim invited the priests and scribes and the elders of the people of Israel— in other words, the members of the Sanhedrin—to a feast and had the priests bless the girl.

Two years later, in the autumn of the year 16 B.C., the three-year-old Mary was solemnly brought to the Temple in fulfillment of her parents' vow. Christian tradition, as was mentioned, has a special feast day commemorating this event, the Presentation of the Blessed Virgin Mary, which is observed on November 21.

The custom of Jewish Temple virgins could go back to the judge Jephthah of Gilead, whose story is related in the Book of Judges. When the Israelite army was waging war against the Ammonites, he made a vow; if he survived, he would sacrifice to the Lord the first person who came out of the door of his house to meet him. It turned out to be his daughter, his only child, who joyfully greeted her father while dancing with a timbrel. It says explicitly that "she had never known a man" (Judg 11:39) and was therefore a virgin. Jephthah was dejected but felt obliged to carry out his vow. The girl, however, asked for two months' time in which to go with her female companions to the mountains and to lament her lost youth before Jephthah "did with her according to his vow which he had made". Did he perhaps offer the girl as a holocaust, as suggested in the German-language Unity Translation of the Bible and in the RSVC (Judg 11:31)? That is out of the question. Since Abraham's day, it was thought that God did not want human sacrifices; and since the time of Moses, they were explicitly forbidden; the Book of Deuteronomy describes it as pagan cruelty, "which the LORD hates[; the Canaanites] even burn their sons and their daughters in the fire to their gods. . . . You shall not do so to the LORD your God" (Deut 12:31). What happened, then, to Jephthah's daughter? She spent the two months that she had "bargained for", not with her beloved parents, but rather in the greatest possible freedom—with her female companions in the mountains. Actually, she did not lament the fact that she would lose her life, but only mourned her "youth", as it says in the Unity Translation, literally: "on account of her virginity". After all, the Torah speaks about a vow of chastity, the *nazirite* vow for women also (Num 6:2); it could be taken for a limited time or else for life (we know, for example, that James, the *brother of the Lord*, took a lifelong *nazirite* vow). A lifelong commitment to service in the tent of meeting (the precursor of the Temple) would have meant that she could no longer marry and, consequently, could not have any children, either. That was a real sacrifice for her father, too; having no offspring, as we said, was regarded by the Jews as a disgrace, and Jephthah's daughter was his only child, which made this doubly painful. In fact, the corresponding passage in the Book of Judges seems to serve not merely as an anecdote but as an explanation for the Jewish custom: "And it became a custom in Israel that the daughters of Israel went year by year to lament the daughter of Jephthah the Gileadite four days in the year" (Judg 11:39–40). The translator adds that these girls go "to the mountains", but that was probably true only of the time before the building of the Temple. Several things suggest that this later became an institution, that parents "sacrificed" their daughter "to the Lord" for a specified time or even for life and that these virgins consecrated to the Lord were described as "Daughters of Israel"—the same expression that we find in the *Proto-Gospel*, too.

There is proof, at least for the early period of Judaism, that there were women who served in the tent of meeting (and later in the Temple). Thus we read in the Book of Exodus about Bezalel, Moses' goldsmith: "He made the laver of bronze and its base of bronze, from the mirrors of the ministering women *who ministered at the door of the tent of meeting*" (Ex 38:8, emphasis added). The fact that such women's service still existed shortly before the founding of the Jewish kingdom in the eleventh century B.C. is proved by the Book of Samuel. Among the many shameful acts that the sons of Eli committed was the fact that "they lay with the women who served at the entrance to the tent of meeting" (1 Sam 2:22); the Lord punished the brothers by letting them die.

So it is more than likely that this female service was later continued in Solomon's Temple. Even though the Sadducees did not allow it initially in the Second Temple, and the Pharisees with their strictly patriarchal way of thinking and their strict precepts of ritual purity perhaps even rejected it, the Essenes, who were well informed about all the details of Jewish worship in the early period, must have advocated it. In Qumran, beside the main graveyard, archaeologists discovered a cemetery with equal numbers of men's and women's skeletons, but no graves of families or children; this indicates that, besides the educated "monastic order", there were also celibate men and women in the community, who lived in the vicinity of the monastery and probably were responsible for its subsistence. In fact, the "second community rule", the so-called *Damascus Document*, also mentions various "camps", one of which was occupied by the priests, the second by the Levites, the third by the celibate "children of Israel", and the fourth by the newly converted. "Virgins" are expressly mentioned as members of the third and fourth groups. When the Roman author Pliny claimed that the Essenes were "a solitary, strange people. They live without women, without money, and in the community of their palm trees alone", then this certainly applied to the Essene priesthood (in contrast to the conventional Jewish priests, who had families), but not to the community as a whole. Nevertheless, the Essenes, too, considered a sexually mature woman to be unclean during her monthly period and in the seven days following it, which made it impossible for adult women to be permanently integrated into the community and disqualified them from serving in the Temple. Therefore, we can assume that service in the Temple, where ritual purity was very painstakingly observed, was reserved for prepubertal girls. If the *Damascus Document* uses "children" as a collective term for the "Sons" and "Daughters of Israel", then this is the same terminology as in the *Proto-Gospel*. Mary, therefore, joined these "Daughters of Israel"! The memory of them died out in Judaism, like so much that we are now rediscovering in Qumran, with the destruction of the Temple; after that, Pharisaical Judaism alone set the tone. This is the only way to explain the fact that even today what is so clearly proved in the Torah and in the Books of Judges and Samuel is unimaginable for many Jewish scholars: that girls performed service "at the entrance to the tent of meeting" and of the Temple and that there were parents who entrusted their daughters to the Lord.

Thus the *Proto-Gospel* of James reports:

> When the child [Mary] turned three, Joachim said, "We should call the undefiled daughters of the Hebrews and have them take torches; let them set them up, blazing, that the child not turn back and her heart be taken captive away from the Temple of the Lord." They did this, until they had gone up to the Lord's Temple. And the priest of the Lord received her and gave her a kiss, blessing her and saying, "The Lord has made your name great for all generations. Through you will the Lord reveal his redemption to the sons of Israel at the end of time." He set her on the third step of the altar, and the Lord God cast his grace down upon her. She danced on her feet, and the entire house of Israel loved her.

Naturally the text exaggerates, even though it was said that the Jewish high priests, like the Essene priests, had the gift of prophecy. The description of how the three-year-old girl "danced on her feet" is just darling; families tell stories like that. But there is a deeper meaning to it, namely, the comparison of Mary with *Sophia*, the Divine Wisdom, which, as Proverbs 8:30 [Douay-Rheims] says, is "playing before him at all times" as God's daughter. It should be taken even less literally when the *Proto-Gospel* goes on to say: "Mary was in the Temple of the Lord, cared for like a dove, receiving her food from the hand of an angel." Maybe she lived with the "unspotted daughters of the Hebrews" in one of the four buildings that made up the "outer court of the women"; it is more likely that she and the others were lodged in a house of the Essene order near the Temple. (The fact that family traditions tend to exaggerate is certainly not exclusively an early Christian phenomenon.) In any case, they commended her "to the community of the virgins, who constantly praised God day and night", as we read in the Jewish-Christian *Gospel according to Pseudo-Matthew*. But besides "singing praises and keeping vigil", their duties also included manual work: "from the third to the ninth hour"—that is, from 9:00 A.M. to 3:00 P.M.—she was "busy weaving. . . . She wove woolen fabric diligently, and what the older women could not manage, she accomplished even at a tender age."

At some time between 10 and 7 B.C., when Herod was celebrating the thirtieth anniversary of his ascent to the throne, the actual new Temple building was completed; for one and a half years, the priests had worked on it under the direction of experienced craftsmen. "[The Jews] feasted and celebrated this rebuilding of the Temple", Flavius Josephus writes. "The king sacrificed three hundred oxen to God, as did the rest, everyone according to his ability." Now they started on the courtyards situated in front of the Temple and finally the Royal Hall, an extensive basilica on the southern edge of the Temple Mount. Not until A.D. 64 was the final work completed; six years later, in A.D. 70, the Temple already lay in rubble and ashes again after the Jewish rebellion was quelled by the Romans.

Shortly after the consecration of the new sanctuary, when Mary was twelve years old (in September of the year 7 B.C.), her service with the "Daughters of Israel" ended. "What then shall we do with her, to keep her from defiling the sanctuary of the Lord our God?" the priests asked as they were holding a council. According to the Book of Leviticus (15:19–31), a menstruating woman would not only defile everything she touched; she would be a catastrophe for the Temple and the whole people. We read there: "Thus you shall keep the sons of Israel separate from their uncleanness, lest they die in their uncleanness by defiling my tabernacle that is in their midst." According to the case law of the Mishnah and the Talmud, a girl was "of age" with the beginning of her periods or on her twelfth birthday, whichever occurred sooner. At the age of twelve years and six months, she was, according to the rabbis' terminology, "mature" (*bogeret*), and it was expected that she would be already married or at least betrothed. Usually a Temple virgin would be sent back home on her twelfth birthday, but by then Mary's parents were already dead; according to the Orthodox tradition, Joachim died at the age of eighty, when Mary was nine years old, and Anne two years later, at the age of seventy or seventy-nine. Only in the West, where this circumstance was not known, were stories told about Saint

Anne having two more husbands and images painted of her together with her daughter and the Child Jesus.

In fact, at that time Mary had only two living relatives, who were already elderly: a married couple, Elizabeth and Zechariah. The latter is described in the Gospel of Luke as a Temple priest "of the division of Abijah". Elizabeth, too, was "of the daughters of Aaron" and was perhaps a sister of Mary's mother, Anne. So it is not surprising when the *Proto-Gospel* says that the council of priests instructed "Zacharias" to make arrangements for the girl's future and to find for her a husband who was willing to take her in but also respected her vow of chastity. The text, which is based on an oral tradition, makes an obvious mistake when it gives the impression that Zechariah himself was the chief priest at the time. He was not, since we know that the high priest until 5 B.C. was named Simon Bar Boethus, as mentioned before. Therefore, Zechariah was not the one who prayed in the Holy of Holies for a sign of what God had in mind for the girl's future, for only the chief priest entered there, once a year, on the Day of Atonement in September. It was much more likely during a sacrificial offering at the altar of holocausts that Zechariah believed that he heard the angel's voice: "Go out and gather the widowers of the people, and have each of them bring a rod; she will become the wife of the one to whom the Lord God gives a sign."

This is reminiscent of an episode related in the Book of Numbers. In order to find out from which tribe God would select his priests, Moses had the leaders of the twelve tribes each bring him a rod on which was written the name of the respective tribe. Then he placed the twelve rods in the tent of meeting before the Ark of the Covenant. When he entered the tent the next morning, one of the rods had turned green; it sprouted, blossomed, and bore almonds. It was Aaron's rod, which represented the tribe of Levi. From that day on, the Levites served as priests.

Of course the *Proto-Gospel* exaggerates when it says that a messenger summoned the widowers from "all the countryside of Judea". It is much more likely that Zechariah looked for relatives who were willing to enter into this unusual liaison. Perhaps there were several "candidates", from among whom he had to select the right one. But since none of the rods brought by the widowers blossomed, Zechariah prayed for another sign. At that moment, a white dove came out of the rod of one of the men and alit on Joseph's head. Maybe he was in

Jerusalem at that time as one of the ten thousand experienced foremen whom King Herod had summoned to construct the additional buildings on the Temple platform. In any case, neither the *Proto-Gospel* nor the canonical Gospels leave any doubt as to his profession: He was a *tekton* ("builder"), which is generally translated as "carpenter", but in Palestine, where wood was scarce, it meant a master builder rather than a woodworker.

Critics like to accuse the *Proto-Gospel* of making Joseph an older widower just to make Mary's virginity appear more plausible. Yet the Gospels, too, indicate that he was in fact considerably older than Mary. In them he is mentioned for the last time when Jesus was twelve years old and went with his parents on pilgrimage to Jerusalem. When the Son of God began his public ministry, at the age of thirty-one, the Gospels speak only about Mary, which probably means that by then she had been a widow for some time. Unless we assume a premature death as a result of illness or an accident (for which there is not the slightest indication), advanced age is the most plausible remaining explanation. This in turn makes a previous marriage more than likely, for among the Jews a young man was usually married by the age of twenty at the latest. "A man who has not married by the age of twenty transgresses one of God's commands and calls down God's wrath upon himself", we read in the *Babylonian Talmud*. But if he had already married, he would also have had children, for childlessness was considered by the Jews as a disgrace, as we saw in the case of Joachim and Anne. The only exception at the time of Jesus was the Essene community, which was acquainted with celibacy for men and women. But there is to date no indication that Nazareth was an Essene colony, even though the descendants of David surely maintained close contacts with the Essenes. Consequently the *Proto-Gospel* offers here again a plausible scenario in a Jewish context. Nevertheless, it is probable that Joseph likewise took an "Essene" vow of chastity, at the latest upon his betrothal with Mary, if he had not already been close to the community for some time. The comment in Matthew (1:19) that he was "a just man" could certainly be interpreted along these lines.

While the *Proto-Gospel* emphasizes that Mary was a descendant "of the house of David", two evangelists, Matthew and Luke, say the same about Joseph. It is certain, therefore, that Mary was entrusted to a relative. Incidentally, it is striking that the genealogies of Jesus in the two Gospels are clearly different. That is peculiar, because it is well known that the Jews were especially careful about their genealogies; as late as the fourth century, as we heard, the *relatives of the Lord* still possessed the tables of their ancestors. Since Luke wrote a few years later than Matthew, we can assume that he was familiar with that Gospel. Why, then, did he not simply copy Joseph's genealogy; why did he run the risk of a contradiction that would necessarily be noticed by any halfway attentive reader? In Matthew, it says verbatim: "Jacob begat Joseph", or, in the Revised Standard Version (Second Catholic Edition):

> The book of the genealogy of Jesus Christ, the son of David, the son of Abraham. . . . Azor [was] the father of Zadok, and Zadok the father of Achim, and Achim the father of Eliud, and Eliud the father of Eleazar, and Eleazar the father of Matthan, and Matthan the father of Jacob, and Jacob the father of Joseph the husband of Mary, of whom Jesus was born, who is called Christ. (Mt 1:1-16)

Everything indicates, therefore, that Matthew is recording the ancestral line of Joseph; incidentally he also tells the Christmas story from the perspective of the foster father of Jesus. Luke, in contrast, wrote:

> Jesus, when he began his ministry, was about thirty years of age, being the son (as was supposed) of Joseph, the son of Heli, the son of Matthat, the son of Levi, the son of Melchi, the son of Jannai. (Lk 3:23-24)

Now there are three possible explanations for the apparent contradiction between the two genealogies, and ultimately they amount to the same thing. Obviously Luke describes the entire infancy narrative from Mary's perspective. Might he therefore have recorded the family tree of the Blessed Virgin, which later copyists erroneously applied to Joseph? A variant appears in later manuscripts (the phrase "the ancestors of Joseph" is *added*), but even in the oldest manuscripts, the foster father of Jesus is described as "the son of Heli". An argument for this interpretation would be that Heli is a short form of the name Joachim, which in Hebrew was actually pronounced *Eliachim*, and we know that that was the name of Mary's father. Nevertheless, we must not make it quite so easy for ourselves if we do not want to miss important indications.

A second explanation comes from the writings of Julius Africanus, a learned Gentile Christian who lived in Jerusalem and Nicopolis (the biblical Emmaus) at the turn of the third century. Since he was not

only a contemporary of the last *relatives of the Lord* but also explicitly
mentioned them, he probably was in direct contact with them. In his
writings, we read that Jewish law governing adoption was the reason
for the different genealogies. According to this hypothesis, Joseph was
an adopted child and therefore had two genealogies, one from his natural father, Jacob, and the other from his adoptive father, Heli, probably a relative who was descended from another branch of the house of
David. The example of Jesus shows that this, too, is possible. Although
all the evangelists agree that Joseph was not his natural father, the "carpenter" became his adoptive father through his marriage with Mary.
Through adoption, even a non-relative could attain the legal position
of a son, with all the prerogatives that that entails. The Jewish *Mishnah* (*Baba Bathra* 8:6) explains this unlimited right to adopt as follows:
"When a man says, 'This is my son', we should believe him." Thus,
theoretically speaking, Jesus would have been a legitimate member of
the Jewish royal house even without Mary's Davidic lineage, just as
according to Roman law Octavian became the "son of the divine Julius
(Caesar)" by adoption alone.

With that, Julius Africanus unfortunately neglects to explain who
this Heli or Eliachim was; apparently he was not that familiar with
the Jewish law of inheritance. For Mary, being the only child of her
parents, was a so-called *daughter-heiress* (see Num 27:8). Consequently
her father's possessions—at least the part that he had not bequeathed
to the Temple and to the Essene Order—were left to her; she, however, was obliged to marry a man from the same tribe, if possible even
from the same clan, just as the Book of Numbers prescribes (36:10–
12): "And [so] their inheritance remained in the tribe of the family of
their father." The husband of a daughter-heiress had to be enrolled in
the lineage of her father and thereby acquired, so to speak, a second
father. We find evidence of this practice in the Book of Nehemiah
(7:63): "Barzillai . . . had taken a wife of the daughters of Barzillai the
Gileadite and was called by their name." But if Joseph had become a
"son of Heli" by this legal act, then Luke actually recorded for us the
family tree of the natural ancestors of Mary and Jesus!

In any case, when Mary had just turned twelve, her uncle Zechariah
entrusted her to Joseph: "You have been called to take the Lord's virgin into your safekeeping." That was the equivalent of a betrothal. According to the Jewish law, the wedding was supposed to follow within
a year of the betrothal; moreover, in order to be married, a girl had to

be at least twelve years and six months old. A Jewish betrothal (*'erusin*) was in itself a legal act, a binding promise of marriage and fidelity. Until the wedding and the ceremony of "home-taking" (*nissu'in* or *likkuhin*), sexual continence was recommended but not obligatory.

But where was Mary to live meanwhile, since both her parents had already died? "See, [Mary,] I have received you from the Temple of the Lord. Now I am leaving you at home, while I go out to construct my buildings; later I will come back to you. The Lord will watch over you", Joseph supposedly said, according to the *Proto-Gospel*. His house was located in Nazareth, it is clear from the Gospel of Luke (Lk 1:26). It was a safe place; the neighbors were his closest relatives, among them the family of his brother Cleophas, with whom his own children may have lived, too. There Mary could learn to do household chores, which had not been among her duties as a servant girl in the Temple. In the winter, her betrothed promised her, they would be married.

And so Mary became the Virgin of Nazareth, who exchanged the splendid Temple of Herod for a simple stone cottage—and there she came closer to God than any human being had ever done before.

～

5

The Holy House

The house in which the greatest miracle in world history came to pass
—the Incarnation of the Son of God—stands today in Italy. But the
story of how it came there and how it lasted for two millennia in the
first place is a miracle, too. At any rate, nowhere on earth can the visitor penetrate so deeply into the mystery of Mary as in the Nazareth
of the Marches, in Loreto.

· Long before Lourdes, Fatima, and Medjugorje, the "Holy House"
(*Santa Casa*) was the most important Marian shrine in Europe. The list
of popes, emperors, and kings, and saints, too, who went on pilgrimage to Loreto is endless; among them are Popes Nicholas V, Paul II,
Pius V, Pius IX, Pius X, John XXIII, Paul VI, John Paul II, and Benedict XVI; the Holy Roman Emperors Charles IV, Charles V, and Fer-
dinand II; King Jan III Sobieski, Don Juan of Austria, the victor at
Lepanto, and Saints Charles Borromeo, Ignatius of Loyola, Francis
Xavier, Francis Borgia, Peter Canisius, Aloysius Gonzaga, Francis de
Sales, Benedict Joseph Labre, Thérèse of Lisieux, Maximilian Kolbe,
and Padre Pio. Yet even more impressive testimony of its importance
is the fact that in many major European cities true-to-scale copies of
the Holy House were built, for example, in Rome, Prague, Cologne,
Munich, and Salzburg—two thousand in all throughout the world.

In fact, no one who has ever been in Loreto can escape the charm of
that place. The visitor who comes by automobile, whether from the
north, driving past Ancona, or from Rome via Pescara, sees already
at a distance the cupola of the shrine, which is enthroned on a hill
and looms over the countryside, visible from afar. It was constructed
right before the Holy Year 1500, sixty-four years after the Cathedral
of Florence and a half-century before Saint Peter's Basilica. Since that
time, it has crowned the basilica that was begun in 1469 and rises over
the Holy House like a protective reliquary. Its white stone, with a light

shade of gray, stands out clearly from the intense green of the fertile
Marches, the endless fields of the farmers, and the deep blue of the sky,
which is reflected in the water of the Adriatic Sea. It is less than two
and a half miles distant from the coast. Consequently, it is so easy to
recognize from the sea that the popes, as the patrons of Loreto, were
concerned early on about the security of the shrine, the pilgrims, and
their sometimes magnificent offerings. Because the Turks made the
Adriatic Sea unsafe in the early sixteenth century, they developed the
Holy Hill of Loreto into a veritable fortress. To this day, the imposing bastion dominates the skyline of the little town, which still has no
more than 11,000 inhabitants. It serves as "a typical example of how a
shrine generates a city", because it came into being only to meet the
needs of the pilgrims. Before the shrine arrived, there was nothing at
all there; the nearest small town, Recanati (population today 21,000)
was located four miles away. Today a grandiose square welcomes the
millions of pilgrims from all over the world; it is flanked on two sides
by an apostolic palace, a work of the great architect Bramante; Pope
Julius II had personally sent him to Loreto in order "to do great things"
there. Toward the east, the square leads to the basilica; its simple, elegant façade does not reveal what it conceals deep within.

There is scarcely any shrine in the Christian world that is more international. In the heyday of devotion to Loreto, at the time of Blessed
Pope Pius IX, Catholics from the major nations were invited to set
up a wreath of altars that was supposed to surround the Holy House
like flower petals. So one finds here chapels designed by the Spaniards,
the Italians, the Germans, the French, the Slavs, the Poles, the Swiss,
the Americans, the Mexicans, and the Indians, each suited to the taste
of the respective country. In the center, however, directly under the
splendidly painted cupola, rises the marble shrine of the Santa Casa.

This marble shrine, too, Bramante's true masterpiece, is merely a
reliquary, albeit the largest and one of the most artistic in all Christendom. The visitor steps into it through a side entrance and is suddenly
in another world and another time—inside the Holy House, the place
where, according to tradition, an angel appeared to Mary, listened to
her *Fiat*, and announced the birth of Christ. Precisely this faith makes
Loreto one of the holiest places in Christendom.

The Holy House, the legend of Loreto maintains, was carried by
angels from Nazareth to the Marches. In 1291, as the Crusaders' last
bastion in the Holy Land fell and the infidels pounced on the Christian

holy places, they lifted it from the ruins of the half-demolished Basilica of the Annunciation that had been built over it and brought it first
to Tersato (today: Trsat), above Rijeka in Croatia. But the Croatians
proved unworthy of this gift from God, the legend says. When they
began to boast that they owned the Holy House, this displeased the
angels so much that after only three and a half years, on December
9, 1294, they carried it off again—this time to the other side of the
Adriatic Sea, to the vicinity of Recanati. In memory of the miracle
and to revere several stones that were left behind, the Croats built a
true-to-scale copy of the Holy House, which over the centuries became
the most important Marian shrine in the land; Pope John Paul II visited
it in 2003 during his hundredth journey abroad.

But during that same night, shortly after midnight on December 10,
1294, something incredible is said to have come to pass in Recanati:
"As deep silence held everything in thrall and the night had reached
the middle of its course, a light from heaven shone all around in the
sight of many who were near the shore of the Adriatic Sea, and a sweet-
sounding harmony of singers urged the drowsy, weary inhabitants to
look at the miracle," so Gottfried Melzer translates an old written account of the legend, "and they saw and gazed at a house, bathed in
bright splendor, supported by angels and carried through the air." So
half of the town came running and witnessed how the angels set the
Holy House down in the nearby forest of Laureta. Because the forest
was too unsafe, it was moved once again, and then a fourth time because the landowners quarreled about the votive offerings. Finally, it
settled into its final location in the middle of a road that led to the sea.

As wonderful and beautiful as this legend may be, there is a hitch to
it: there is no contemporary evidence for it. The earliest report mentioning such a miraculous conveyance of the Holy House was penned
by a supervisor of the shrine by the name of Pier Giorgio Tolomei,
also known as Teramano. It was written sometime between 1465 and
1472, which is a good 170 years after the event. Before that, there
were only the visions of Saint Catherine of Bologna (1413–1463), a
mystically inclined abbess, who was perhaps even the main source for
the alleged transport by air. A witness questioned by Teramano, a certain Rinalduccio, declared, on the other hand, that his grandfather had
heard from his grandfather that the Holy House had come to Loreto
"like a ship on the waves of the sea". Shortly thereafter, in 1485, the
scholar Giovanni Battista Petrucci remarked that the Holy House had

been "removed by force" from Nazareth, had crossed the sea and come into the possession of the Illyrians first and then of the inhabitants of the Marches, without angelic assistance. Thus the earliest depictions of the Holy House also show how it crosses the Mediterranean Sea on a ship. For this reason alone, the popes did not commit themselves, either, to the legend about its conveyance; although Pope Paul II was convinced "that this church came about in a miraculous way" (quoting verbatim a Bull from the year 1470), even Julius II, who had Bramante design the sanctuary for the Holy House, spoke in this regard only about "pious belief and legend" ("ut pie creditur et fama est"). No one disputes the fact that a church of Santa Maria de Laureto is first mentioned in the year 1313. At that time, several brigands were tried in court for having stolen monetary offerings and votive gifts from it, among other things the crowns of the statue of the Madonna and Child. There are even testimonies of German pilgrims from that time (1310–1318) who swore that they would travel "to see the miraculous Holy Virgin of Loreto". By this they meant the statue of the "Black Madonna", supposedly a work by Saint Luke, which was said to have come from Nazareth along with the Holy House.

Is it possible, though, that the legend has a grain of historical truth? The fact is that pilgrims to Nazareth since the sixth century have explicitly mentioned a house of Mary in which relics of the Blessed Virgin's garments were also venerated. "Saint Mary's house is a church, and people receive many beneficial effects from her clothing", wrote the pilgrim from Piacenza, who around the year 570 still encountered relatives of the Holy Family, Jewish Christians one and all, in Nazareth. Some of the handwritten notes of his *Itinerarium* are even more specific, adding: "The house is at the place where the large basilica is." A hundred years later (around 760), the Frankish bishop Arculf also reported from Nazareth that that was the place where "the house was built, which the archangel entered to greet Blessed Mary". We owe the most detailed description to the Cretan monk John Phocas, who visited the Holy Land between 1177 and 1185. He not only confirms that there was "a magnificent church" over the house of the Annunciation but also reveals its precise location: "Its left side, for instance, near the altar, is a cave, which does not open into the depths of the ground but, rather, appears to be [on the same] level. . . . And entering by this mouth into the cave, one descends a few steps and then sees the former house of Joseph, in which . . . the archangel announced

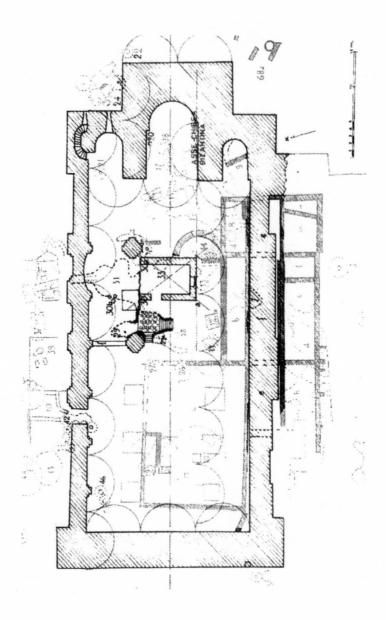

Ground plan of the Crusaders' Basilica of Nazareth and of the Byzantine structure that preceded it: The Holy House was situated precisely in the middle of it.

the good tidings (to Mary)." Then Phocas becomes even more precise: "To resume, there is in the place of the Annunciation a cross of black stone cemented into white marble and, over it, an altar, and on the right of this altar is shown a little room (*oikískos*), in which dwelt the Ever-Virgin Mother of God. On the left of [the place of] the Annunciation is seen another chamber, without light, in which Christ our Lord is said to have lived, after the return from Egypt, till the beheading of the Precursor [that is, of Saint John the Baptist]." Latin descriptions of this "house"—the word *domus* is always used expressly, while the adjoining Grotto of the Annunciation is described as a *spelunca*, a "little cave"—have been left by a whole series of pilgrims from the time of the Crusades; Saint Louis is said to have prayed there in 1251 after his release from imprisonment, and it is explicitly related that Francis of Assisi, during his pilgrimage to the Holy Land in 1219, came to Nazareth "in order to venerate the house in which the Word was made flesh." The last eyewitness account is the one by Ricoldo di Montecroce, a missionary of the Dominican Order, who visited the Holy Land in 1288, before he set out for the interior of Asia Minor. He found the Crusaders' Basilica of the Annunciation in terrible condition; at the command of the Sultan Bibars, it had been torn down by his troops in 1263. Apparently only the Holy House had been spared by the Muslims; after all, the Annunciation to Mary is mentioned in the Qur'an as well. Thus the friar reported that "of the almost completely demolished church nothing of the earlier buildings is left standing except a cell where Mary heard the angel's message; the Lord preserved it as a reminder of humility and poverty." Reports from this time were the basis of the *Libro d'Oltramare* ("Book about Overseas", as the Crusaders used to call the Holy Land) written by the Italian Poggibonsi in the year 1345, which still says: "Within (the city) there was a very beautiful church right at the place where our Lady's house stood when the angel greeted her. But now the church has been destroyed, with the exception of our Lady's room. Said room is very small and adorned with mosaics, and the house abutted against the grotto of rock."

But long ago that ceased to be the case, as we learn from Wilhelm von Baldensel, a German nobleman who came to Nazareth in 1332 as a pilgrim. He, too, found the church destroyed, but instead of the house or the room of the Blessed Virgin, only a lone pillar stood at the place of the Annunciation: "There, near a certain marble pillar, (the

Saracens) assure the visitor, the venerable mysteries were accomplished whereby God was made man." But what had become of the "cell" or the "room" that Ricoldo visited, the "house against the grotto of rock" of which Poggibonsi had heard? Evidently it had disappeared without a trace sometime between 1288 and 1332!

That there might actually be something to the—admittedly fantastic —story of the Holy House was determined as early as 1531 by building contractors, when they removed the supporting wall of bricks that surrounded its original walls. This in itself is already proof of the great honor in which the original walls of the Holy House were held even in the early fourteenth century and shows that the inhabitants of Recanati spared no expense in order to secure and preserve it. An ordinary pilgrimage church would have been torn down and rebuilt more magnificently! As the workers took out the floor, in order to lay the foundation for the heavy marble covering of Bramante, they discovered to their astonishment that the *Casa Santa* itself had no foundation whatsoever. It actually stood in the middle of an old road, while one part of its walls had crushed the hedges and bushes that once grew at the side of the road. A rosebush had even grown sideways toward the road beneath the wall of the house that rested upon it. This was confirmed in 1751, when Benedict XIV, one of the most learned and sagacious popes in Church history and a great devotee of Mary as well, ordered a new investigation. At that time, when the bishop of Loreto reached with one arm under the walls, he brought out acorn and hazelnut shells along with one dry nut. In 1921 a fire ravaged the interior of the Holy House and destroyed its precious *Black Madonna*—it was replaced with a copy, carved out of cedar wood from the Vatican Gardens. Afterward, when the architect Frederico Manucchi was commissioned to investigate the structure and to renovate the shrine, he noted in his report with astonishment: "Although the Holy House has no foundation walls and stands on soft ground without any solidity, which was also overloaded, albeit partially, by the weight of the vault that was built over it to replace the earlier roof, nevertheless it has outlasted the centuries without the slightest indications of settling or other damage to the stonework— this fact is surprising and extraordinary." Finally, in the years 1962– 1965, the Franciscans commissioned an extensive archaeological investigation of the Holy House, during which an underground passage was also excavated beneath its walls. Yet once again the finding from 1531 was confirmed: the *Santa Casa* does in fact stand without foundations on a medieval road.

This disproved at least the hypothesis of the critics of Loreto who considered the shrine to be a simple rural chapel, in which there may have been a Marian statue that was revered as miraculous. The very material out of which the house is built is evidence to the contrary. For in the Marches there are no quarries but, instead, plenty of good clay; thus people in the region formerly built almost exclusively with bricks. They used bricks even to pave the streets. The Holy House, however, at least the lower part of the three main walls, is made up of almost unhewn natural stones. That was how they used to build in the Holy Land, but not in the Marches! This fact struck Pope Pius IX, also; he was from Senigallia in the Marches and was particularly devoted to Loreto. As a young man, after fervent prayer in the Holy House, he was cured of the epilepsy from which he had suffered since childhood. So in 1857 he commissioned the Roman prelate and scholar D. Bartolini to investigate the building material used in the Holy House. For this purpose, the Roman official obtained stones and mortar from Nazareth and Loreto and submitted them to the chemist Professor F. Ratti with the request to analyze their properties and composition. Without knowing where the samples came from, Ratti determined that they were identical—both were composed of calcium carbonate with iron deposits. Not until March 2006 did the author Professor Giorgio Nicolini publicize the results of a more recent archaeological-geological study that the architect Nanni Monelli had conducted at the request of the Congregation of the Holy House in Loreto. The "apostolic altar" of the Holy House proved to be made of the same stone as the Grotto of the Annunciation in Nazareth; the material of which it is built displays the same chemical "signature" on the table of elements.

Yet the most remarkable findings had already been brought to light by the archaeological investigation in the 1960s. At that time the excavators found in a hollow between the stones of the *Santa Casa* five red cloth crosses, which proved to be an extremely significant discovery. For such cloth crosses were worn only by knights who went on a Crusade. They vowed that if they reached their destination safely, they would leave them in thanksgiving at one of the holy places in Jerusalem or Nazareth. The cloth crosses in themselves are therefore a clear indication that the Holy House originated in Palestine (the era of the Crusades ended with the eighth and last Crusade in 1270–1272, when there was no shrine yet in Loreto). But they are not the only proof for the authenticity of the Holy House. As the archaeologists determined, the natural stones of its three main walls showed traces of having been hewn in a zigzag pattern, which is typical of the masonry work of the Nabateans. In Herod's day, the technique made its way into Israel as well, for the king liked to employ construction workers from his mother's native region. More relevant, though, are the numerous letters and symbols ("graffiti") that were obviously scratched onto the stones by pilgrims. There are crosses, chi-rho symbols, alpha and omega and other Greek letters, and even the Greek inscription: "O Jesus Christ, Son of God". They were even able to identify two Hebrew characters, but not one single word in Latin or Italian, the languages that were spoken in the Marches. Capuchin Father Giuseppe Santarelli, who devoted his life to research on the Holy House, demonstrates in his excellent book *La Santa Casa di Loreto* [1999] that they are identical to the pilgrims' graffiti that were found in Jerusalem and Nazareth—some of them even on the site of the Basilica of the Annunciation!

In 1620, this plot of land had come into the possession of the Franciscan Order, which had to battle for over a century with the Ottoman rulers until it finally obtained permission to build a new church there. It was now focused entirely on the Grotto of the Annunciation, the cave in front of which the Holy House had once stood. It was smaller than the Crusaders' basilica and had been built in such haste and in adverse circumstances that it was not only bursting at the seams with the throngs of pilgrims in the postwar period but also had become dilapidated. So in 1954, the Order decided on a radical solution: the church dating back to 1730 should be torn down, and in its place an impressive, spacious new edifice should be built. Israeli construction firms received the contract for the job, as a sign of the reconciliation of Christians and Jews. But it was designed by two Italians: the brilliant architect Antonio Barluzzi provided the first sketch, which Professor Giovanni Muzio adapted to the local requirements. The grayish-white cupola was to be visible from afar, announcing the miracle of the Incarnation of the Son of God. Thus it resembles a closed lily flower, surrounded by two rings, which are reminiscent of a filigreed diadem and allow light to stream into the interior of the basilica. There could be no more successful combination of heaven and earth, light and matter.

But before the cornerstone to this masterpiece of modern architecture was laid, they took advantage of the unique opportunity to examine the entire site archaeologically.

The first things found by the Franciscan archaeologists, under the direction of Father Bellarmino Bagatti, were traces of extensive agricultural activity. Oil presses, cisterns, cellars, and silos, often interconnected by underground passages, were carved here into the soft limestone. Just a few yards north of the traditional Grotto of the Annunciation, there was a winepress chiseled into a rock. The grape clusters were trod in a trough, the must drained off into a small basin, and from there it could be conducted into an underground grotto or "wine cellar"; in its floor they found holes to accommodate amphoras. A small cave was used as a stall, and a manger or feed trough was carved into the wall. A series of rooms was partially chiseled out of the rock, partially built of stonework; a stone bench and an oven were located in one. Obviously an extended family had once lived there, which earned at least part of its living by farming. Shards of pottery revealed when that had been the case; the oldest came from the time of Herod. The Holy Land expert Gerhard Kroll summed up the results of the excavation as follows:

> It yielded conclusive proof that this site had been settled during the turn of the first century A.D. Therefore, the house in which Mary lived, which was built adjoining a cave, could have stood here. Even today there are dwellings in Nazareth that consist of two parts: a small cottage with a flat roof built up against a rocky slope and behind it a grotto hewn into the rock.

We can also quickly ascertain the place on which such a cottage must have stood, for the center of the whole site was obviously located in front of what was later called the Grotto of the Annunciation. The fact that it is wide open strongly suggests that it once had a structure in front of it, even though there are no remnants of it today. That must be because they are located now in Loreto. The tract of land around the present-day Basilica of the Annunciation was in fact part of the village of Nazar, or Nazareth, two thousand years ago, and stone houses very probably stood here: this is proved by a finding from the very recent past.

In November 2009, when the Mary of Nazareth International Center was about to be built by the French firm Chemin Neuf (New way)

right opposite the Basilica of the Annunciation, the construction workers made a spectacular discovery: they ran into ancient walls.

As the law of the State of Israel requires, the Israeli Antiquities Authority (IAA) was immediately informed, and it sent its archaeologist
Yardenna Alexandre to Nazareth. On site, as Alexandre inspected the
remains of the walls, the significance of this chance discovery was immediately clear. So she ordered construction work to be interrupted for
one month in order to use this time for excavations. Four weeks later,
on December 14, 2009, the archaeologist announced the results of her
investigations at a press conference on the site. Present were Barshod
Dror, director of the Northern District of the IAA, an expert represent-
ing the Franciscans, and a Latin-rite prelate stationed in Nazareth, then
Auxiliary Bishop Giacinto-Boulos Marcuzzo. This high-profile panel
gives some impression of the significance of the discovery and of its
importance for Christendom: For the first time in Nazareth, builders
had stumbled upon the remains of a house that was definitely from the
time of Mary and Jesus.

"The house was small and unassuming and therefore surely typical
of the town of Nazareth", the archaeologist declared. It had only two
rooms, which were arranged in an L-shape around a small courtyard.
Its walls consisted of slightly hewn limestone. The pottery shards that
they found were Herodian, but another discovery was even more relevant. Alexandre had found a series of fragments of ancient limestone
vessels, which in archaeology are considered a "Jewish index fossil".
Huge jars were carved out of limestone to store water that was used in
ritual purification; stone "measure jars" were used to draw water. But
this was so only in one clearly defined period of Judaism, when people
were conscious that the coming of the Messiah must be imminent:
after King Herod had announced the new construction of the Temple.
"Purity erupted in Israel", is how the Jewish *Tosefta* describes the situation then: the downright obsession of the Jewish people with questions of ritual purification, as it was defined in the *Halakha*. It ended
abruptly in A.D. 70 with the destruction of the Herodian Temple. The
discovery proves, therefore, that orthodox Jews of modest means who
kept kosher lived in Nazareth between 20/19 B.C. and A.D. 70. They
were obviously the immediate neighbors of the Holy Family, perhaps
even related to them. "Jesus would certainly have known this place
and this house", Yardenna Alexandre also declared.

Beside the house there was a small cistern, just as on the neighboring property around the Grotto of the Annunciation. Moreover, the archaeologists hit upon a well-concealed entrance to a cave. It was probably designed as a place of refuge, when Roman troops were deploying in Galilee in A.D. 67 to crush the Jewish uprising. The house apparently survived that time unscathed, for ceramic from the second century was found there, too. In its size and in the materials used, it is not significantly different from the Holy House in Loreto. Now the excavations are supposed to be incorporated in the Marian Center so that future visitors can see them. They will surely be part of the obligatory sight-seeing tour for all future pilgrims to Nazareth.

But what distinguishes the house that once stood in front of the Grotto of the Annunciation from this discovery and other possible future findings in Nazareth is the early cult venerating it, which the Franciscan archaeologists were able to prove. Their discoveries show that it had been transformed into a Judaeo-Christian shrine as early as the second or third century. Probably this happened after 135, when the *Lord's relatives*, like all the Jews, were driven out of Jerusalem and returned to the property of their family in Galilee. The fact that Jewish priests from the priestly class Pizzez also settled in Nazareth at that time is proved by a third-century Hebrew inscription that was discovered in Caesarea Maritima. It is also the first written evidence that confirms the existence of this town, aside from the inscription over the Cross of Jesus (the *titulus Crucis*, preserved today in the Basilica di Santa Croce in Gerusalemme in Rome). This alone allows us to conclude that the Mosaic laws were followed strictly in Nazareth at that time, by the Jewish Christians and the Lord's relatives, too.

At that time, the original residence of the Holy Family was obviously preserved but incorporated into a larger structure; the only remaining evidence of it today are the remains of one wall that runs parallel to the opening of the Grotto of the Annunciation at a distance of about forty-three feet. Within these walls there was a *mikveh*, a Jewish purification bath, that may have been used already by the Holy Family; in any case, it was now expanded into a baptismal pool. The archaeologists discovered a second, identical *mikveh*, which likewise had been repurposed as a baptismal pool, on the site of the neighboring Church of Saint Joseph. In both cases, steps had been added to the original design until there were exactly seven that led down into the pool. Furthermore, they were newly plastered, and signs were scratched in the still wet plaster: a cross with three points, little boats, a fisherman's net, a plant. These were

sacred symbols of the Jewish Christians, who were still quite familiar
with the mysticism and symbolism of the Essenes. Thus they believed,
according to the Church Father Irenaeus of Lyon (135–202), that the
Word of God descends from the seventh heaven and the soul ascends
to God in the seventh heaven. Bishop Cyril of Jerusalem (315–386)
has even handed down to us their baptismal formula: "Boldly you cross
then over the Jordan and climb up through the seven heavens into the
Promised Land. After you have tasted its milk and honey, you receive
the anointing of spiritual baptism." So it is not surprising that even
Saint Jerome in the late fourth century writes about the inhabitants of
Nazareth that they were "neither Jews nor Christians: with the former
they share their everyday customs and, with us, their faith." Not until
the early fifth century, after Emperor Theodosius had declared Christianity to be the state religion, did Byzantine Christians take control
also over the holy places of Nazareth. Now a monastery was built on the
site with a basilica, the alignment of which can be explained only with
reference to the Holy House. Without this "intermediate structure",
it would run parallel to the Grotto of the Annunciation at a distance
of sixteen feet, which really would make no sense. Another indication
that the *Santa Casa* was incorporated is the magnificent mosaic floor of
the Conon Grotto, a smaller cave west (to the left) of the Grotto of the
Annunciation. This was a memorial to the martyr Conon (or Konon),
who suffered martyrdom in the year 250 under Emperor Decius after
declaring: "I am from the town of Nazareth in Galilee, a relative of
Christ, whom I serve, as my ancestors did before me." It is possible
that he once lived in this grotto and looked after the Jewish-Christian
synagogue, and it is conceivable that he was also buried here; what is
certain, however, is that the Jewish Christians had already established
a *martyrion*, a memorial at this place. A certain woman named Valeria,
who probably came from Pamphylia, where Conon was executed, had
it artistically painted as a veritable garden of paradise with patterns of
ornamental plants and provided a dedicatory inscription. This must
have happened before the end of the third century, as the concept, the
style of painting, and the paleography prove, which allows us to ask
whether she was perhaps an acquaintance or a relative of the martyr.
Another Conon, who identified himself as a "deacon in Jerusalem",
had the courtyard in front of the grotto of his patron saint decorated
a century later with a magnificent mosaic. This mosaic extends a bit
farther in the direction of the Grotto of the Annunciation, until it

suddenly ends six and a half feet before the entrance to it. What else could have stopped it but the wall of the Holy House? If one projects the *Santa Casa* of Loreto onto the site and places it directly in front of the Grotto of the Annunciation, then the mosaic would come right up to its entrance—a meaningful and beautiful connection between the two shrines.

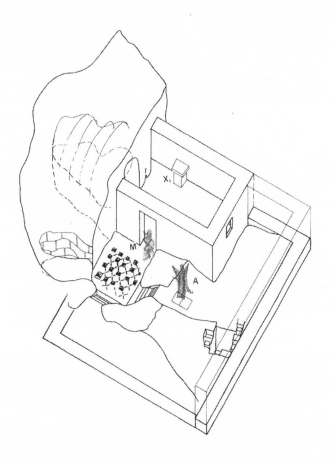

The Holy House fits perfectly in front of the Grotto of the Annunciation in Nazareth and would fill the intervening space between the preserved walls of the Jewish-Christian shrine and the rock face. A and M designate the position of the Mother of God and of the angel according to the account of the Proto-Gospel; X marks the spot of the "apostolic altar".

Another Byzantine mosaic that adorned a hall of the adjoining monastery was carefully removed by the archaeologists. In doing so, they made the most sensational discovery of the whole excavation. For the ground beneath it was filled with columns, capitals, and ornaments of the sort typical of Galilean synagogues in the second and third centuries. They counted eighty different architectural elements, which obviously came from the Jewish-Christian synagogue that once stood here and was later torn down by the Byzantines. These fragments were completely covered with graffiti, scratch marks, and mostly Greek letters, which resembled the ones that were found on the stones of the House in Loreto. Here they were again, the crosses and chi-rho symbols, the "M" or "MA" of Mary, the "Alpha" and "Omega", Christ's name in all variations, the names of pilgrims, and also short prayers and invocations that testify to Marian devotion long before the Council of

Jewish-Christian graffito from Nazareth, fourth century: "(Kneeling?) beneath the holy place of M(ary) I wrote there her (name and) venerated her image (eikos)." This is the earliest evidence of the veneration of a Marian icon!

Ephesus in A.D. 431. Thus a pilgrim, probably in the fourth century, scratched the Greek words XE MAPIA into the pedestal of a column; this is the abbreviated form of "XAIPE MAPIA" (*chaire Maria*), Greek for the angel's greeting. Another Greek graffito, scratched into the ornamentation of a column, even testifies to the veneration of a Marian icon in the fourth-century Jewish-Christian synagogue: "(Kneeling?) beneath the holy place of M(ary) I wrote there her (name and) venerated her image (*eikos*)."

If the plan of the Byzantine monastery church makes sense only with reference to the Holy House, this is even truer of the Crusaders' basilica. If the Holy House and the Grotto of the Annunciation supposedly were located in a crypt, as we gather from the reports of pilgrims, then the main altar of the church stood directly over the Holy House. The grotto, in contrast, lay beneath the left aisle at a not very prominent place. The Baroque pilgrims' church from the year 1730 situated it in the center for the first time—and set up its main altar over it.

But how precisely did the Holy House fit in the free space in front of the Grotto of the Annunciation, at the place where the so-called Angel's Chapel and the new altar are located? That is difficult to determine today, because in building the Baroque church, they ventured to make several encroachments. Fortunately for us, however, an exact report from the time before its construction has been preserved, specifically from the year 1625, when the final remains of the ruins from the period of the Crusades had to be carted away because of the danger of collapse. In the process, they came upon the original foundations of the house of Nazareth, as a formerly skeptical Franciscan, Father Obicini of Novara, notes in his bone-dry "Report on the acquisition of the Shrine in Nazareth" (*Relatio acquisitionis sanctuarii Nazareth*). Of course the Italian had heard about the Loreto legend and had already experienced all sorts of "doubts and hesitation"; for at first glance the *Santa Casa* seemed much too large for the intervening space in question. But let us listen to him:

> It seemed impossible to me that a wider object could fit into a narrower space. Therefore I proposed, in the presence of all these pilgrims and friars, . . . to carry out a thorough investigation, since I had with me a reliable plan of the Holy House of Loreto, which was printed in Rome in the year 1619. By no means could I harmonize the real, original space in Nazareth with this ground plan, for the former was around

four spans (36 inches) shorter in length and width. Whereas the Holy House of Loreto is reportedly 40 spans (30 feet) long, this space is only 36 spans long (27 feet); the former is 18 spans (13.5 feet) wide, while the latter is only 14 spans (10.5 feet) wide; as a result, I found no proportion and no agreement in such a serious, important matter. Therefore, although in all other points I was quite certain, I still had doubts and hesitation about this space. But God . . . supplied what was impossible to grasp and discover without faith. Since Father James of Vendome, the first Guardian of the new monastery of Nazareth, intended to renovate the part of the Angel's Chapel that was about to collapse—the part that had been located toward the west and the south, near the (former) door of the house—he had them excavate the old structure down to the foundations. Upon closer inspection thereof, they found that the foundation of the Holy House lay two spans wide apart from the other foundation. According to our discovery, the latter, likewise two spans wide, constructed of hewn stones, had been added by the early Christians on the inside to support the structure and to decorate the interior of the house.

When we disregarded the latter and started from the old and true foundation, drawing a straight line of measurement from it, the space in Nazareth was, to the great joy of all, found to be perfectly equal, as if a footprint, to the Holy House of Loreto, and by the grace of God the investigation yielded as its unerring result the exact correspondence of the measurements between the foundation and the walls, place to place, site to site, space to space, that is to say, between Nazareth and Loreto.

Therefore the *Santa Casa* in Loreto fit on the foundation in Nazareth as perfectly as an egg in an egg cup. Its three walls—the fourth wall is clearly an addition—and its windows and doors make sense only when we imagine the Holy House as a structure built in front of the Grotto of the Annunciation in Nazareth. Then the original door faces west, in order to catch the last rays of the sun before the onset of darkness, whereas the window for light and air is located on the south side, where it serves its purpose longest. In Loreto, in contrast, the door faces north and the window faces west, which is thoroughly illogical. But if it was in fact originally from Nazareth, and everything indicates that it was, then how did it come to Loreto, and by what route did it travel the exactly 1,384 miles as the crow flies?

The pretty legend that angels carried it halfway across the Mediterranean Sea, as we have seen, was first attested rather late and at that time was also in competition with another story: not angels but human beings accomplished the crossing, and they did so, not through the air, but rather, quite conventionally, on a ship. Evidence for this "reading" of the legend is provided by woodcuts and frescos from the fifteenth and sixteenth centuries, which show the Holy House on a ship, gliding through the waves or carried by angels who float over a ship. And in fact the solution to the riddle was in the Vatican. We owe it to Dr. Giuseppe Lapponi, the personal physician of two popes (Leo XIII and Pius X). He was originally from Osimo near Loreto and was more than eager to learn the historical truth about the transportation of the Holy House. Finally, Leo XIII allowed him to conduct research in the Vatican Secret Archives. On May 17, 1900, Lapponi informed a French priest-friend of his, Maurice Landrieux, later bishop of Dijon, in a confidential letter that he had made a valuable discovery. He had held in his hands proof that not angels but members of a Byzantine imperial family, the Angeloi, had rescued the remains of the Holy House of Nazareth from the Turks and brought them to Italy. In 1905 he entrusted the same information to the historian of antiquity Henri Thédenat and added that he had even discovered a whole file with documentary proof of this operation. In any case, the reigning pope, a strict defender of the tradition of Loreto, forbade the publication of his findings.

Not until 1985 was a purportedly long-lost document published that confirmed Lapponi's statements. The *Chartularium culisanense* was a collection of records of the Byzantine noble family of the Angeloi, of which the emperors of the Eastern Roman Empire in the years 1183–1203 were descendants. After the disastrous Fourth Crusade in 1204 and the conquest of Constantinople by the Franks and the Venetians, they moved back to Epirus (a region consisting of today's northwestern Greece and a large part of Albania), which they ruled as despots until 1318. Through the marriage of the Angeloi Princess Helena with Manfred of Sicily, one branch of the family had settled in Palermo, where the family archive was housed in the Palazzo dei Despoti in Collesano. Only when the line died out in 1860 were the documents handed over to the national library of Palermo, where unfortunately they were destroyed in a bombardment by the Americans in 1943. Luckily, though, a copy is extant, which Benedetto D'Acquisto, bishop of Monreale, was allowed to make in 1859 in the presence and with the permission of the last of the Angeloi, Prince Ortensio II de Angelis. The bishop was not only a learned Byzantine scholar but also the grand chancellor of a chivalric order that had been founded by the Angeloi. Through him, the handwritten copy finally arrived in the archive of the Santa Caterina Monastery in Formiello, whose abbot likewise belonged to that military order. There they would have sunk almost into oblivion had not the Italian historian Gian Marco Rinaldi tracked them down during his search for clues to the provenance of the Shroud of Turin.

But the handwritten copy of page 181 of the *Chartularium culisanense* proved to be at least as explosive. At first glance, it appears to be an inventory of the dowry that Nikephoros Angelos, Despot of Epirus, provided when his daughter Ithamar married the son of the king of Naples, Philip II of Taranto. But the second entry on the list already catches the reader's attention. He mentions "the sacred stones that were carried away from the house of our Lady, the Virgin Mother of God". Even more interesting is the time of the wedding: between August and October 1294, which means only two to four months before the appearance of the Holy House in Loreto!

In fact, while investigating the *Santa Casa* in 1962–1965, archaeologists discovered two medieval coins that were still stuck in the floor, one of them directly beneath one of the side walls. These were the only coins that originated at the time of the arrival of the Holy House, thereby confirming its traditional dating. They had been minted by Guy de La Roche, Duke of Athens from 1285 to 1308. Guy was the son of Helena Angeloi, the niece of Nikephoros and cousin of Ithamar Angeloi, who ruled the duchy when her son was not yet of age—that is, from 1287 to 1294. Was she responsible for the transportation of the Holy House? Were the "sacred stones" perhaps "temporarily stored" in the harbor of Rijeka before they were brought to their final destination? Did the Croats use the opportunity to keep a few stones as a "toll", so to speak, and to build their own Marian shrine according to the dimensions of the Holy House, before the ship left their harbor again? Or did the legend refer only to the fact that the precious relics remained *somewhere* in ancient Illyria for three years after they were salvaged from Nazareth in 1291? Actually, the Italian name for Rijeka, namely, *Fiume* (literally "river"), is first mentioned in a document from the year 1530, so we cannot rule out a misunderstanding. After all, there was another *Fiume*, in Greek *Potamo*, on the Island of Corfu, which was part of Epirus.

But why in the world was the Holy House brought in 1294 to Loreto, of all places? Dr. Lapponi gave a clue to the solution of this riddle when he explained that documents concerning its transportation are stored in the Vatican Archive. Quite obviously Philip II did not keep the precious dowry of his wife; in any case, no trace of these *sacred stones* is to be found in Taranto. Perhaps, though, being a very good Catholic, he wanted to give them to the pope. Now in July 1294, after a two-year *sede vacante*, a hermit was elected as the Successor of Peter. After his election, Celestine V, as he called himself, traveled on a donkey to the city of L'Aquila in the province of Abruzzo, and then Charles II brought him to Naples and built a wooden monastic cell for him there; he would never set foot in Rome. On December 13, 1294, three days after the "appearance" of the Holy House, he abdicated. His successor was the ambitious Boniface VIII, perhaps the "most Roman" of all the medieval popes.

The Vicar General who conducted papal business during the absence of the saintly and equally unworldly Celestine V, a Monsignor Salvo, was at the same time bishop of Recanati—the small town near which the "miracle" is supposed to have taken place. Is it all that preposterous to assume that he thought first of his own episcopal see when Philip II tried to sign over to the pope the *sacred stones* of the house of Mary of Nazareth? Since Recanati was part of the papal states, the donation remained on the pope's territory, after all, and no one could accuse Bishop Salvo of having enriched himself without authorization. Of course such an important shrine guaranteed streams of pilgrims in perpetuity, of which his otherwise utterly insignificant diocese could only dream. Perhaps he even started the legend of the miraculous transportation of the Holy House so as not to have to render an account in the future of why the precious relics remained in Recanati. After all, there was some truth to it: "Angels" did in fact bring the Holy House from Nazareth to Epirus and from there to Recanati. For the Greek word for "angels" is *angeloi*, just like the name of the Byzantine noble family.

This theory even gives a plausible answer, which is quite consistent with the legend, to the question of why the Holy House stands right in the middle of a road. The legend says that it stood at first on a hill overlooking the rural road, on land which belonged to the two noble brothers from Recanati. They, however, fought so fiercely over the donations and *ex voto* gifts of the pilgrims that the angels reacted abruptly and carried the house off once again; 164 yards away, right on the road to the sea, they set it down. These noble brothers were not just anyone; their names were Simon and Stefano, and they were the sons of the same Rinaldo Antici who accompanied Emperor Frederick II to the Holy Land in 1228, was appointed commander of the town of Nazareth, and perished while defending the town. Had Bishop Salvo for that reason entrusted to them initially the honorable task of protecting the Holy House of Nazareth, until they proved utterly unworthy of it?

Whatever really happened back in those days, the visitor to the Shrine of Loreto can be sure, in any case, that he is standing in front of an authentic relic. The stones of the Holy House, which obviously was rebuilt according to the true dimensions, are in fact originally from Nazareth. Here, just as there, the miracle of the Incarnation, whereby God became man, is perceptible; here, just as there, the words taken from the Gospel of John hold true: HIC VERBUM CARO FACTUM EST: Here the Word was made flesh!

~

6

A Virgin Shall Bear a Son

If we are to believe the *Proto-Gospel*, the Holy House was by no means the first or the only place of the Annunciation. Moreover, we learn from it something about the accompanying circumstances, which Luke withholds, limiting himself to the essentials.

One detail reveals to us that we are in fact chronologically in the years (or months) immediately after the completion of the Temple in Jerusalem. Only in that way does it seem plausible that a "council of priests" was held, as the *Proto-Gospel* says, at which they decided: "Let us make a curtain for the Temple of the Lord." This costly curtain protected the Holy of Holies, which only the high priest was allowed to enter once a year, in the sight of the ordinary priesthood and the people. Since the Temple was God's house, it had to be especially magnificent, but above all ritually clean: only unspotted virgins were allowed to work at it, and there had to be seven of them, corresponding to the sacred number. There were six Temple virgins immediately after Mary's departure, but no seventh; therefore, the high priest remembered her and commanded her "to weave the scarlet and the genuine purple". That must have been shortly before her trip to Nazareth, perhaps immediately after her betrothal, and perhaps also when she made a pilgrimage with her new family to one of the great Temple feasts. Commissioned handcrafted work such as spinning and weaving, according to Jewish custom, could be done only by a woman in her own home, while the remuneration belonged to her husband or fiancé. So Mary was supposed to take the precious materials with her and to do her work at home and then to deliver the finished fabric back to the Temple on her next pilgrimage to Jerusalem.

In Nazareth there was only one well, from which the whole village drew its fresh water, and it still exists today. It is located around half a mile north of the Grotto of the Annunciation at a square that then as now was the center of the town. Its water comes from a spring that wells up around 164 yards northwest of its present-day outlet in a cave eleven yards underground. A channel, nineteen yards long, conducted it to the oldest place in the village to draw water, and we can be sure that Mary, too, used it. She must have come there on every day that she lived in Nazareth.

Standing over the well today is a Greek Orthodox Church that is dedicated to the Archangel Gabriel. To spare the Muslim population of Nazareth the trouble of visiting this sacred place, a new well was built farther south, in the middle of the town square; in 1862, it was renovated and since then has been called Ain Sittna Mariam, "Mary's well".

The present-day church over the authentic Marian well was not built until 1750, but its history goes much farther back. Thus we find in the treasury of the Cathedral of Monza a ceramic plate with a depiction of Mary at the Annunciation and the Greek inscription: "Blessings from the rock of the water of the Mother of God", clearly a pilgrim's souvenir from the sixth century. Bishop Arculf, who visited Nazareth around the year 670, described not only the Basilica of the Annunciation over the Holy House but also another church "in the middle of the town built on two elevations . . . and arches set up between them. Underneath, between the two hills, it contains a very clear spring, which the entire populace visits, to draw their water from it. The water is drawn up in vessels by a windlass into the church that is built over it." Since the bishop from Gaul was unacquainted with the *Proto-Gospel*, he thought that that was where the house stood "in which our Redeemer was raised" and that it was obviously different from the house of the Annunciation.[1] Only later was the Russian Abbot Daniel, who came to Nazareth in 1106, able to make some sense of its tradition:

> We found a remarkable and rather deep well, whose water is very cold and to which one descends by steps. A round church named after the Archangel Gabriel covers this well . . . there the Blessed Virgin received the first greeting of the archangel.

---

[1] In any case, it is possible that Arculf referred, not to the Church of the Well, but rather to a cistern west of the Church of the Annunciation, the remains of which were excavated beneath the convent of the Sisters of Nazareth; over it a church was built fairly early, because the house and the grave of Saint Joseph were traditionally located there.

This church, too, was destroyed by the Turks at the end of the Crusaders' rule, but its ruins were incorporated into the masonry of the succeeding structure.

Today a miraculous icon from the eighteenth century shows what happened at this place. But it does not alter the fact that this authentic holy place is ignored by most Western pilgrims. Thus we find here, besides Greeks, predominantly Russian Christians, who in recent years have discovered the Holy Land. The fact that the Greeks like to call their shrine "The Church of the Annunciation" too, and the Arabic-speaking Orthodox even call it *bet Maryam*, "Mary's House", does not contribute to its popularity in Catholic circles but, rather, gives it the appearance of senseless competition, although it is not that at all. For even according to the *Proto-Gospel*, the actual event took place in the Holy House in front of the Grotto of the Annunciation. The visitor who walks through the middle nave of the Church of the Well, which is decorated with frescos by Rumanian icon writers, has to climb down six steps before he stands in the vaulted crypt. At the end of it, beneath a marble altar stone, there is a circular hole above the well, into which visitors like to throw coins. Others bring bottles with them and fill them with the blessed water. You can hear its gurgling, and it sounds like an echo from another era.

> Mary took a pitcher and went out to fetch some water. And behold, she heard a voice saying, "Greetings, you who are favored. The Lord is with you. You are blessed among women." Mary looked around, right and left, to see where the voice was coming from. She then entered her house frightened and set the pitcher down. Taking up the purple, she sat on her chair and began to draw it out.

So we read in the *Proto-Gospel*, which in the wording of the angel's greeting is almost identical to Luke's account. The reader of the English translation misses a lot, though. For the word *chaire*, which appears also in Luke's original text, is much more than an everyday greeting, more than the usual *shalom*, or "Peace be with you", that was conventional in the East; for it means "Rejoice" and provides proof of the uniqueness of this moment. In other scriptural passages, too, God's gracious action is announced by angels. In the Greek text, a pretty play on words follows, when it reads: "Chaire, kecharitomene", a word with the same root: *charis*—grace, favor, gift. No wonder Mary runs back into the house perplexed, indeed frightened, not suspecting what all that is supposed to mean. Only there did the angel whose voice she had heard appear to her; he spoke to her:

> "Do not fear, Mary. For you have found favor before the Master of all, and you will conceive a child by his Word." But as she listened she was asking herself, "Am I to conceive from the living Lord God and give birth like every other woman?"
>
> The angel of the Lord said to her, "Not so, Mary. For the power of God will overshadow you. Therefore, the one born from you will be called holy, the Son of the Highest. And you will name him Jesus, for he will save his people from their sins."
>
> Mary replied, "Behold the slave of the Lord is before you. May it happen to me as you have said."

We cannot be certain whether the author of the *Proto-Gospel* took the Gospel of Luke as his model here and deliberately changed the text of the Annunciation or whether we are dealing here with a parallel tradition. In any case, not only the points in common but also the differences are striking. For instance, in the account of "James" [whose name is the same as "Jacob"], the announcement that Jesus would "reign over the House of Jacob for ever" is missing. Maybe this happened so as to avoid the image of a "political" Messiah-king, which Jesus never intended to be, but perhaps also as an adaptation to the actual situation: for Jesus never really did begin his reign over the Jewish people, although he did so over the "new Israel", the Church. That is the only thing that the angel could have meant when he spoke about reigning "for ever": "and of his kingdom there will be no end" (Lk 1:33), whereas all worldly rule, even that of King David, ended with the monarch's death. But actually no such explanation is needed, for his name alone was agenda enough: Jesus, in Hebrew: *Jehoshua*, and in the Aramaic vernacular: *Jeshu*, means much the same as "God (Yahweh) saves." The same name was borne by Moses' deputy (we call him Joshua), who led the people of Israel into the Promised Land. And the Essenes, too, were hoping for another such Joshua, for a new annexation of territory and a new, sanctified Israel, when they founded their "desert camp" at Qumran. But what astonished Mary even more than the promise that the Messiah desperately awaited by all Israel would be born was the idea that the miracle of the Incarnation, God becoming man, was to

take place in her virginal body. For her as a young Jewish woman, this
was the real miracle, the unexpected, indeed, unprecedented thing that
was ultimately to distinguish Jesus from all who falsely claimed to be
the Messiah. It was also to become for posterity the "stumbling block",
even more inconceivable than the Resurrection, a *skandalon* that was
unacceptable for many. Thus, as early as the second century, as Irenaeus
of Lyon reports, aghast, a group of Jewish Christians who did believe
in Jesus as the Messiah nevertheless rejected the Virgin Birth. The fact
that they called themselves *Ebionites*, "the poor", points to an Essene
origin, for in the Dead Sea Scrolls the same name is used repeatedly
as a self-designation. They considered Jesus to be "the child of the
normal union of a man with Mary", the Father of the Church reports.
Perhaps the *Proto-Gospel* originated as a direct response to their heresy.

Mary's own doubts about the manner of her conception are at any
rate understandable, and they should be seen against the backdrop of
the Greco-Hellenic culture with which she must have come into contact in one way or another, both in Jerusalem and also in Galilee. Would
the LORD God then perform the act of begetting in a carnal form, as was
claimed about Zeus, for example? Of course not, the angel answered,
and to explain he used an ancient Jewish image. "The power of God
will overshadow you" sounds ominous only in English, whereas the
word choice in Hebrew points to an Old Testament parallel: it recalls
the cloud that hovered over the tent of meeting during the exodus of
the Israelites and indicated God's presence. Thus Mary in fact becomes
the tabernacle of the New Covenant, the "new Temple", the fulfillment of Israel, and the beginning of a new era of salvation. Nowhere
else is it so clear, to quote Joseph Ratzinger, that "the image of Mary
in the New Testament is woven entirely of Old Testament threads";[2]
the fact that all this supposedly happened while she was weaving the
Temple curtain makes this colorful image shine even more intensely.
This is the same Temple curtain that was torn from one end to the
other in the earthquake at Jesus' death (Mt 27:51), in order to reveal
the terrifying and equally gladdening truth: the Holy of Holies was
empty! God no longer rested upon his Mercy Seat in the Temple, on
the rock of Mount Moriah; he was hanging on the rock of Golgotha

---

[2] Joseph Cardinal Ratzinger, *Daughter Zion: Meditations on the Church's Marian Belief*,
trans. John M. McDermott, S.J. (San Francisco: Ignatius Press, 1983), 12.

on the Cross! And all that was made possible only through Mary's *Fiat* in the Holy House of Nazareth:

> Then Mary said: "I am the handmaid of the Lord; let it be to me according to your word." (Lk 1:38)

Never until then had a human being spoken words that had more momentous consequences—*Fiat mihi secundum verbum tuum*, in Latin. *Fiat*—"Let it be", "Let it be done"—was also the word with which God created heaven and earth in the beginning: "And God said, 'Let there be light'; and there was light" (Gen 1:3). Thus Mary's words lead us back not only to the beginnings of the New Covenant but to the creation of the world, and they make this moment in Nazareth a new creation. Now, the reversal of the angel's greeting *Ave* to *Eva* works only in Latin, of course, and was certainly not intended by the Greek-speaking Luke; nevertheless, it expresses a mystery that from the second century on (since the days of Polycarp of Smyrna, a disciple of the apostle John, and Justin Martyr, who died in 165) was understood by Christians: Mary became the new Eve. Through her obedience, she made it possible for us human beings to be redeemed from original sin, the disobedience of our first mother, Eve.

Justin Martyr, who was originally from Shechem in Palestine, wrote around the year 150 and, thus, at about the same time as the *Proto-Gospel* was set down in writing:

> We know that [Jesus] became Man by the Virgin so that the course that was taken by disobedience in the beginning through the agency of the serpent might be also the very course by which it would be put down. For Eve, a virgin and undefiled, conceived the word of the serpent and bore disobedience and death. But the Virgin Mary received faith and joy when the angel Gabriel announced to her the glad tidings that the Spirit of the Lord would come upon her and the powers of the Most High would overshadow her, for which reason the Holy One being born of her would be called the Son of God.

This doctrine, which in the second century had become a permanent article of the Christians' faith, was summed up as follows by Irenaeus of Lyon, a disciple of Polycarp: "The knot of the disobedience of Eve was untied through the obedience of Mary." Or, even more succinctly, in Saint Jerome's formula: "Death through Eve, life through Mary!" Pope Pius IX drew the logical conclusion from this teaching in 1854, when he defined the dogma of Mary's Immaculate Conception. As the "new Eve", Mary had to be as sinless as the Mother of all the living; she was already redeemed in advance through God's grace.

Yet the most provocative statement about Mary is itself missing from the *Proto-Gospel*. It is so subtly formulated that its wording was probably lost over the course of the oral tradition or else was reinterpreted as a simple question as to whether she was to bear a child like any other woman. We can trust Luke here, who was only half as far removed in time from the event itself when he quoted Mary as saying:

"How shall this be done, because I know not man?" (Douay-Rheims)

If we read only the Gospel of Luke, this sentence seems to be difficult to understand. Granted, Luke also reports that she was still a virgin, but concerning her previous history he reveals only this: she was "betrothed to a man whose name was Joseph, of the house of David". That sounds at first as though she were a completely normal country girl, specifically from "a city of Galilee named Nazareth". It would be expected of her that she would marry within a year and then have children, too—quite in keeping with the *mizwah*, the obligatory commandment of the Jews, among whom childlessness was generally considered a disgrace, as an offense against God's order to mankind: "Be fruitful and multiply" (Gen 1:28). In this context, however, her question would be more than astonishing, because one could actually assume that with the imminent wedding, nothing now stood in the way of the birth of a child. But Mary's surprised question by no means refers to the past, to the fact that she had thus far "known no man", but rather sounds strangely categorical. Precisely as if she would "know no man" as a matter of principle. Only in this way is it suggested to the reader of the Gospel that Mary was quite different after all. But why? The *Proto-Gospel* gives a plausible answer when it alludes to a lifelong vow of chastity and has Mary's mother, Anne, promise at the angel's annunciation of the birth of her daughter: "Whether my child is a boy or a girl, I will offer it as a gift to the Lord my God, and it will minister to him *its entire life*" (emphasis added).

But was such a vow imaginable in Judaism in the first place? This very question was disputed for a long time by critics of the *Proto-Gospel*. Yet there is certainly precedent for it in the Old Testament, in the First Book of Samuel; it occurs, moreover, in the story of Anne's namesake, Hannah, the wife of Elkanah. She, too, had no children, since "the LORD had closed her womb" (1 Sam 1:6), and so in her distress she "went up to the house of the LORD", that is, to the tent of meeting, where the priest Eli was keeping watch. He witnessed as Hannah swore: If God would send her male offspring, "then I will give him to the LORD all the days of his life, and no razor shall touch his head" (1 Sam 1:11). Finally God heard and answered her pleading; when Elkanah "knew" his wife again, she became pregnant and bore a son. She named him Samuel and entrusted him to the priest Eli, who raised him and instructed him in the faith. Thus Samuel finally became one of the great prophets of Israel, but also one who "as long as he lives . . . is lent to the LORD" (1:28), in other words, someone consecrated to God, a celibate.

The reference to the "razor" reveals that this was more than an individual decision: it was about a Jewish institution, the *Nazirate*. This involved an oath of continence that was usually temporary and only in rare cases lifelong, which also entailed renouncing haircuts and shaves. The rules for it are set down in chapter 6 of the Mosaic Book of Numbers, where it explicitly states that a woman, too, can make "the vow of a Nazirite, to separate [her]self to the Lord" (from the Hebrew *nezarim*: "consecrated man", "holy one of God"). A Nazirite had to give up not only wine, beer, and cutting his hair but also all contact with anything that makes a person unclean, such as dead bodies and bodily fluids, which naturally also implied sexual continence.

Such a vow of continence could also be perpetual or lifelong; this is demonstrated not only by the example of Samuel and other prophets, who likewise lived as single, chaste men, but also by chapter 30 of the Book of Numbers, entitled "The Keeping of Vows", which even gives an explicit, detailed description of women's vows:

> Or when a woman vows a vow to the LORD, and binds herself by a pledge, while within her father's house, in her youth, and her father hears of her vow and of her pledge by which she has bound herself, and says nothing to her; then all her vows shall stand, and her every pledge [of continence] by which she has bound herself shall stand. . . . And if she is married to a husband, while under her vows . . . , and her husband hears of it, and says nothing to her on the day that he hears; then her vows shall stand, and her pledges [of continence] by which she has bound herself shall stand. (Num 30:3–7)

Consequently, the Law of Moses, the Torah, already laid down, in a manner that is binding on all Jews, that even a married woman can remain faithful to a vow of chastity if her husband approves of it. Thus the consecrated life has priority over the duty to reproduce, even in Judaism!

The Temple Scroll of the Essenes, which was found in Cave 11 of Qumran, proves that this law was relevant in Mary's time, too. In column 53, it repeats the words from the Book of Numbers:

> A woman who makes me (God) a vow or binds herself with a formal pledge (of continence) in the house of her father with an oath, in her youth, and her father hears the vow or the formal pledge with which she bound herself, and her father says nothing about it, all her vows will remain in force and all the pledges with which she bound herself will stay in force.

After a lacuna, the scroll says what happens if this young woman marries:

> the oath of continence: her husband can declare it valid, (or) her husband can (also) annul it on the day that he hears of it.

If Joseph, as a widower who had already fulfilled his duty to propagate (or perhaps as an Essene?), had declared Mary's vow to be valid—and the fact that after her betrothal she still categorically ruled out the possibility of ever "knowing" a man allows no other conclusion—then Mary was bound by it for her whole life and was in fact *aeiparthenos*, "ever-virgin", as the Fifth Ecumenical Council in Constantinople in 553 declared as binding in faith for all Christians.

Actually, there are numerous indications in the Gospels that Mary "knew no man" even after the birth of Jesus. For instance, only Mary, Joseph, and the twelve-year-old boy Jesus seem in fact to have taken part in the pilgrimage to the Temple; brothers and sisters are not mentioned. Incidentally, for a mother there was no obligation whatsoever to undertake this pilgrimage; it involved an absence of at least fourteen days from home, a time during which she could never leave underage children alone back at the house. To the wedding feast in Cana, too, only Mary and her son, Jesus, were invited, who came accompanied by his disciples, but there is no talk about other members of her family. We have already noted the fact that the "brothers and sisters" mentioned in Nazareth and Capernaum were cousins; at any rate, the Gospels are careful enough to hand down to us also the names of their fathers and mothers. There is a reason, of course, for the fact that they occasionally accompanied Mary, too, for instance during the visit to

Capernaum: in Judaism it was unthinkable for a woman to travel alone
or even to leave her village or town unaccompanied. Moreover, it may
be that the relatives of the Lord left Nazareth together as a protest (or
were driven out) after their fellow townsmen nearly stoned Jesus. The
clearest proof, however, as we already said, was the situation beneath
the Cross. Naturally Jesus, as Mary's firstborn, had the duty of taking
care of the widow's future. Had there been other sons, this duty would
automatically have fallen to them; instead, though, he entrusted her to
the youngest of his disciples, John. It makes no difference that Luke
writes that Jesus was Mary's "first-born son" (Lk 2:7), for that was
true even though there was no second birth. In fact, the first son in
Judaism always bore the title *bekor* ("firstborn son"), even if no other
children followed. One proof of this is the Greek burial inscription of
a Jewish woman from the year 5 B.C., which was discovered in 1930
in the Egyptian Leontopolis, which reads: "During the birth pangs of
my firstborn child, fate brought me to the end of my life." The same
argument applies to the verse in the Gospel of Matthew that says that
Joseph did not "know" Mary (the usual biblical term for sexual relations) "until she had borne a son" (Mt 1:25). For in Semitic languages,
and also in Greek, the word "until", even after a negation, "very often
indicates only the limit within which the main action is being considered, without necessarily implying that something changed afterward",
as the linguist Klaus Beyer observes.[3] Thus, the Book of Genesis cites
God's promise to Jacob: "I will not leave you until I have done that
of which I have spoken to you" (Gen 28:15), without suggesting that
he would be abandoned by God afterward.

Nevertheless, critics of the Christian tradition like to maintain that
the theme of Mary's virginity was an invention of the evangelists
Matthew and Luke, based on an incorrect translation of the Bible.
In fact, Matthew—and he alone, since the reference is missing from
Luke!—sees the birth of Jesus as the fulfillment of the prophecy of
Isaiah to King Ahaz, who did not dare to ask on his own for a sign
that would restore hope to Israel:

> Therefore the LORD himself will give you a sign. Behold, a virgin
> shall conceive and bear a son, and shall call his name Immanuel. (Is
> 7:14)

Now, at the point where we read "virgin", the original Hebrew text
has the word *alma(h)*, which can mean both "virgin" in the biologi-

---

[3] *Semitische Syntax im Neuen Testament* I/1 [Göttingen, 1962], 132, n. 1.

cal sense and "young woman". Another Hebrew word, *betulah*, also has this double meaning. The difference is that an *alma(h)* is a virginal young woman who may be betrothed, while *betulah* designates a virgin who is not betrothed. In contrast, the word *isha* would be used for a married woman. When seventy (or seventy-two) Jewish scribes were commissioned by the Egyptian King Ptolemy II to translate Sacred Scripture into Greek for the famous library of Alexandria, they chose to render *alma(h)* with the Greek word *parthenos*, "virgin". According to this argument, that was the only reason why the early Christians, who were notoriously capable of anything, attributed to Mary a virginal conception and simply invented the pretty story about the annunciation by the angel for that purpose. What are we to make of this assertion?

First, we have to ask ourselves what Isaiah meant to say. Upon closer inspection, his prophecy consists of two parts, a long-term perspective that is supposed to encourage the harried king and concerns the future appearance of the Messiah and, then, a short-term perspective that would first fill him with "dread" and would "lay waste the land". Since the prophet was speaking about a special sign from God, he would hardly have meant a conventional birth. He did not mean an event in the near future, in the first place, otherwise he would have recorded the fulfillment of the prophecy; the queen did not have a son named Immanuel, nor did any person with that name appear during the prophet's lifetime. In the very next chapter of his book, the prophet refers to Israel as "the breadth of your land, O Immanuel" (Is 8:8). This is remarkable, because usually in the Old Testament, and of course in Isaiah also, Israel is considered solely as "the LORD's land" (14:2). This contradiction can be explained only if we identify Immanuel with God, the Lord. Actually, the prophet leaves no doubt about it: this Immanuel is the Messiah: "The government will be upon his shoulder, and his name will be called 'Wonderful Counselor, Mighty God, Everlasting Father, Prince of Peace.' Of the increase of his government and of peace there will be no end" (9:6–7). Besides, every day young women bring children into the world, and around half of them are sons. In contrast, very seldom does it happen that a virgin conceives a child—which in fact would be a miracle and a sign from God. The scribes who worked on the Septuagint must have looked at the verse in a similar way when they very deliberately chose the Greek word *parthenos*, "virgin", as the most accurate translation.

Some Jews who ridiculed the Gospels, but also Kelsos (or Celsus), a

Greek opponent of Christianity, were quick to explain away the "son of the virgin" as the "son of Panthera", who in legend soon morphed into a Roman soldier. Thus in the early twentieth century, there were still dyed-in-the-wool ideologues who claimed to identify a certain archer known as Panther mentioned on a Roman tombstone in Bingerbrück am Rhein as the alleged father of the Son of God, who thus was recognized as an "Aryan". As recently as 2006, the American Bible scholar James Tabor warmed over this, the oldest of all the "black legends", in order to spice up his thesis of a Jesus Dynasty and of a family tomb in Jerusalem with a scandalous whopper. But that only unmasks the malicious improvisation in the obvious anagram (the transposition of letters in the word *parthen-os* to make the taunting name *Panther-a*).

Actually, Christians were the first to refer Isaiah's prophecy to the Messiah. No traditionally Jewish source had ever dared to draw this conclusion; nowhere does it say explicitly that the Messiah would be the son of a virgin. Only the Essenes appear to have believed that the Messiah would be God's Son in an immediate sense. In any case, the *Rule of the Congregation* (1QSa 2:11–12) mentions that "God begets the Messiah", and in the *Aramaic Apocalypse* (or *Vision of the Son of God*) (4Q246), we even find an anticipation of the angel's words: "He will be called son of God, and they will call him son of the Most High", but in a negative context: the text refers to the Syrian tyrant Antiochus IV Epiphanes ("appearance of God"), who is thus declared to be the Anti-Messiah, so to speak. Yet generally speaking, it is typical of Matthew that he almost compulsively strives to discover Old Testament prophetic announcements of Jesus' deed. Often he succeeds very well, whereas in other passages the "predictions" seem somewhat arbitrary. But the very fact that he needed to "bend" the Old Testament evidence into shape reveals his intention: he wanted to prove to the Jews at all costs that Jesus is the Messiah, precisely because in many respects he was so completely different from what people had expected: for instance, a warrior to liberate them from the Romans. In his effort, the evangelist would never have dared to change the life of Jesus; too many eyewitnesses were still alive and knew very well what had happened. Instead, he interpreted the events in the light of the prophecies, convinced as he was that they can only have referred to Jesus.

But the best proof that Matthew and Luke did not come up with the Virgin Birth on account of Isaiah is found in the oldest Gospel, in Mark. There the inhabitants of Nazareth ask, after Jesus appears in their synagogue: "Is not this the carpenter, the son of Mary . . . ?" (Mk 6:3). This contradicts the Jewish custom of identifying a man as the son of his father, but not just that: Jesus is the only male Jew in all of Jewish literature who is named in terms of his mother! It is quite possible that in the Gospel of John, which originated independently of the Synoptic Gospels and often enough corrects them, there is another confirmation of the Virgin Birth. For even though John 1:13 in most modern translations refers to the "children of God" and reads in the plural ("who were born, not of blood nor of the will of the flesh nor of the will of man, but of God"), there is a second version in the singular, which a series of exegetes consider to be the original: "to him, who was born not of blood nor of the will of the flesh nor of the will of man, but of God". The fact that this version is attested already in the second century in widely separated regions of the ancient Church makes their argument plausible. The objection that the Gospels took as their model Greek and Near Eastern mythology, which is swarming with demigods and sons of gods, is swiftly refuted. For all the legends talk only about a sexual act of begetting in which a god assumes the form of a man or an animal in order to lie with a woman, who was perhaps a virgin before that night, but never afterward. A conception through the Holy Spirit, on the other hand, is unique in all of human history and mythology.

But when was it; when did the Annunciation take place? The traditional feast day, March 25, of course leads straight to the Feast of the Nativity of Our Lord, December 25. At any rate, in my book, *Jesus von Nazareth: Archäologen auf den Spuren des Erlosers*, I demonstrate that this date is neither attested early nor probable. The mere presence of shepherds in the field rules out a point in time between early November and early March, since in those months the sheep remained in the sheepfolds. Based on astronomical considerations—namely, the identification of the Star of Bethlehem with the supernova that was visible in the constellation Aquila ("the Eagle") in the northern sky from early March until mid-May in the year 5 B.C.—I dated the birth of Christ to the first half of March in that year. Given a normal pregnancy lasting forty weeks, the Annunciation must have occurred around the end of May or in early June of 6 B.C. This not only fits nicely with the old tradition of "May, the month of Mary" but also explains why Joseph was not at home, for construction work went on from spring until autumn. Probably Mary was entrusted to his care when he came as a pilgrim to Jerusalem for the Passover, like all believing Jews. She may even have spent the interval between her twelfth birthday (in September?) and the Passover feast, a good half year, with her uncle Zechariah and her aunt Elizabeth, to whom she later hurried immediately to tell what had happened to her. That squares well with the Jewish custom that a twelve-year-old girl had to be at least betrothed, which Zechariah would then have arranged.

Moreover, Luke gives the impression that, after the Annunciation, Mary decided on her own to travel to visit her relatives, when he writes: "In those days Mary arose and went with haste into the hill country, to a city of Judah" (Lk 1:39). That was, nevertheless, a distance of eighty-four miles, which was usually covered in three days, which a young woman in those days would never have ventured to travel without companions. It is much more likely that she took the occasion of an upcoming Temple feast to join a caravan of pilgrims from Nazareth and in that way to reach Jerusalem safely. That is likely because in the year 6 B.C., the Feast of Weeks, Shavuot, our Pentecost, fell on June 3. The *Proto-Gospel* adds that she had to go to Jerusalem anyway, in order to deliver to the Temple the scarlet and purple that she had finished weaving. Only after the priest had praised her for her work did Mary visit Elizabeth, who was pregnant.

Clearly, the *Proto-Gospel* assumes familiarity with the canonical Gospels and is concerned only with supplementing them. So we seek in vain the prehistory of Elizabeth's pregnancy with which Luke begins his Gospel. From then on, though, the two texts mesh like gears, and only when taken together do they give a complete picture.

As in the *Proto-Gospel*, so, too, in Luke an elderly married couple is at the center of the action at first, namely, the priest Zechariah and his wife, Elizabeth, and it says explicitly that she, like her husband, was a descendant of Aaron. Zechariah, we learn also, was "of the [priestly] division of Abijah". Consequently, he was not a Sadducee, a member of the priestly aristocracy that resided in Jerusalem, but rather belonged to the great majority of the priesthood who lived on the land and stayed in Jerusalem only during their weeks of service. Since the income of these priests was insufficient to feed a family, he must have pursued a secular career on the side, maybe as a vine-grower or the owner of a small herd.

Since the days of the Temple of Solomon, the priesthood had been made up of twenty-four *classes* or *weekly divisions*, each of which had a weeklong service twice a year, besides the three major Temple feasts. These priestly divisions are traced back to the twenty-four grandsons of Aaron, among whom the service in the Temple was originally divided (1 Chron 24) and who bequeathed the privilege to their descendants. After the Babylonian Captivity, when only four of the old priestly families returned, the original twenty-four priestly divisions were "replicated" among their members. The eighth one was Abijah (1 Chron 24:10), whose service fell in the months of May (8–14 Sivan, to be precise) and November (24–29/30 Cheshvan [or Marcheshvan]).

Every *weekly division* had from four to nine subdivisions, the so-called *houses of the fathers*, each of which, at least theoretically, performed service in the Temple for one day and thus formed a *daily division*. Every daily division assigned the various duties to its members in the early morning by lot. First, it was determined who would slaughter the lamb and sprinkle its blood and who would clean the altar of incense and the candlesticks. Then, in a second round of drawing lots, it was determined which priests had to bring the individual parts of the slaughtered lamb to the altar platform. The offering of the incense sacrifice, which was determined by the third lottery, was considered the most honorable task; the one making this sacrifice was allowed to enter the Temple, directly in front of the richly embroidered curtain that separated the Holy of Holies from the outer world. There, in the immediate and yet still veiled presence of God, beside a table for the showbread and the golden, seven-branched candlestick, stood the altar of incense, on which the priest who had been selected placed the incense. The fourth lottery then decided who would throw this part of the sacrifice from the altar platform onto the altar of holocausts.

At the time of Herod, there were an estimated 7,200 priests in the Temple, and so each priestly division had on average three hundred members. Therefore, usually a priest had the privilege of offering incense only once in his lifetime; once someone had drawn the lot, he did not participate again in the lottery for this duty. Rarely did it happen that this privilege was granted to an individual several times and only for very special reasons.

The incense offering was presented in the morning before the burnt offering and in the afternoon after it. The *Mishnah* depicts it for us in extensive detail. The priest who had drawn the lot took the large golden bowl, in which there was a small bowl with the frankincense, which was made out of 368 ingredients. He handed the bowl over to a brother priest, while he, after an admonition to be careful, entered the sanctuary. Inside the Temple, he devoutly placed the frankincense on the glowing coals of the altar. Then he threw himself down prostrate on the floor to worship God. In the courtyards, the people accompanied his prayer: "May the God of mercy come into the sanctuary and be pleased to accept the sacrifice of his people."

Finally he emerged from the Temple. There he was received by the four priests selected by him who had prepared his offering previously. Together with them, he raised his hands and pronounced the blessing over the people:

> The LORD bless you and keep you: The LORD make his face to shine upon you, and be gracious to you: The LORD lift up his countenance upon you, and give you peace. (Num 6:24–26)

When the lot fell to him to burn incense, Zechariah was already an old man. He and his wife, who was not much younger, had remained childless, just like Joachim and Anne, supposedly because Elizabeth was barren. In any case, Zechariah in the presence of God was probably praying also for a belated blessing of children, when, in the middle of the sanctuary, "on the right side of the altar of incense", an angel appeared. The elderly priest was frightened, but the angel reassured him:

> "Do not be afraid, Zechariah, for your prayer is heard, and your wife Elizabeth will bear you a son, and you shall call his name John." (Lk 1:13)

But Zechariah doubted these words. Too long he had prayed in vain; nothing had ever happened. And now, at her advanced age, his wife was to become pregnant? The heavenly messenger punished him for his disbelief by striking him dumb. When Zechariah went back out and tried to bestow the blessing on the people, he could no longer utter a word. Only through signs could he make it clear what had happened. That must have been on 29 Cheshvan, or by our reckoning on November 3, 7 B.C. Soon afterward, by our reckoning in December of the year 7 B.C., "his wife Elizabeth conceived" (Lk 1:24). Forty weeks later, in September of the year 6 B.C., shortly before the Jewish Feast of Atonement, Yom Kippur, John the Baptist was born. For every orthodox Jew, this feast is the conclusion of the ten days of contrition and repentance with which the Jewish year begins. But for little John it was the beginning of a mission centered on the call to contrition and repentance.

Three months before that, in June, Mary had come to the hill country of Judah. After her release from Temple duty, she herself had witnessed the events surrounding Zechariah, as the *Proto-Gospel* expressly emphasizes ("At that time Zacharias became silent"). The angel in Nazareth had cited the pregnancy of Elizabeth, who was now in her "sixth month", as proof that "with God nothing will be impossible." Who would be a better conversation partner, then, for the young woman who was still upset about what had just happened to her? Surely she sought also the counsel of her wise priest-uncle, who now could only write his answers on a slate.

The place where this is said to have happened is still today one of the most beautiful and peaceful spots in all Israel.

~

7

The First Advent

Ein Karem, "the spring of the vineyard", is located only four and a half miles away from Jerusalem. One hill farther on, we find the Holocaust Memorial Yad Vashem, which every German pilgrim to the Holy Land should have visited, if only to understand contemporary Israel. Before the horror of the Holocaust, that nadir of human history, all words fail. No one will ever comprehend the cruelty, the barbarity of which the henchmen of the godless Nazi regime were capable. The only comprehensible thing will be the determination of the survivors and of their posterity, their oath, to prevent it at all costs from ever happening again. There, before the eternal flame that commemorates the six million victims, Pope Benedict XVI laid a wreath on May 11, 2009, and recalled the names of the dead, whose "cry raised against every act of injustice and violence . . . still echoes in our hearts". These were gentle, almost poetic words, which he pronounced timidly, almost hesitantly, and at times with his voice breaking. Yet it was also an unequivocal statement that culminated in the words: "May their suffering never be denied, belittled, or forgotten!" Only someone who had hardened his heart would be unmoved by this appeal by the pope.

On that same day, I set out in search of the place where the *Magnificat* was proclaimed. So I drove to Ein Karem, with which I immediately fell in love. Anyone who wants to find peace in the Holy Land should travel to this blessed valley. Already from a distance I could see the golden domes of the Russian monastery gleaming on the hillside, which is separated from the slim tower of the Church of the Visitation only by a cypress grove a little below it. Then before me lay the hollow, surrounded by gentle hills covered with a pine forest, and in the middle of the low ground sprawls the town, stretched out in front of the church marking the birthplace of Saint John the Baptist. Small, tidy stone houses are surrounded by gardens, in which olive, almond, and orange trees, palms and pines grow. Vineyards were planted, at least in former times, on artificially constructed terraces. Paradise cannot have been a more delightful garden.

Actually Luke does not say a single word about Ein Karem. He speaks, as we noted, only about "a city of Judah" in "the hill country" (Lk 1:39). The Jerusalem calendar of feasts for the year 638 mentions "the town Enquarim" and "the church of the righteous woman Elizabeth" for the first time. Nonetheless, Theodosius knew around the year 530 that the place "where Saint Elizabeth, the mother of John the Baptist, lived" was less than five miles distant from Jerusalem, which is true of Ein Karem. But how reliable is the tradition that this was the place where Mary visited her aunt, where three months later John the Baptist was born?

The Franciscans who have resided at this locality since 1621 wanted to know that, too. In order to investigate the question archaeologically, they conducted extensive excavations on the site of the Church of Saint John the Baptist. As early as 1895 the friars had come upon the ruins of a three-aisled chapel, whose Greek inscription ("Hail, ye martyrs of God!") identified it as a chapel commemorating martyrs, without any clear indication as to which witnesses to the faith were meant. The cave tombs located under the rectangular apse went back to the Roman era, in any case. In 1941, the Franciscan archaeologist Father Sylvester Saller discovered to the right of the Byzantine chapel the ruins of a small church with a mosaic floor. It had been erected over stone terraces and an ancient wine press. A basin hewn out of the rock, with steps leading down into it, might have been a *mikveh*, a Jewish ritual bath, which would have been indispensable in a priest's house. To the left of it, under the walls of a Byzantine monastery, the ruins of a Roman building came to light. The oldest shards of pottery found there dated back to the Herodian era. Thus everything indicated that even before the birth of Christ there was a small farm on this spot, where vineyards were tended. There is no evidence to rule out the possibility that the priest Zechariah and his wife, Elizabeth, could have lived there. The earliest church probably stood over this place in the fourth century.

The most spectacular find that Father Saller made, however, was from the Roman era. In a rectangular excavation, he unearthed the marble torso of a woman. The fragment, twenty-eight inches long, was part of a ritual image of Aphrodite, the goddess of love, and was modeled on a statue by the Greek sculptor Praxiteles. The archaeologist knew that the Roman Emperor Hadrian had had a similar statue set up on Mount Golgotha in Jerusalem in A.D. 135. It was part of his policy of systematically paganizing Jewish and Judeo-Christian holy places in Palestine, in order to nip in the bud any Messianic movements among the Jews. The fact that a statue of Aphrodite was set up in Ein Karem also suggests that the site of the present-day Church of Saint John was considered a shrine as early as the second century either by the Jewish Christians or by the followers of John the Baptist. Of course, it will never be definitively determined whether the cave in the crypt of the church is in fact the place where Elizabeth brought her son into the world, where Zechariah regained his voice and, filled with the Holy Spirit, began to speak prophetically. It is plausible, in any case, because Elizabeth, too, would have sought out for herself during the time when she was "unclean" a separate room, perhaps a storage chamber.

Ein Karem, as further excavations by Saller and by the British archaeologist G. Ernest White showed, has been inhabited since the Middle Bronze Age. That is not surprising, since it is located near a spring, and where there are springs, human beings have always settled, too. Probably it is identical to the Karim that is mentioned in the Book of Joshua (15:59 NAB) as one of the towns "in the hill country" in the territory settled by the tribe of Judah. As Beth-Karim or Beth-haccherem ("house of the vineyard", so called in Jer 6:1), it became in the Iron Age the capital of the highland west of Jerusalem. But that might solve the riddle of why Luke does not mention the city by name but only vaguely speaks about the "hill country" (in Greek, *oreine*). For we know from Flavius Josephus that Judea was divided into eleven *toparchies*, or districts. According to Pliny, the author of the *Natural History* composed around the year 77, the name of the district bordering Jerusalem on the West was in fact *Orine*, Hill Country. Therefore, it was evident that a city of "the hill country . . . of Judah" could only mean the old capital of the district, Or(e)ine, Beth-Karim, modern Ein Karem.

The ancient spring that provided the locality with drinking water is today enclosed within a mosque. According to an old tradition, this was where Mary met her aunt Elizabeth, who, filled with the Holy Spirit, exclaimed: "Blessed are you among women, and blessed is the fruit of your womb!" (Lk 1:42). At that moment, the child in her womb leaped for joy, for he was right opposite his future Redeemer.

Mary, however, uttered one of the most beautiful prophetic prayers of all times, the *Magnificat*:

> My soul magnifies the Lord,
> and my spirit rejoices in God my Savior,
> for he has regarded the low estate of his handmaiden.
> For behold, henceforth all generations will call me blessed;
> for he who is mighty has done great things for me,
> and holy is his name. (Lk 1:46–49)

I stop for a moment and allow Mary's words to take effect within me. If she really pronounced this prayer and composed this hymn by herself, then Mary was not only inspired by the Holy Spirit but also had an extraordinary theological education. The latter is not impossible, although Jewish girls did not go to the synagogue school and as a rule could not read or write. Yet the surroundings in which she grew up, the Temple, and her kinship with the priestly tribe of Aaron and her wise uncle Zechariah perhaps made her an exception; at any rate, traditional Judaism was, after all, much less hostile to women than the Pharisaical rabbinate of a later age. On the contrary, in the Old Testament, we even find a whole series of strong, educated women, indeed, even prophetesses; Miriam, the sister of Moses, was only the earliest, while Esther was a more recent example. There was even a Jewish queen, Salome Alexandra from the dynasty of the Hasmoneans, who reigned from 76 to 67 B.C., a time considered to be one of the most peaceful and fortunate periods of Jewish history. Women were allowed to go to the synagogue, too, although while there, as Saint Paul noted in the First Letter to the Corinthians, they had to "keep silence in the churches [assemblies]" (which is unfairly held against him, since he was only citing a well-known Jewish rule). Thus, there were different opinions and interpretations: whereas the first-century Rabbi Eliezer, for example, maintained: "Anyone who teaches his daughter the Torah teaches her intemperance", his contemporary, Rabbi Symeon Ben Azzai, declared: "A man is obliged to teach his daughter the Torah." There were also women who could read and write, and this did not depend on their social status. So it is quite possible that Mary was acquainted with the song of praise of Hannah, the mother of Samuel (1 Sam 2), to which the *Magnificat* bears a certain resemblance. At least we can say that its "author" was not only her mother's namesake but also served as a great example for her. The magnificent song is also filled with quotations from the psalms and the writings of the major prophets and testifies to the greatness of the moment when Mary perhaps for the first time truly realized that she was privileged to have a part in God's plan of salvation. From now on the "handmaiden of the Lord" would crown the series of the servants of God in ancient Israel. Forever her words resound in this blessed valley, which reminds us of paradise lost and likewise of the future kingdom of God.

But another reaction is interesting, too: "When Elizabeth heard the greeting of Mary, the child leaped in her womb" (Lk 1:41). The verb "to leap" that Luke uses here is the same as the one that describes David's joy in the presence of the Ark of the Covenant (1 Chron 15:29). It is also always used in other passages of the Old Testament to express enthusiastic joy about the coming of God (for instance, in Ps 114:4, Wis 19:9, Mal 4:2). Thus the baby John, an unborn child in the sixth month, is in fact the herald of Christ: the first human being who recognized Mary as the new Ark of the Covenant, as the Temple of the God-made-man, indeed, as the cause of joy for all creation. And Elizabeth's amazement, too, has its parallels in the Old Testament. For when she asks: "And why is this granted me, that the mother of my Lord should come to me?" (Lk 1:43), this echoes the words of King David: "How can the ark of the LORD come to me?" (2 Sam 6:9). Now Mary was the new Ark of God's Covenant.

Here, then, at the well of Ein Karem, the Mother of God drew water for three months for her aunt, who was far along in her pregnancy. Here she herself probably reflected often on what plans God still had for her. Certainly as she walked she uttered one anxious prayer or another, but ultimately her heartfelt *fiat* always won out: "Let it be done to me according to your will!" Probably she stayed until the baby John was born; she witnessed how her uncle regained his voice; or perhaps she traveled back shortly before that. "Day by day her own belly grew. Mary then returned home in fear and hid herself from the sons of Israel." So the *Proto-Gospel* describes her homecoming.

After "three months", an interval that is specified in both sources, would mean in early September. Probably she participated in the Feast of Booths, too, so as to join a group of pilgrims afterward, with whom she traveled safely to Galilee. It was around her thirteenth birthday, even though some versions of the *Proto-Gospel* read: "She was (now) sixteen years old." The mistake is easy to explain. In Roman numerals, "13" is written "XIII" and "16" as "XVI". In a handwritten copy (and that

was the only sort at that time), the numeral III could easily become VI
and establish an incorrect reading from then on. Yet there was another
reason why this second reading was preferred, even though in a Jewish
context it was completely impossible (according to Jewish law, Joseph
could not wait for three and a half years for their wedding; it had to
take place within a year after the betrothal): Christians, unlike Jews
and pagans, were from the start against marriages that were too early,
which often enough were the result of parental agreements. Instead of
others making decisions "over their heads", girls should reach a certain
maturity and then select a husband themselves (or decide on a life of
consecrated continence). Since Mary was the model par excellence for
every Christian maiden, a higher age had to be assigned to her at her
wedding, for pedagogical reasons, so to speak. In that way, at least they
kept her from being cited as the star witness for child marriages.

At this point, there is a break in Luke's account, and he takes up the
narrative again with the Christmas story. Thus he spares us the details
about the premarital drama that played out a good three months after
Mary's return to the Holy House of Nazareth, when Joseph found
his chaste fiancée six months pregnant. On the other hand, Matthew
starts here, and of course the *Proto-Gospel*, too, in which we find an
even more detailed report: "When she was in her sixth month, Joseph
returned from his buildings. As he came into the house he saw that she
was pregnant", it begins. According to our calendar, it would have been
in December, when the winter rain starts in Israel and the construction
workers in fact could go back home for three months. Matthew depicts
his dumbfounded reaction rather cautiously: "Her husband Joseph, being a just man and unwilling to put her to shame, resolved to send her
away quietly" (Mt 1:19). For it was not merely a question of Mary's
good name; since he was betrothed to Mary, a relationship with another man would have been adultery according to Jewish law and, thus,
a crime punishable by stoning. Thus the author of the *Proto-Gospel* describes his reaction more dramatically ("Striking his face, he cast himself to the ground on sackcloth, weeping bitterly") and his misgivings
rather realistically, recording his inner debate as follows: "If I hide her
sin, I will be fighting the law of the Lord; if I reveal her condition
to the sons of Israel, I am afraid that the child in her is angelic, and I
may be handing innocent blood over to a death sentence. What then
should I do with her? I will secretly divorce her."

Actually, according to Jewish law, Joseph had two options in this situation; both are recorded in the Torah, or, more precisely, in the Book of Deuteronomy. If a man who had married a wife observed that she was no longer a virgin, then he could report this to the elders of his city. They confronted the bride's father first with the charge and gave him the opportunity to prove the contrary by presenting the bridal garment from the wedding night. If he could not furnish proof, "then they shall bring out the young woman to the door of her father's house, and the men of her city shall stone her to death with stones, because she has wrought folly in Israel by playing the harlot." In the case of rape, though, the assailant would be sentenced to death and the young woman would go free. In the case of a false accusation, on the other hand, the accuser was to be whipped and sentenced to pay a stiff fine of a hundred shekels (silver pieces), "because he has brought an evil name upon a virgin of Israel" (Deut 22:13–21). But since Mary had not been raped, any charge of adultery would have meant certain death for her.

The second possibility was divorce, which was expressly permitted by the Torah, "when a man takes a wife and marries her, [and] then she finds no favor in his eyes because he has found some indecency in her" (Deut 24:1). In this case, he simply had to write her a *bill of divorce*, which made it possible for her to remarry, even if the two were only betrothed, for betrothal was for the Jews the real legal act. In this document, he would not only certify his "dismissal" of the woman but also settle all financial questions. Jewish bills of divorce that have been found in Egypt prove that such divorces often took place with the mutual agreement of both partners. As Matthew implies, Joseph probably decided initially on this course of action, before the vision of an angel in a dream instructed him about a better one. The angel's words are handed down by Matthew and the *Proto-Gospel* in almost identical form:

Matthew: "Joseph, son of David, do not fear to take Mary your wife, for that which is conceived in her is of the Holy Spirit; she will bear a son, and you shall call his name Jesus, for he will save his people from their sins."

Proto-Gospel: "Do not be afraid of this child. For that which is in her comes from the Holy Spirit. She will give birth to a son, and you will name him Jesus. For he will save his people from their sins."

When Joseph awoke, the matter was clear to him: "He did as the angel of the Lord commanded him; he took his wife" (Mt 1:24), which can only mean that he married her. When this happened is left uncertain, in any case; the *Proto-Gospel* describes Mary even at the time of Jesus' birth as "his betrothed". "Mary the virgin has borne a child less than two months after she was married", says the *Ascension of Isaiah*, an apocryphal work that was composed around A.D. 100. Matthew, on the other hand, seems to suggest that Mary was not married even at the time of the flight into Egypt, when he quotes the angel as saying to Joseph: "Rise, take the child and his mother" (2:13; the same wording is found in 2:14: he "took the child and his mother by night, and departed"), instead of ". . . and your wife". Prior to this, in any case, the *Proto-Gospel* adds, there was another unpleasant scene.

Annas, who according to James was "a scribe" and probably the ruler of the synagogue in Nazareth (the likewise apocryphal *Infancy Gospel of Thomas* relates that Jesus played with his son), visited Joseph one day during this time to find out why he had not appeared in the synagogue. Joseph blamed everything on his weariness after the long journey, until Annas caught sight of the pregnant Mary. Immediately the austere man of faith suspected a scandal. When the men of Nazareth set out in December for Jerusalem for the Feast of the Dedication of the Temple (*Hanukkah*), he reported Joseph to the high priest: "He has defiled the virgin he received from the Lord's Temple." Sexual relations between the betrothed were not even forbidden in Judaism; it was regarded at worst as a premature act of consummating the marriage. But evidently Mary and probably Joseph, too, had taken a vow of chastity. For married couples, that was possible only among the Essenes (and then it was even frequently the case), but at least Mary, as we noted, came from an Essene background. The second problem was that both of them emphatically denied having "known" each other. When brought before the high priest, each one individually declared his innocence. Who was lying, then? Mary, because she had committed adultery? Or both, because they had broken their vow? Finally, the high priest remembered an old jealousy ordeal from the Torah that is described in the Book of Numbers (Num 5:16–31):

> "The priest shall bring [the wife] near, and set her before the LORD; and the priest shall take holy water in an earthen vessel, and take some of the dust that is on the floor of the tabernacle and put it into the water. . . . Then the priest shall make her take an oath, saying, '. . . if you have gone astray, though you are under your husband's

authority, and if you have defiled yourself, and some man other than your husband has lain with you, then . . . [may] the LORD make you an execration and an oath among your people, when the LORD makes your thigh fall away and your body swell; may this water that brings the curse pass into your bowels and make your body swell and your thigh fall away.' And the woman shall say, 'Amen, Amen.' "

The high priest subjected not only Mary to this ordeal but also Joseph, who was likewise accused. In order to keep them from defiling Jerusalem, the city of the Temple, he even sent them into the desert after they had drunk "the Lord's water of refutation". But both came back well, which was a sign of their innocence: "But if the woman has not defiled herself and is clean, then she shall be free and shall conceive children" (Num 5:28), the Torah declares. And so, too, the high priest exonerated Mary and Joseph: "If the Lord God has not revealed your sins, then neither do I judge you."

Despite the high priest's exoneration after a "divine judgment", the suspicion was still in the air later on, when Jesus' opponents accused him of being a *mamzer*, a bastard, which would automatically have made him an outcast from Jewish society. We find this polemic in the Gospel of John, which consequently also confirms at least that Joseph was not the father of Jesus: "They said to him, 'We were not born of fornication' " (Jn 8:41). But there was no sequel to the insinuation; in Jesus' trial, his social position made no difference. On the contrary: his Davidic lineage was now taken by his accusers as an indication that he was an insurrectionist making claims to the throne. Finally, the Sanhedrin could not annul the judgment of an earlier high priest that had confirmed Mary's innocence. So he died, exalted over all, as "Jesus of Nazareth, King of the Jews", on the Cross. Only the second-century Jewish polemic rehashed the charge of illegitimacy with the slogans about *Ben Panthera*.

But no sooner had they come through all these difficulties than Joseph was confronted by a new challenge: the census. The announcement of it is the second of the three events "anchoring" the Gospel of Luke in history. The first is the mention of Herod (in Lk 1:5), which reveals to us that the promise of the birth of John the Baptist took place sometime between 37 and 4 B.C. (according to our chronology, in November of the year 7 B.C.). The third dates the Baptist's first public appearance in the "fifteenth year of the reign of Tiberius Caesar", which most probably means in A.D. 27 (Tiberius was appointed co-regent by Augustus in the year 13). At that time, Jesus and John (the latter was only a half year older) were "about thirty years of age" (Lk 3:1, 23), which, combined with the first indication, places their birth in the years immediately before Herod's death, and therefore around 7–4 B.C. (according to our chronology, September in the year 6 B.C. and March of 5 B.C.). Whereas all that is fairly clear, the aforementioned second anchor in history seems at first glance problematic:

> In those days a decree went out from Caesar Augustus that all the world should be enrolled. This was the first enrollment, when Quirinius was governor of Syria. (Lk 2:1–2)

The problem is that the Jewish historian Flavius Josephus, our most important source for the history of the Holy Land until the destruction of Jerusalem in A.D. 70, mentions a census under Quirinius, too. It, however, took place, not during the time of Herod, but rather after the dethronement of his son and successor, Archelaus, in A.D. 6, when Judea became a Roman province under the governance of an imperial prefect. Such fiscal stock-taking occurred in every new province, so as to be able to estimate future tax revenues. For that reason alone, this census met with vehement resistance among the Jews, who did not want to be subject to any foreign rule. Thus it led to the rise of a resistance movement of the so-called Zealots, especially in the northern part of the country. Their leader was Judas the Galilean, and alongside him stood a priest named Zadok, which certainly could suggest a Messianic character of the Jewish *Résistance*. Of course the possibility that Jesus was not born until that point in time is ruled out, for that would mean that in A.D. 27, instead of being "about thirty", he would have been just twenty-one years old; too young to be addressed as *Rabbi* ("Master") by the Jews. After all, in Judaism a man had to be at least thirty in order to participate in disputes about the Torah, and none of Jesus' opponents accused him of being too young; although they did scoff at him, saying that he was "not yet fifty years old" and claimed to have seen Abraham (Jn 8:57). What was the census under Quirinius doing, then, in the Gospel? Biblical criticism made quick work of the riddle: Luke had arbitrarily incorporated the census into his story about the birth of Jesus as an excuse for having the Holy Family travel to Bethlehem, where, according to the Jewish tradition, the Messiah was to be born. And if he was already spinning tales, then is it not easy to conclude that other elements of the narrative are, to put it politely, "legendary" and that Jesus in reality was born quite unspectacularly in Nazareth?

Now what occurred in A.D. 6 was not a general census but, rather, as we said, an initial assessment of a province, as it was to take place every fourteen years from then on. A simultaneous tax appraisal throughout the empire, as readers like to imagine in reading the Nativity Gospel, never happened anyway; the sheer size of the realm governed by Rome would have made it unfeasible. But Luke does not say that all the inhabitants of the *Imperium Romanum* were assessed at the same time; he just mentions the "decree" of Augustus, which was valid for all imperial citizens. And that did in fact exist, as contemporary chroniclers attest. Thus, the Roman Tacitus reports in his *Annals* that Augustus had made a careful accounting of "the national wealth, the number of enrolled citizens and allies, of the fleets, kingdoms, and provinces, of the taxes and tributes". Dio Cassius, too, notes: "Augustus sent some men here, and others there, to record the personal property and that of the cities." This was confirmed by the *Res gestae*, the emperor's statement of accounts, which was stored in the Temple of Vesta in Rome; he had copies of it posted in all the Augustan Temples in the empire. One of them, discovered as early as 1555 on the walls of the Augustan Temple in Ankyra in Galatia (modern Ankara in Turkey), is preserved to this day. Its very first words are reminiscent of Luke: "The deeds of Augustus, through which he subjected the entire world to the rule of the Roman people". Three censuses are explicitly mentioned, which he ordered in the years 28 B.C., 8/7 B.C., and A.D. 14. At any rate, they concerned only Roman citizens, of whom there were more than four million throughout the empire. Besides this there were counts of all who were obliged to pay tax, in the provinces as well as in the vassal states (those subject to taxation!) and, therefore, also in Herod's kingdom. Thus we know, for example, that in the neighboring state, the Nabatean kingdom, which had the same legal status, around the year 6 B.C. a certain Fabatus went to work, whom our source— Flavius Josephus—expressly describes as *dioketes*, as a Roman tax collector. There is no reason to assume that the kingdom of Judea was treated differently. In fact, the Roman advocate and Christian apologist Tertullian, who did research in the late second century in the Roman state records, confirmed that such a census took place in Judea under the governor Gaius Sentius Saturninus (8–5 B.C.). Flavius Josephus not only mentions this Saturninus but also describes him as Herod's "superior". How dependent Herod was on Rome as *rex socius* was evident in 8 B.C., when he fell into disfavor with Augustus. Without asking the emperor first for permission, he had undertaken a lightning-fast military campaign against the neighboring kingdom of the Nabateans, another vassal of Rome. This resulted in a severe censure: Augustus conveyed to him the message that until then "he had regarded him as a friend, but in the future he would treat him as a mere subject." Even when he wanted to put his own sons along with the Hasmonean Princess Mariamne on trial for high treason, he had to obtain the emperor's permission first. The trial was finally held around the year 7 B.C. in Berytos (Beirut), with the aforesaid governor Saturninus presiding. The sons of Mariamne were then found guilty and executed, and Herod's son Antipater was declared the sole heir to the throne. Then, at the very latest, Herod in return must have conceded to allow a census.

Indeed, Flavius Josephus tells of an oath of loyalty to "the Caesar (Augustus) and his King (Herod)", which the entire Jewish people had to take sometime between 6 and 5 B.C. Six thousand Jews refused and were therefore fined, which indicates how systematically they had proceeded. There must have been lists of names, therefore, and the oath must have been taken by each Jew individually in the presence of witnesses—officials of the king. It goes without saying that they were interrogated about their property and lineage, and maybe the oath itself was only a propagandistic pretext to show the people, but not too clearly, that the sellout of their homeland to Rome had long since begun. In any case, in Josephus we read that immediately after Herod's death in March of 4 B.C., the emperor granted the Samaritans tax deductions; therefore, definite numbers must have been available long before then.

The question about Quirinius remains. Did Luke perhaps mean in the original text: "This was the first enrollment, *before* (instead of *when*) Quirinius was governor of Syria"? The original Greek text of course does not read "governor" (*hegemon*) but, rather, *hegemoneuon*, which is by no means the same thing. Both titles are derived from the Greek word *hegemonía*, "command", "sovereignty", and can designate the supreme governmental authority or "hegemony" as well as the military high command. There must be a reason why Luke uses the word *hegemoneuon* instead of the term *hegemon*, which is usual in his Gospel (for example, for Pilate), for the evangelist is very precise linguistically. Therefore, it must have referred to some other office than that of the governor, and the augmentation indicates that it was a higher office. But is that possible at all in the Roman context? And does it fit an office that Quirinius held during the governorship of Saturninus?

In 1764, an ancient fragment of an inscription was discovered in Tivoli [classical Tibur] in Latium, which the great German historian Theodor Mommsen identified in 1883 as part of the tomb inscription of Quirinius; today it is found in the Vatican Museums. It says that he "was for the second time legate of the deified Augustus with propraetorian authority in Syria and Phoenicia".[1] In 1997, the renowned ancient historian from Heidelberg Geza Alföldy confirmed that the inscription in fact must have referred to Quirinius, whose name unfortunately is not preserved. If in A.D. 6 he was employed in Syria "for the second time . . . with propraetorian authority", when was the first time?

Now at least something is known about this man's biography. In 15 B.C., while still an *eques*, or knight, he was appointed proconsul of the province of Creta et Cyrene (the Island of Crete and modern Libya). When he conquered the Garamantes, a warlike Saharan tribe, he was celebrated in Rome and elected consul in 12 B.C. In that year, Marcus Agrippa died, whom Augustus had appointed in 23 B.C. vice-Caesar for "the lands beyond the Ionian Sea". During that same year, the emperor relieved Quirinius of his duties as consul, which was highly unusual, and sent him away to the East, evidently as successor of Agrippa. He received the supreme command over three Legions, the *legio III Gallica*, *legio VI Ferrata*, and *legio X Fretensis*, which were stationed in Syria, and began a campaign against the rebellious Homonadenses, a tribe in the mountainous region in southern Central Anatolia. In 5/4 B.C., after a brilliant victory, he was appointed governor of the wealthy province of Asia, until he transferred in 2/1 B.C. to the staff of Augustus' grandson Gaius Caesar. Gaius, then eighteen years old, was considered a potential successor to the throne; the emperor had appointed him vice-Caesar for the east of the empire, but for that very purpose he needed an experienced counselor. Immediately after the early death of Gaius Caesar as a result of an injury (A.D. 4), Quirinius again received command over the three legions stationed in Syria and was at the same time

---

[1] A *propraetor* was a Roman who had served as praetor at Rome and then was sent as governor to a province.—TRANS.

governor of Syria, and thus he now held both offices. That is what the Tivoli inscription probably refers to when it speaks about his twofold activity in Syria. Whereas the first time Saturninus was *Legatus Augusti pro praetore* in Syria, while Quirinius commanded the legions, the latter must already have held a superior rank at the time. Probably he was *Orienti praepositus*, that is, commander-in-chief in the East, and thus he was the *hegemoneuon* (supreme commander), exactly as Luke writes, while Saturninus was the *hegemon* (governor).

Another inscription proves that this is not mere speculation. The tombstone of the prefect of a cohort of the First Augustan Legion, Quintus Aemilius Secundus, was acquired in Beirut in 1674 by Venetian merchants and shipped off to the lagoon city. Its Latin inscription says that the officer fought under Quirinius, "Caesar's legate in Syria", against the mountain tribe of the Itureans in Lebanon and conducted a census in the mighty, independent city state of Apamea, which at that time had 117,000 inhabitants. Now Flavius Josephus also reports in his *Jewish Antiquities* (16, 9) about the "robberies" of the tribes in the rugged north, which also spread from the Trachonitis to Iturea and all of Coele-Syria. He expressly emphasizes that this was when Saturninus was governor of Syria. The tomb inscription did not need to mention him, since as a soldier Aemilius was under the command of Quirinius; and so this not only proves that the latter was already active in Syria between 8 and 4 B.C. but is also evidence of a census in the free state of Apamea on the Orontes (in modern Syria) during those years. Probably the assessment in Herod's vassal kingdom took place at about the same time. But the period can be demarcated even more exactly; usually the census took place in December, but in Judea it probably would have been undertaken at the same time as the collection of the half-shekel Temple tax that took place every year from 15–25 Adar (in the year 5 B.C., then, from February 24 to March 6).

Now in the Roman era there were two taxes, a head tax and a property tax. From the province of Syria we know that men had to pay the head tax from the age of fourteen until sixty-five, while women had to pay it from the age of twelve until sixty-five. For that reason alone, it was imperative that families appear in their entirety before the census official, so as to determine who was obligated to pay the head tax in the first place. The place of taxation was always the place where one owned land, for the property tax was determined at the same time.

Archaeologists found proof of this praxis in 1961 in the so-called

Cave of the Letters on the western shore of the Dead Sea. There Jews had hidden their private archives before the renewed advance of the Romans during the Bar Kochba Revolt in A.D. 132. Among the documents, there was a certified copy of the tax declaration of a Jewish woman by the name of Babatha, which she had submitted in 127 during the last provincial census. Although she herself lived in Maoza, for that purpose she had to come personally to Rabbath-Moav, which is twenty-five miles away, because she owned property there. Her husband accompanied her, of course; not only because he could not send his wife alone on the day's journey but also because legally he was her *tutor*, or guardian, and families were always assessed together. The fact that Babatha for the most part used the same vocabulary as Luke shows, incidentally, how familiar the evangelist was with the contemporary tax practices.

So around A.D. 104, during the provincial census, the Roman governor in Egypt called on all those "who for any reason were outside the district . . . to return to their native place, so that they might attend to the customary business of assessment". Also from Egypt, from A.D. 47/48 (and thus nearer in time to Luke!), comes the order: "Whoever owns land in another community must submit his declaration in the community within whose boundaries the property is located. For one must pay the land tax to the community in whose territory one owns property." In the year 5 B.C., the rule was no different, and even then this already led to veritable mass migrations.

Mary and Joseph were both of Davidic lineage, and Bethlehem was the ancestral seat of their family. Thus the author of the first Church history, Eusebius of Caesarea, citing Hegesippus, observed that in the time of the Emperor Domitian (A.D. 81–96), property around Bethlehem still belonged to descendants of David. The fact that these people were at the same time *relatives of the Lord*, who owned at least one field covering between twenty-five and thirty-five acres makes this note even more interesting. Still, it is rather unlikely that Joseph was the landowner; in that case, would he have earned his money as an itinerant master builder? More probably it was Mary's "dowry", inherited from her wealthy father, Joachim, who as a cattle breeder from the house of David surely owned pastureland near Bethlehem. We have already noted that she, being the only child of her parents, was a so-called "heiress-daughter", as defined in the Jewish Law (Num 27:8). This was Mary's land, therefore, probably leased to the local shepherds. For that reason alone, the very pregnant woman, accompanied by her fiancé and legal guardian, had to make the three-day journey, and under those circumstances there was no way around it.

The *Proto-Gospel* says nothing about the land tax, but its author is quite familiar with the "head tax". At any rate, Joseph also brings his underage sons along to "register" them; we learn that one of them was named Samuel (the sons of Joseph are therefore not identical with the "brother of the Lord" James, Simon, Joses, and Judas!): "He saddled the donkey and seated her on it; and his son led it along, while Joseph followed behind." So they came to within three miles of Bethlehem.

There is an old tradition that comments on the Holy Family's journey to the "City of David" and was archaeologically confirmed just a few years ago. For at that place, three miles from Bethlehem, Mary supposedly was filled with pain, only to laugh happily a moment later. When Joseph asked her what was the matter, she explained that before her inner eye she saw two peoples, "the one weeping, the other laughing". Immediately afterward, her labor pains began. At that the carpenter helped her down from the ass and went into Bethlehem in search of lodgings.

Apparently the place of this episode was determined early on. Thus, Cyril of Scythopolis, a cleric from modern Beit Shean, tells us that in 456 the wealthy widow Ikelia founded a splendidly decorated church and a monastery at the spot where Mary had once rested on the journey to Bethlehem. They named the shrine Kathisma ("seat", "chair") after the rock on which she rested. Saint Theodosius is said to have been trained as a monk there. At the latest in the eleventh century, during the persecution of Christians by the insane Sultan al-Hakim, the complex must have been destroyed. What remained was a cistern where, the story goes, Mary once quenched her thirst.

Like so many discoveries in the Holy Land, this one, too, was owed to chance. In the fall of 1992, the road from Jerusalem to Bethlehem was supposed to be widened. But as the bulldozer began to tear up the ground in an olive grove, only 186 yards from the Mar Elias Monastery, he suddenly hit a Corinthian capital and the remains of a mosaic. Immediately the construction work was stopped and the Israeli Antiquities Authority was alerted. The competent head archaeologist, Vassili Tsaferis, authorized the young archaeologist Rina Avner to conduct an emergency excavation. What she uncovered proved to be an archaeological sensation. Beside the sealed cistern, she ran into the foundation walls of a once octagonal church. Its interior was ornamented with extensive mosaics. They display geometric figures in some parts and decorative depictions of plants in others. In the center of the octagon, however, was the rock on which, according to the legend, Mary once rested. The building was forty-nine yards wide and surrounded by four chapels, which were flanked by three entrances and the main apse to the east. Here, until the construction of the church over Mary's tomb, Christians commemorated the Dormition of the Mother of God on August 13 or 15 (today the Solemnity of the Assumption of the Blessed Virgin Mary).

In terms of the history of architecture, the discovery was spectacular, because everything indicated that it served as the model for the Muslim Dome of the Rock on the Temple Mount. Inscriptions uncovered in the church prove that it was in use even after the Islamic invasion. They had even set up a prayer niche for Muslim pilgrims, probably so that the freestanding shrine would be respected by the new masters, also. A mosaic shows a date palm; in the Qur'an it says that Mary rested under such a palm tree when her labor pains started.

In 1997, it was possible to complete the excavations successfully. At that time, the Greek patriarch planned to build a new pilgrims' center there, but then the second Intifada intervened. Israel reacted to the terror and sealed itself off; since then, an ugly concrete wall runs through the biblical landscape and divides the feuding sons of Abraham. The stone on which Mary rested lay too close to the prohibited area between the fronts, not far from the wall. So the site was at first not made public—and is awaiting better, more peaceful times.[2]

While Mary was recovering there from the hardships of the long journey, Joseph looked for lodgings in Bethlehem. "He found a cave there and took her into it. Then he gave his sons to her [for protection] and went out to find a Hebrew midwife in the region of Bethlehem," the *Proto-Gospel* relates. That is surprising at first glance. Does not every child know that Jesus was born in a stable, like the one that stands under every Christmas tree and in every church at Christmastime? But our astonishment just betrays the fact that we are Europeans: for a Jew in biblical times, there was no contradiction here, for in a land where wood is scarce and stone is soft, people used natural and manmade caves

---

[2] It is found right on Derech Hevron Street, above a bus stop right before the Mar Elias Monastery.

as stables and storage rooms, in Nazareth as well as in Bethlehem.

The Holy Family had to make do with a cave stable "because there was no place for them in the inn", Luke explains (2:7). But Joseph certainly did not expect his very pregnant fiancée to bring a child into the world in a shabby caravanserai. In fact, the original Greek text of the Gospel of Luke does not read *pandocheion*, "inn", but rather *katalyma*, which can perhaps best be translated as "upper room" or else "guest room". As descendants of David, both Mary and Joseph surely had close or distant relatives in Bethlehem and first tried to find lodgings with them. However, there was a problem according to the Jewish Law, and that was Mary's pregnancy. According to the Book of Leviticus, a woman who bore a son was considered unclean for forty days, and, along with her, everything that came in contact with her (Lev 12 and 15:19–30). Hence the problem was probably not that there was "no room" left, but that there was "no place for her", as Luke subtly differentiates. In those days, plain houses had only one main room, in which the occupants worked all day, ate together, and rolled out simple reed mats to sleep on. Adjoining it were side rooms, as a rule for storage purposes. In better houses, in contrast, the storage rooms were located on the ground floor, whereas people lived in the story above it: that is also where feasts were celebrated and guests were lodged. This is what Luke meant by *katalyma*. Of course, under normal circumstances, the relatives could have taken Mary and Joseph in; they would simply have placed the sleeping mats a little closer together. However, the high feast of Passover was just around the corner. How could they have celebrated it if a pregnant woman defiled the house? And so the Holy Family had to put up with a cave stable, which may even have been located on Mary's property. It would be empty now, since the sheep had been driven out to pasture on the first of Nisan.

This cave of Bethlehem, the place of the first Christmas, was never forgotten afterward. In fact, it is attested since the beginning of the second century as one of the earliest Christian shrines. Justin Martyr, who was originally from Shechem in Palestine, mentioned the "cave in the vicinity of the town" around 135. His very precise description of its location allows us to conclude that he either visited it himself or was acquainted with the *Proto-Gospel* (which then must be older than scholars like to claim); for if it says there that Joseph went from the cave *to* Bethlehem, then at best it could have been situated at the edge of the town. Today, of course, the Basilica of the Nativity is found in the center of the city. Later archaeological excavations, however, showed that Justin and "James" were right: the biblical Bethlehem lay to the east of the cave.

If Justin (born around 100) was there while Judas, a relative of the Lord, still presided over the Jewish Christians of Jerusalem as their bishop, then this site must be authentic, and then neither Matthew nor Luke invented their Christmas story in order to make Jesus appear as the long-awaited Messiah. In fact, the tradition was so strong that Emperor Hadrian, as part of his "paganization program", felt it was necessary to transform the cave of Jesus' birth into a cultic grotto for the pagan god Adonis, around which he had a sacred grove planted. But that in no way changed the fact that the locals still knew, as they had always known, who really came into the world there. "What is displayed there is familiar to everyone in the vicinity. Even the pagans tell anyone who will listen that a certain Jesus was born in said cave", Origen wrote around the year 220. Later, Saint Helena, the mother of Constantine the Great, had a church built over it in 325 during her pilgrimage to the Holy Land. But the Cave of the Nativity, which can still be visited today, is only part of a whole network of old caves, each one of which has its own history. Saint Jerome, one of the greatest theologians and Fathers of the Church in late antiquity, lived in one of them from 385 until his death in 420; there, commissioned by Pope Damasus, he prepared the Latin translation of the Bible, the *Vulgata*, which to this day is regarded as *the* Catholic Bible. As he worked, he wanted to be as close as possible, physically too, to the origin of the Christian faith. And so he was, since his cave was located right beside the old entrance to the Cave of the Nativity, which today is under the Franciscans' Church of Saint Catherine; the steps by which the visitor enters and leaves it today were added later. Right beside the Church of the Nativity is the Milk Grotto, also called the "Grotto of the Lady Mary" by the Arabs. The faithful tried to explain its unusually white limestone by saying that a drop of Mary's milk fell to the ground as she was nursing her Child. From the early Middle Ages on, this stone, ground to a powder and poured into bottles or little tubes, used to be considered a special relic (which today is often ridiculed): *de Lactis Beatae Mariae Virginis*, "from the milk of the B.V.M.", it was called. Perhaps the Holy Family resided there when Mary was ritually clean again after forty days and for that reason had to leave the Cave of the Nativity.

The midwife brought by Joseph, after he had left Mary behind with his sons in the cave stable, played another special role in the *Proto-Gospel*. For when she arrived, the Divine Child was already born—an event that the text describes as a *theophany*, an Old Testament revelation of God:

> Right away the cloud departed from the cave, and a great light appeared within, so that their eyes could not bear it. Soon that light departed, until an infant could be seen. And it went and took hold of the breast of Mary, its mother.

At that moment, a second midwife named Salome showed up; probably someone, after hearing that Joseph was looking for a woman to help with a birth, had informed her. Her colleague told her what she had just seen, but Salome could not and would not believe that a virgin had given birth there. She, like the apostle Thomas thirty-five years later, demanded palpable proof: "If I do not put my finger in and investigate, I will not believe." So she went in, examined Mary, and literally burned her fingers. Only after she prayed to God and touched the Child was she healed. Then she proclaimed: "In truth, a great king is born for Israel." Thus she became the star witness for Mary's perpetual virginity, and her statement gave rise to unending theological debates. But she also obeyed the voice of an angel who commanded her to keep silence.

The ecclesiastical author Origen, who lived in the early third century in Caesarea on the Mediterranean coast of the Holy Land, records an anecdote from the life of Mary that we find neither in the Gospels nor in the extant apocrypha; probably it was related in the circles of the Lord's relatives. It concerns a visit to the Temple by the Mother of God shortly after the forty-day period of her ritual uncleanness, probably on the occasion of Shavuot (Pentecost) of the year 5 B.C.:

> After the birth of our Redeemer, Mary went to worship (in the Temple) and stood on the side of the virgins. Those who knew that she had borne a son tried to drive her away from that place; but Zechariah said to them: "She deserves the place of the virgins, for she is still a Virgin."

So even after the birth of Christ, she was to go down in history as the Ever-Virgin. The icons of the Eastern Church to this day show Mary with three stars, two on her shoulders and one on her forehead, which symbolize her virginity before, during, and after giving birth. Thus the Holy Night was the accomplishment of the miracle of the Incarnation that had begun with the Annunciation. And since the Lamb of God came to earth in a cave stable, in which sheep had been sheltered just a few days earlier, it is no wonder that the shepherds were the first to whom angels announced the birth of the Messiah and the beginning of the heavenly kingdom of peace among "men of good will" (Lk 2:14, Douay-Rheims). Soon afterward, Gentiles, too, "wise men" or "astrologers from the East", followed the bright star that blazed amid the vernal constellations on that first Christmas night. "But Mary kept all these things, pondering them in her heart" (Lk 2:19).

~

8

The Redeemer's Birth

When Marco Polo, the seventeen-year-old son of a Venetian merchant, set out in 1271 for the second time with his father, Niccolo, and his uncle Maffeo for the Far East, in order to deliver to the Great Khan a message from Pope Gregory X, his itinerary led through the heart of Asia, past the cradle of civilization. Only twenty-four years later did he return to Venice with precious gems that were sewn into his clothing and fantastic stories from faraway lands, which even then no one really believed. In the naval battle against Genoa, he had been taken prisoner and shared a cell with Rustichello da Pisa, a writer of popular romances about chivalry. We do not know whether the garrulous Polo, with his boasting about the Khan's treasures and his own wealth, rightly got on the author's nerves or whether the latter immediately saw genuine bestseller potential in his cellmate. At any rate, he had nothing better to do, and he offered Polo his services as a ghostwriter. The Venetian, who never let a deal slip through his fingers and whose vanity was flattered by the idea of a literary monument, enthusiastically agreed. And so came about *The Book of the Marvels of the World*, which became one of the most widely read works of its time. In Venice, though, it appeared under another title, which had become Polo's favorite nickname: *Il Milione*. Although people even in those days accused him of copying from other sources, on his deathbed the Venetian still swore: "I have not told half of what I saw."

The most fascinating of his travel stories plays out in Persia, where, after a visit to the colorful bazaar in Tabriz, he learned a real secret:

In Persia is the city of Saba [Sava], from which the Three Magi set out when they went to worship Jesus Christ; and in this city they are buried, in three very large and beautiful monuments, side by side. And above them there is a square building, carefully kept. The bodies are still entire, with the hair and beard remaining. One of these was called Jaspar [Caspar], the second Melchior, and the third Balthazar.

Evidently he visited their tombs but could learn nothing more about the identity of the three astrologers from the Muslim populace. Only after three days of traveling, when he reached Cala Ataperistan, were his questions answered:

> The people there . . . relate that in old times three kings of that country went away to worship a Prophet that was born, and they carried with them three manner of offerings, Gold and Frankincense and Myrrh. For, said they, if he take the Gold, then he is an earthly King; if he take the Incense, he is God; if he take the Myrrh, he is a Physician.

Then they came to the child, who was "some thirteen days" old, adored him, and presented their gifts to him. He took all three and in thanksgiving handed them a small closed box. After that, they set out on their journey home:

> And when they had ridden many days, they said they would see what the Child had given them. So they opened the little box, and inside it they found a stone. On seeing this, they began to wonder what this might be that the Child had given them, and what was the import thereof. Now the signification was this: when they presented their offerings, the Child had accepted all three, and when they saw that, they had said within themselves that He was the True God, and the True King, and the True Physician. And what the gift of the stone implied was that this faith which had begun in them should abide firm as a rock.

The three wise men, however, did not grasp what the stone was supposed to mean. When they came to a well, they took it out of the little box and threw it into the water. At that moment a blazing fire fell from heaven into the depths of the well. The three were awestruck; they took some of the fire, which they later brought to their temple and kept burning continually from then on. Hence this locality was also called, translated from Persian, "The Castle of the Fire-Worshippers".

This is a strange and uniquely charming story that Marco Polo brought back with him from modern Saveh in Northern Iran, ancient Media south of the Caspian Sea. Certainly it is a pretty legend to which we would not lend too much credence except that it has a kernel of truth. At any rate, that is what the Canadian journalist and author Paul William Roberts found when he traveled in the footsteps of Marco Polo in Iran. His adventurous and equally witty travel book *Journey of the Magi* describes this search. Finally someone brought him to an old mosque that loomed over the remains of a fire temple of the followers of Zarathustra. But beside an ancient fire altar, he found traces of Christianity, also: polished limestone slabs decorated with a chi-rho, which especially in the fourth century was the sign by which disciples of Jesus recognized one another. Through underground vaults and chambers they led him to a large, windowless room, the walls hung with green and red fabrics and the floor covered with inexpensive carpets. This was a place, he learned, where local women would often come to pray. Everywhere he saw symbols of three religions: Christianity, Islam, and Zoroastrianism. It was quite possible that the shrine, which today serves as a mosque, was two thousand years old. And then Roberts found what he had been looking for: outside, in front of the mosque, on an adjoining plot of land, which at first glance looked like a garbage dump, right beside the outer walls of the ancient fire temple, stood a cube-shaped house, not quite twenty-three feet wide and tall, topped by a dome. It was situated perhaps twenty-two yards distant from the ruins of the ancient city wall. Two entrances must once have led into it, one on the northern wall, the other to the east. Both had been bricked up at one point, but the eastern entrance was later broken open again; here a wooden door that was only four feet tall led now into the interior of the cube. "Tomb", Roberts' guide exclaimed, and unbolted the door. The Canadian stepped into the square room and saw two stone sarcophagi set up right next to each other along a line running from East to West, and so not facing Mecca. A statue must have stood once in a niche. There was plenty of room for a third sarcophagus, the floor had obviously been renovated, and so no one knows whether Marco Polo had merely invented the third "King" or whether it had originally been a tomb for three.[1] It is even less certain who was once buried in the sarcophagi, which are empty today, and whether the Venetian ever saw the bodies or just relied on local legends. But Roberts had found out this much: there was a kernel of truth to his report. Cala Ataperistan, too, was not a fantasy, but merely a transcription of the Persian *Qal'ah-i Atasparastan*. A local

---

[1] So it is quite possible that their remains were transported in the third or fourth century via Edessa to Milan and from there eventually arrived in Cologne.

historian, Dr. Morteza Zokaii, led the Canadian to the foothills of the Zagros Mountains, west of Sava [Saveh]. There it stood, an extensive, ancient castle built of dark, reddish-gray stone, topped with one large and six smaller arches, a distinctive feature of Zoroastrian architecture; they stand for the supreme god, Ahura Mazda, and his "six immortal spirits" or angels. Coins discovered there prove that this castle already existed in the second century B.C. But did the "Wise Men" come from here, too? That is quite possible. For in Cologne, Germany, where the remains of the "Three Kings" have been venerated since 1164, they know about this city. "In *Sewa*", it says in an old *Martyrologium* in Cologne, which Roberts cites, the three astrologers, who meanwhile had been baptized, are said to have met once again in the year 54 "to celebrate Christmas". Shortly thereafter they died: "Saint Melchior on January 1 at the age of 116; Saint Balthasar on January 6 at the age of 112, and Saint Gaspar on January 11 at the age of 109." That is of course a pious legend, since Christmas demonstrably was celebrated only from the fourth century on, but it does anchor *Sewa* = Sava, Saveh in Christian tradition even before Marco Polo. The lovely Christmas story that the Venetian recorded for us was definitely not invented by him. Probably it goes back to a local legend, which likewise has a kernel of truth: It identifies the "three Wise Men" as "fire-worshippers" and, thus, as Zoroastrians. Consequently, the accounts in Matthew and the *Proto-Gospel* appear in a completely different light. For not only Romans and Jews but also the members of the "sixth world religion" waited longingly for the Messiah.

Its founder is the most mysterious of all the prophets. No one knows for sure when or even where Zarathustra lived; probably his home was in the northeast of modern Iran. In the few sources about his life that exist, there is talk about him laughing at his birth, about wild animals that guarded him as a baby, and about his early miraculous deeds. Diogenes Laertius, author of biographies of Greek philosophers, maintains that he lived 48,863 years before Alexander the Great. More realistic traditions date him to "258 years before Alexander" and by that mean his victory at the Battle of Gaugamela in 330 B.C., but that still leaves open whether they are referring to the prophet's birth, death, enlightenment, or first public appearance. The last-mentioned occurred when he was forty-two years old; at the age of twenty, he had left his parental home, at thirty, he had had a vision that revealed to him the "true" or the "good religion". In the next twelve years, he converted only one person, his own brother. But then came the breakthrough, when he introduced himself at the court of King Vishtaspa of Bactria, who is probably identical with Hystaspes (ca. 588–521 B.C.), the satrap of Bactria and father of Darius the Great. The "king" ordered two *magavan*, or magi, members of the Median [Old Persian] priestly caste, to test him. When he utterly overwhelmed them with his knowledge and wisdom, Vishtaspa/Hystaspes accepted the new faith on their recommendation. In fact, his son Darius (522–486 B.C.) went down in history as the first Zoroastrian king of the Persian Empire. Quite in keeping with this new faith, his inscriptions call Ahura Mazda the "only God".

Zarathustra's teachings are compiled in a holy book, the *Avesta* or *Zendavesta*, which contains his psalm-like *gathas*, or "songs", which were collected by his disciples. In the opinion of religious historian Mary Boyce, they show that Zoroastrianism "has probably had more influence on mankind, directly and indirectly, than any other single faith". Its dualistic world view of God and his adversary, heaven and hell, the resurrection of the dead, angels and demons, the Holy Ghost, a savior and redeemer, and the apocalyptic battle between good and evil or light and darkness before the last judgment found its way not only into Judaism and Christianity but also into Islam, Mahayana Buddhism, and Hinduism. Thus the changes in Judaism after the Babylonian Captivity and its sudden fondness for apocalypses and its belief in hierarchies of angels, which find expression especially in the writings of the Essenes, can be explained only through intensive contact with the new doctrine. Daniel especially, the favorite prophet of the Essenes, was suspected by the Persians of being a disciple of Zarathustra. The Jews countered by declaring Zarathustra a disciple of Daniel; Abu al-Faraj, a thirteenth-century Syrian-Orthodox polymath, was likewise convinced of it. There is no question that Daniel himself had already been appointed by King Nebuchadnezzar "chief prefect over all the wise men of Babylon" (Dan 2:48), whereby the Septuagint, the Greek translation of the Old Testament, translated "wise men" as *magoi*. Flavius Josephus, too, in his *Jewish Antiquities*, describes how closely Daniel collaborated with the "Chaldean magi" and how forcefully he spoke up for them when the king on one occasion, indignant about their failure, ordered their execution. And so his prophecies enjoyed great favor among the magi after the days of the Babylonian Empire, which by then was already doomed to decline.

"One of Zarathustra's most revolutionary concepts", writes the

British scholar of religious studies Peter Clark, "is that of the savior, the 'bringer of benefit' or the benefactor known in the Gathas as the *Saoshyant*. . . . [It] was later to have such a dramatic effect on the development of postexilic Jewish theological thought." This "savior" —for that is precisely what *Saoshyant* means—would be born of a virgin at the beginning of a new era after she bathed in a lake of pure water and thus conceived. His task would be to destroy evil, to teach justice, and to usher in a new, eternal world; then the dead would arise. Clark writes: "It is evident, though, that Zarathustra was either anticipating the apocalyptic event in the near future or at least that he was hoping for it. . . . In a sense he establishes, alongside an 'official' sacerdotal class, a preaching vocation of all believers (Ashavans), who would work with him toward the final event." The *Ahuna Vairya* prayer (Yasna 27:13), which Zarathustra taught his disciples, reads:

> For he (*Saoshyant*) is the Chosen One among men; from him goes forth judgment from truth itself on the deeds and good works of men; his is the power, which was entrusted to him by Ahura Mazda, who called him to be the shepherd of the poor.

He made the *magavan*, or magi, responsible for the new teaching; they were members of the Old Persian priestly tribe, comparable to the Levites of the Jews. Their headquarters was Ecbatana, modern Hamadan. There they cultivated their ancient tradition, which resembled that of the Vedic Indians: they revered the four elements, especially fire, and explored the mysteries of nature. The city was ringed with seven walls, the Greek historian Herodotus tells us, and each one was painted a different color: they symbolized the seven known planets of the solar system. Herodotus was able to report many other things about the *magavan*, whom he called *magoi* in Greek (*-van* is a plural ending in Old Persian). He described them as wise men, interpreters of dreams, oracular priests, and counselors of the king with an outright legendary reputation. Even centuries later, somebody merely had to call himself a *magus* or a disciple of *magi*, and those seeking advice would stand in line. Of course charlatans soon took advantage of this, and gradually they ruined the reputation of "magicians" irremediably, at least in the West (that is, the Roman Empire).

Nevertheless, Matthew leaves no doubt as to who the "wise men" or "astrologers from the East" were (as they are called in various translations), who at first asked in Jerusalem about the "newborn king of the Jews" (cf. Mt 2:1-2)—for in the original Greek text, he explicitly designates them as *magoi* and thus uses the same term as Herodotus. Later Christian exegesis turned them into "kings"; after all, Isaiah and Psalm 72 speak about kings bringing gifts: "May the kings of Tarshish and of the isles render him tribute, may the kings of Sheba and Seba bring gifts! May all kings fall down before him" (Ps 72:10–11). But Matthew himself, who is often accused of having invented Mary's virginity for the sake of a misinterpreted prophecy, would never have taken the liberty of suddenly transforming magi into kings; Tertullian (circa 200) was the first to hit on this absurd idea, and his contemporary Origen counted three of them, based on the gifts that are mentioned, and an Alexandrian manuscript, likewise from the third century, first mentions their names: *Bithisarea, Melichior,* and *Gathaspa,* which at least sound more Persian than the Latinized version: Kaspar, Melchior, and Balthasar. The earliest images in the Roman catacombs of the Adoration of the Magi, from the second and third centuries, sometimes show two, sometimes three, or even four of them.[2] Here, too, they wear Old Persian apparel, but especially, as an unmistakable identifying feature, Phrygian caps. The same can be seen on the colorful mosaics in the Roman Basilica of Saint Mary Major (fifth century) and in Ravenna (sixth century). Granted, this makes them look a little like garden dwarves or Smurfs, but for the viewer in antiquity the message was clear: these were genuine magi, "priests in the robes of the Persian race", as King Antiochus of Commagene called them when he had them sculpted in stone on the Nemrut Dagi with the same colorful cloaks and pointed caps, only a few decades before the birth of Christ.

A whole series of early Christian writers understood the message and knew about their belief in Zarathustra's prophecy. Thus we read in the apocryphal *Arabic Infancy Gospel,* which probably dates back to the fourth or fifth century:

> And so it happened, when the Lord Jesus was born in Bethlehem in Judea at the time of King Herod, behold, there came magi from the east to Jerusalem, *as Zardusht had foretold;* and they had brought gifts, gold, frankincense and myrrh [emphasis added].

As late as the thirteenth century, Abulfaragius, a Christian Arab, wrote that Zoroaster had told his disciples about a star that would announce

---

[2] In apocryphal texts, there is even talk about twelve, probably as a pagan counterpart to the twelve apostles.

the virgin birth of the savior Saoshyant: "You, my sons, will notice its rising before all other nations. Therefore, as soon as you see the star, follow it wherever it leads you, revere the mysterious child, and with the most profound humility offer him gifts."

The magi were in fact particularly well versed in astronomy and astrology, as the design of their capital reveals. When Xerxes observed an eclipse of the sun during a military campaign, he was so uneasy that he immediately called for them. They assured him, according to Herodotus, that it signified nothing and in any case would instill fear in the enemy; the moon that was slipping in front of the sun would protect the Persians. Their horoscopes were legendary, and they specialized in reckoning favorable times for important undertakings. Consequently, they were still active throughout the Near East long after the downfall of the Persian Empire. The horoscope for the ascent to the throne that they prepared for King Mithridates I of Commagene in 109 B.C. was immortalized by his son Antiochus on the monumental burial mound of Nemrut Dagi; the so-called "lion horoscope" is considered the oldest preserved horoscope in the world. This makes it all the more plausible that they applied their astrology also to forecast the coming of the Saoshyant. After all, in the two years that preceded the Incarnation of Christ, several things happened in the night sky that caused them to watch attentively.

It all began on May 27, 7 B.C., when Jupiter and Saturn converged in the night sky, a phenomenon that in astronomy is called a *conjunction*. Jupiter traveled farther, became retrograde on July 17, and met Saturn a second time on October 6, while Saturn was in Pisces. On November 13, Jupiter "turned" once more and again moved forward, so that on December 1 it came to a third and last conjunction with Saturn. (At this point in time, the prelude of the Incarnation of the Son of God began with the conception of John the Baptist.)

It is certain that this triple conjunction of Jupiter and Saturn made the magi curious. "The astrology that they taught was fundamentally different from that of the Hindus and the Greeks. They were familiar with aspects of the heavenly bodies, the major cycles of Jupiter and Saturn, and all these systems of planetary interactions that they had puzzled out", writes contemporary astrologer Rob Hand. An eighth-century Jew named Masha'allah, who had studied with the last great Persian astrologers, even maintained that Jupiter-Saturn conjunctions at the end of a cycle could announce the coming of great prophets and new religions. According to another interpretation, the conjunction of

the royal "star" Jupiter with Saturn, the "star" of the Western lands
(*Amurru*) or of the Jews (who keep Saturn-day, the *Sabbath*, holy), indicated the birth of a Jewish king. Yet whatever interpretation they
chose, the heavenly sign, which repeats itself on average every 120
years,[3] was not all that spectacular.

Things got more interesting the following year (6 B.C.), when a triple
conjunction of Jupiter, Saturn, and Mars took place in the constellation Pisces. But the magi definitely paid attention on February 20,
5 B.C. For then two conjunctions occurred simultaneously: the moon
and Jupiter on one side of the winter sky, Saturn and Mars on the
other side. Astrologically, that could mean that "a great king is born
and arises in order to rule over Israel and combat evil." Did this perhaps refer to the Saoshyant? I can imagine that the magi in those days
held council together and excitedly discussed what was going on in
the heavens. And then something happened that exceeded their wildest
expectations. "We saw a magnificent star shining among the stars and
overshadowing them, so that the other stars disappeared", the *Proto-
Gospel* quotes them as saying. However much it may be exaggerated in
other passages, however often it may cross the line into legend, in this
passage its statement is quite scientific, sober, and precise. For sometime in the first third of March, a star exploded in the night sky that
previously had been so distant, so small and insignificant, that probably
no one had noticed it before, but suddenly its brightness increased a
millionfold, until it was as bright as an entire galaxy. In astronomy,
this is called a *supernova*. The fact that from the beginning or middle
of March until the end of May in the year 5 B.C., close to the star
Theta Aquilae in the constellation of the Eagle, a supernova was observed for seventy-six days is proved indisputably by the records of
Chinese and Korean astronomers (namely, in the book *Ch'ein-han-shu*
and the chronicle *Samguk Sagi*), as the British astronomer Mark Kidger
points out in his book *The Star of Bethlehem*, which was published by
the renowned Princeton University Press. This "new", brightly shining heavenly body, brighter than any other star in the sky, moreover,
in Aquila, the symbol and constellation of their god Ahura Mazda—
this must be the sign for which the magi had waited since the days of
Zarathustra, which announced the coming of the Saoshyant!

Of course they knew where they had to search for him. Regardless

---

[3] The last Jupiter-Saturn conjunction in the constellation Pisces took place in 126 B.C.;
at that time the Hasmonean King Alexander Jannaeus was born.

of whether Daniel and Zarathustra had known each other personally, an encounter had indisputably taken place between Judaism and Zoroastrianism, resulting in mutual influence. The Assyrians had already settled the captured inhabitants of the northern kingdom of Israel "in the cities of the Medes" (2 Kings 17:6). The prophet Daniel belonged to the court of Darius the Mede, who resided every summer in Ecbatana. According to Flavius Josephus, this king not only "praised that God whom Daniel worshipped and said that he was the only true God and had all power" but also made Daniel the "principal of his friends" and his counselor. At that time, the Jewish historian related, Daniel "built a tower at Ecbatana, in Media . . . a most elegant building, and wonderfully made", as a sort of mausoleum in which "the kings of Media, Persia, and Parthia" would be buried: "he who was entrusted with the care of it was a Jewish priest, which thing is also observed to this day." The wife of King Ahasuerus (485–465 B.C.), Queen Esther, even founded a Jewish colony in Ecbatana, which soon was highly respected. Esther's tomb is still revered in Hamadan today. The Acts of the Apostles (2:9) also mentions "Parthians and Medes and Elamites" who went on pilgrimage to Jerusalem for the Feast of Weeks and became witnesses of the Pentecost miracle. Not only were contacts with Jews practically unavoidable for the magi; no people in the world prized them and their religion as much as the Persians and Medes. Cyrus the Great, the conqueror of Babylon, not only allowed the Jews to return to their homeland; he also gave back to them the Temple treasure that the Babylonians had plundered; indeed, he even financed the rebuilding of the Temple. This esteem was gratefully reciprocated on the part of the Jews, as shown by the reaction of the prophet Isaiah; he expressly called Cyrus "the anointed of the LORD" (cf. Is 45:1) and thus ascribed to him the title of Messiah! Since the time of Daniel, Jews occupied leading positions at court, including the most important position of trust, that of the cupbearer, which Nehemiah held (it was usually reserved for one of the closest relatives of the great king), and even the rank of queen (Esther!). When the Maccabees fought against the Seleucids, they were supported by the Persians, who formed a second front; finally the Greeks withdrew their troops from Judea. Antigonus, too, the last Hasmonean king, returned to the throne only with the help of the Persians, at least until Herod arrived with the even mightier troops from Rome. When Emperor Trajan advanced against the Parthians, there were uprisings of Jews throughout the empire; the campaign had to be discontinued. Even in the seventh century A.D., the Jews of the

Holy Land were allied with the Zoroastrian Sassanids, in the hope that together they could shake off the Byzantine Christians who were in power. People even believed for a time that a Persian conquest would precede the coming of the Messiah. If ever in history there was a people that orthodox Jews respected the most, then it was the Persians, and this respect was based on reciprocity. It is no accident, therefore, that the journey of the magi led to the city of the Jewish Temple, to the place where someone could reveal to them where tradition expected the coming of the Messiah.

After the magi had traveled the approximately 998 miles between Ecbatana and Jerusalem (or the 1,120 miles from Saveh) on the caravan roads of the Silk Route, their first stop was at Herod's palace at the west end of the capital city. Even at a distance they were greeted by three skyscraping towers of the fortress, which had been built strategically in front of the most splendid palace of its day (only a century later did Nero, who after all was Caesar of the Roman Empire, outdo Herod with his Golden House). Obviously they knew little or nothing at all about the man who was then seated on the throne; otherwise, it would have been clear to them that their lives, too, were in danger. For with the passage of years, the second most passionate master builder in antiquity (after Emperor Hadrian) had become a cruel tyrant, who mercilessly destroyed everything that could endanger his power. The more he realized that he could not buy the love of the Jewish people, not even with the most magnificent buildings in their history, the more visibly embittered he became. Besides, he had always had a remarkable instinct for gaining power without the least scruples, and anyone who threatened to become a serious rival fell victim to his schemes. So a trail of blood runs through the thirty-three years of his rule: first he murdered the sixteen-year-old Hasmonean Aristobulus, whom he had just appointed high priest at the request of his wife, Mariamne; probably the cries of jubilation over him were too loud. Mariamne herself followed him to the grave seven years later, accused of plotting a conspiracy. His brother-in-law Kostobar and his alleged accomplices were killed during the following year. When his secret police prevented a genuine attempt on his life in 27 B.C. and the accused were executed along with those who were behind the plot, Herod thought at first that he was finally sitting safely in the saddle. He had put to death all the Hasmoneans who could become dangerous to him; most of the descendants of David lived in Galilee and were not interested in the throne. Only fifteen years later, when his sons from his marriage with Mariamne were grown, did his old fear flare up again. Herod had them indicted before the emperor but could produce no evidence against them, was reconciled, and then four years later indicted them once again on account of high treason. Since he could now call "witnesses", he succeeded in winning a conviction; both sons were executed in 7 B.C. and with them at the same time three hundred officers and court officials, who were accused of being part of the conspiracy. The new successor to the throne, his son Antipater, followed them to the scaffold three years later (in March of the year 4 B.C.); Herod thought that he was trying to poison him. "It is better to be Herod's pig than his son", was Augustus Caesar's cynical comment on the cruelty of his vassal, for pigs are not slaughtered by Jews.

Flavius Josephus depicts incisively the extent to which Herod already suffered at that time from a veritable persecution complex:

> Herod . . . sent spies abroad privately, by night and by day, who should make a close inquiry after all that was done and said; and when any were but suspected [of treason], he put them to death, insomuch that the palace was full of horribly unjust proceedings; for everybody forged calumnies, as they were themselves in a state of enmity or hatred against others; and many there were who abused the king's bloody passion to the disadvantage of those with whom they had quarrels, and lies were easily believed, and punishments were inflicted sooner than the calumnies were forged. He who had just then been accusing another was accused himself and was led away to execution together with him whom he had convicted; for the danger the king was in of his life made examinations be very short. He also proceeded to such a degree of bitterness that he could not look on any of those that were not accused with a pleasant countenance, but was in the most barbarous disposition toward his own friends. (*Wars of the Jews*, bk. 1, chap. 24)

Most of all Herod was now afraid of the Jewish belief in a Messiah. Flavius Josephus relates that immediately before the "oath of loyalty" to the emperor and the king, that is, in March of 5 B.C., there was unrest on account of the tax assessment that accompanied it. The Pharisees, who "had the reputation of possessing the divine gift of prophecy", then foretold the birth of the Messiah; "Herod and his descendants would . . . lose dominion by a divine decree." The chronicler does not tell us whether the supernova, the bright new star, led them to this conviction, but we can assume that it did. Immediately Herod had the Pharisees declared guilty and executed, which the historian Walter Otto even regards as the "cause for the development of the legend of the slaughter of the innocents in Bethlehem". I think, rather, that this prophecy was the trigger for the most notorious bloody deed of the nearly insane king.

The arrival of the magi must without question have caused him to go on high alert. For him, religion was always an instrument of politics. Who, then, had sent these odd priests, and what did it mean for his kingdom? He had already had to flee once, when the Parthians attacked the land in order to put their ally, the Hasmonean Antigonus, on the throne. Was this fate threatening him again, now that he was almost seventy years old? Of course he was able to distinguish between Parthians and Medes. They were related peoples, sharing a common religion, language, and culture, but in the last few decades in particular, Media had often enough played a separate role and was even allied for a time with Greater Armenia and Rome, before it definitively became part of the Parthian Empire in the first century A.D. But Augustus had solemnly concluded peace with the Parthians, too, in 20 B.C. So a hasty preventative measure like the murder of the magi was utterly unthinkable if he did not want to incur the emperor's enduring wrath. His only other option was to find out where the potential pretender to the throne was staying, so as then to strike mercilessly after they had left. That is why he received the magi as guests of state, immediately offered them his help, summoned priests and scribes to answer their questions, and meanwhile coaxed from them a promise to inform him immediately when they had found the long-awaited redeemer. Finally one of the learned Jews had an idea where that might be and cited the prophet Micah, whom we cite here in the original wording, because it is more complete and beautiful, and not in Matthew's version:

> But you, O Bethlehem Ephrathah, who are little to be among the clans of Judah, from you shall come forth for me one who is to be ruler in Israel, whose origin is from of old, from ancient days. Therefore he shall give them up until the time when she who has labor pains has brought forth. . . . And he shall stand and feed his flock in the strength of the LORD, in the majesty of the name of the LORD his God. And they shall dwell secure, for now he shall be great to the ends of the earth. (Mic 5:2–4)

The very next morning, when it was still dark, the magi set out on the road to Bethlehem, which lies five miles south of Jerusalem.

They did not have to search for long, for as Matthew reports, "the star which they had seen in the East went before them, till it came to rest over the place where the child was" (2:9). That sounds like a miracle only to a layman unacquainted with astronomy. For according to the laws of celestial mechanics, a star that arose in the east would appear in the sky a half hour earlier every week, until after two months it stood exactly in the south. Therefore, on their journey from Jerusalem to Bethlehem, the magi must in fact have had the star directly ahead of them, until finally, right over the cave stable or the Milk Grotto, in front of which Joseph may meanwhile have built a hut,[4] it disappeared over the horizon.

That must have been around the middle of May, 5 B.C., when the supernova had already been visible for two months and would remain so for only a few more days. From their homeland to Bethlehem it is "a journey of fifty-three days", wrote the (perhaps fictional) medieval pilgrim Sir John Mandeville in his travel account, which is a realistic figure; over the course of fifty-two days, they would have had to cover twenty-two miles per day, which in antiquity was considered a good average for caravan leaders. If we add from seven to ten days for travel preparations, it was in fact two months.[5] During that time, the Holy Family had many reasons to stay in Bethlehem. After eight days, the Child had been circumcised, probably shortly before Passover, which in that year began on March 22. In late April, the Holy Family once again visited the Temple, in order to consecrate Mary's firstborn son to the Lord according to the Law of Moses (Num 18:15-16). On such an occasion, a sacrifice was offered, for wealthy Jews a lamb, which was supposed to be a reminder of Abraham's sacrifice, but for poorer ones a pair of turtledoves or two young pigeons. Interestingly enough, Luke does not mention that Jesus' parents paid five shekels in order to redeem the Child Jesus from Temple service. According to the Torah, only Levites were exempted—which could also be a sufficient explanation in this case, since we know about Mary's priestly, that is, Levite relatives. But it may also mean that she deliberately "sacrificed the child to the Lord", as Joachim and Anne had once done with Mary, and dedicated Jesus even then to a life consecrated to God, a Nazirate.

[4] Or was Mary, who meanwhile had been ritually "purified", allowed to move into the house of her relatives? Matthew at any rate speaks about a "house".

[5] Marco Polo's statement that it was only thirteen days obviously relies on the Christian liturgical calendar, specifically the interval between December 24 (Christmas Eve) and January 6 (Epiphany).

Two old people were living in the Temple at that time, Simeon, who is described as a "righteous" man with the gift of prophecy—it had been revealed to him that he would live until the Messiah came—and a "prophetess" by the name of Anna. They both recognized the baby named Jesus as the Savior who had been prophesied, the "light for revelation to the Gentiles" (Lk 2:32). But some exegetes think that Simeon was an Essene, for he foretold something else, turning to Mary: "And a sword will pierce through your own soul also" (Lk 2:35). She could not imagine how these words would one day come true. Joseph and Mary would probably have celebrated Shavuot, the Feast of Weeks (on May 10 that year), in the Temple also, before he prepared for the return journey to Nazareth. At least the *Proto-Gospel* talks about a departure, when it says: "And behold, Joseph was ready to go into Judea. But there was a great disturbance in Bethlehem of Judea. For wise men came." That must have been around May 15.

Herod, though, waited for their return and their report; one day, maybe two. Only then would he have sent his spies to Bethlehem, who learned that the foreigners had already returned by another way to their homeland. He reacted to that by resorting to the major preemptive strike that made him for two thousand years the worst villain in history (until an Austrian postcard painter vied with him for that title):

> He sent and killed all the male children in Bethlehem and in all that region who were two years old or under, according to the time which he had ascertained from the Wise Men. (Mt 2:16)

Since Flavius Josephus does not mention this foul deed, many historians and exegetes consider it "another" invention by Matthew, so that he could once again cite here a suitable prophecy, this time from Jeremiah. But why "two years"? How could Herod have learned the boy's age from the magi before they had found him in the first place? This passage yields its meaning—and then appears to be astonishingly precise—if we take the astronomical events into consideration. For of course the priest-astronomers reported to the king what they had observed, beginning with the first sign in the heavens, the Jupiter-Saturn conjunction in May of 7 B.C.—exactly two years before their arrival in Jerusalem!

How else could Matthew have thought of "two years" unless there was a direct tradition, an authentic source? But then what happened afterward is also plausible, which Josephus may simply have missed among the many crimes of Herod. What with the mass execution of the Pharisees, the trial against his plotting son Antipater, and the popular uprising of young Torah students, who tore down a golden eagle that Herod had set up over the Temple gate, the mention of around twenty children (for it could hardly have been more than that) murdered in a village like Bethlehem would have seemed almost anticlimactic. Ultimately the king had the youthful ringleaders burned alive and all their fellow travelers put to the sword. And then, while already lying on his deathbed in Jericho, he issued his most horrific order. He summoned the "most prominent Jewish elders", at least one man from each family, and had them confined to the grounds of a race track and surrounded by soldiers. Had his sister not prevented it, they would all have been murdered after his demise by a rain of arrows from his archers, so as to assure that the whole people would be in mourning at the death of the king.

But the inhabitants of Bethlehem did not forget the massacre of the innocents, either. No sooner had Herod been interred with great pomp in a mausoleum on the slope of the Herodium, his favorite castle at the edge of the desert, than they attacked the tomb. They pounded his sarcophagus into a thousand pieces, the fragments of which were not discovered until early 2007. A Jewish document from the time around A.D. 70, *The Assumption of Moses*, also hints at the foul crime. It mentions a "bloody command" by Herod, "as it came to pass in Egypt"— by which was meant Pharaoh's order to kill all newborn Jewish boys.

One indication of the persistence of this memory is the fact that as late as the fourth century, the Feast of the Innocent Children of Bethlehem was celebrated in Jerusalem and Bethlehem on May 18— an absolutely plausible and probably authentic date. This is reported not only by the pilgrim Egeria, who participated in the ceremonies in the year 383 and describes them in detail in her travel account; it is also on an old Armenian calendar of feast days. Yet there is a third reference to this date, which we owe to the *Proto-Gospel*. It takes us again to the enchanting site of the *Magnificat*, to Ein Karem.

On the other side of the valley, beyond the Church of the Birth of Saint John the Baptist, looms another church, evidently the work of Italian architects. Its façade is decorated with a splendid mosaic showing Mary's arrival. When the visitor steps into its inner courtyard, past an artistic wrought-iron grille, he is greeted by Mary's song of praise, which was posted here in forty-four languages during the Marian Year

1954 and since then has never again ceased to resound in this church. Ruins of walls prove that houses of worship stood here already in the Byzantine era and during the Crusades. In a stone crypt beneath a vault of Gothic arches there is a well—which testifies to a pertinent misunderstanding. For of course the *Magnificat* was spoken, not here, but rather at the main well in the middle of the town. Only when the Muslims built a mosque there were the Christians forced to create for themselves a substitute shrine. Earlier, though, quite a different episode was commemorated here, which we find not in Luke but in the *Proto-Gospel*.

Thus the Russian Abbot Daniel, who visited the Holy Land immediately after the First Crusade (in 1106/1107), told not only about the "house of Zechariah, in which the Blessed Virgin greeted her cousin Elizabeth . . . in this house John the Forerunner was born . . . in a little cave", thus unambiguously identifying the Church of Saint John as the site of Mary's Visitation. He knew also about another shrine: "A half *verst* (one-third of a mile) away, on the other side of a valley full of trees, is the mountain to which Elizabeth ran with her son and exclaimed, 'Take in, O mountain, this mother and child.' And the mountain opened and gave them shelter. . . . To this day one can see the place of this event in the rock. Over it stands a little church, beneath which there is a little grotto. From this grotto flows a spring of water."

Indeed, the *Proto-Gospel* ends with the persecution of John's parents by King Herod. It says there that he did not only command the slaughter of the innocents in Bethlehem. He must also have learned about the events surrounding the priest Zechariah, whose son he likewise wanted to have killed, just to be safe. When Herod's soldiers drew near, Elizabeth took the baby John out of the crib and fled. "She went up into the mountains, looking for a place to hide him." In her despair, she prayed for a miracle—"and straight away the mountain split open and received her." But perhaps she merely came upon one of the many old burial caves that archaeologists found in the area surrounding the Church of the Visitation. This story was quite popular among the early pilgrims; proof of this is a medallion made of fired clay that archaeologists discovered in the Italian town of Bobbio; apparently someone brought it back as a souvenir from Ein Karem. It shows how the mother and child slipped into the rock. Over them hovers an angel, while a soldier with drawn sword stands as though rooted at the spot. "The Lord's blessings from the refuge of Saint Elizabeth", reads the Greek inscription. Two parchment manuscripts from the seventh century also mention the cave shrine. The only evidence left today is a stone, apparently taken from the rock on the mountainside, which rests behind bars in a niche of the crypt of the Basilica of the Visitation and displays something like an imprint. "In this rock, Elizabeth is said to have hidden John", says the Latin inscription made of gilded mosaic stones.

But with that the *Proto-Gospel* is not yet entirely over. When Herod's men returned from Ein Karem without accomplishing their mission, the king ordered them to interrogate Zechariah. Just then he was again performing his Temple service, but he had someone tell the soldiers that he did not know where his son was. Then the soldiers forced their way into the Temple and stabbed the elderly priest beside the Lord's altar of incense. For three days the people are said to have mourned him.

This passage is often cited as proof of how historically unreliable the *Proto-Gospel* is. While Luke keeps to the facts and knows that a particular priestly class served only twice a year and that the priest who presents the incense offering was carefully selected by lot, in the account by *Pseudo-James* it appears at first glance as though the incense offering was Zechariah's regular duty. Of course that would be completely impossible.

But it becomes interesting when we remember that the priestly class of Abijah served twice a year, specifically in November and May. The time of service in May fell during 8–14 Sivan, which in 5 B.C. would correspond to May 13–20. As mentioned earlier, the Feast of the Holy Innocents of Bethlehem was still celebrated in the fourth century. Is it mere chance that this date, May 18, falls precisely in one of the only two weeks in which Zechariah actually performed his service in the Temple? And might it not be, then, that after the marvelous deeds that God had done for him, his priestly class allowed him to present the incense offering once again (or from then on)?

Maybe Jesus was even alluding to his deceased great-uncle when he accused the Pharisees and scribes: "You build the tombs of the prophets whom your fathers killed . . . from the blood of Abel to the blood of Zechariah, who perished between the altar and the sanctuary" (Lk 11:47, 51). Usually this passage from Scripture is referred to Zechariah son of Jehoiada, about whom we read in 2 Chronicles 24:21: "But they conspired against him, and by command of the king they stoned him with stones in the court of the house of the LORD." This stoning did take place on the Mount of Solomon's Temple, but surely not in the restricted space "between the altar and the sanctuary" of which Jesus spoke. The evangelist Matthew, on the other hand, is thinking of "Zechariah the son of Barachiah", who wrote the Book of Zechariah; but in it we do not find the slightest hint of a violent death. Since Jesus was describing a long arc, from the first murder of a prophet (Abel) to the last, one would rather think of an incident from the recent past. Of course anyone can maintain that the *Proto-Gospel* tailored its version of the death of Zechariah to fit this saying of Jesus exactly. But it is equally possible that Jesus was referring to the murder of a priest from his own family. Not until 2003 was it discovered what "monument" he may have been thinking about in that connection.

In the Kedron Valley of Jerusalem, along the path from the well of Siloam to the Mount of Olives that Jesus so often walked, three monumental tombs from the time of Herod are found in a rock wall. I always liked this path, because for a few yards it led directly back into the time of Jesus. On the left side rises Mount Moriah, with the mighty walls and the Temple platform, whose golden brown battlements stand out against the blue of the sky. On the right side, the ancient tombs lean on the rock face from which they were once carved out. The roof of the first one resembles a pyramid, while the roof of the third one projects like the inverted bell of a trumpet into the steely blue sky. They stood here when Jesus used to withdraw to one of the caves on the Mount of Olives in the evening; they kept watch as he, together with the disciples, came from the Last Supper; they were witnesses to his arrest, when in the glow of the torches he was dragged off in chains in the opposite direction, to the place at the foot of Mount Zion where the high priest's palace was located. Since that time, the path has remained almost unchanged; at the edge of it many shards from biblical times have been found. It made me all the more wistful, therefore, when I saw that it was being leveled and in places filled up as an access road to the tract of land in the Kedron Valley where Pope Benedict celebrated a Mass on May 12, 2009.

In the light of the setting sun, which casts unusually long shadows and thus brings hidden things to light, an Israeli archaeologist had discovered six years earlier a hitherto unnoticed inscription. It is found over the entrance to the largest of the three tombs, Absalom's Tomb, as it is called, and consists of forty-seven Greek characters in two rows, each one around four inches tall. "This is the tomb of Zechariah, martyr, a very pious priest, father of John", the text reads. In the opinion of Emile Peuch, an expert in epigraphy from the École Biblique of the Dominican Friars in Jerusalem, it dates back to the fifth century, when the Byzantines endeavored to determine the location of places in and around Jerusalem that are mentioned in the New Testament. Of course the late date makes it rather unlikely that Zechariah was in fact buried there, but the possibility cannot be ruled out. Supposedly James, the *brother of the Lord*, was also buried there later.

Perhaps the stone tower at the side of the ravine that was so closely connected with Jesus' fate was in fact a monument to a murdered prophet, another victim of Herod, who at all costs wanted to prevent the true "King of the Jews" from growing up within his sphere of influence.

~

Digression: When Was Jesus Born?

There are various reasons why in my book *Jesus von Nazareth* I dated the birth of the Savior to the first half of March, 5 B.C.—not only because I identified the supernova that flared up at that time in the constellation Aquila with the Star of Bethlehem.

The fact is that the first Christians were almost indifferent about Christmas. No early Christian author mentions celebrations on the anniversary of the Lord's birth; on the contrary: Origen even considered the observance of birthdays a "pagan" practice. Thus, the early Christians never celebrated the birthdays of their saints and martyrs, either, but always the day of their martyrdom, when they were "born in heaven". Accordingly, we find in the Gospels very specific indications about the day of Jesus' death and the time of his Resurrection—but other than that, only a note that he was then, in A.D. 30, more than thirty years old. Matthew and Luke agree that he was born during the reign of Herod the Great, and that is the only reason we are certain that he came into the world before March of 4 B.C. The reference to the shepherds in the fields, moreover, definitively rules out the months of November through February; at that time the sheep were still in the sheepfolds.

The earliest record about the historical "date of Christmas" comes from Clement of Alexandria (150–215); not surprisingly he neglects to mention December 25:

> And there are those who have determined not only the year of our Lord's birth, but also the day; and they say that it took place in the twenty-eighth year of Augustus, and in the twenty-fifth day of [the Egyptian month of] Pachon. . . .
>
> Others say that He was born on the twenty-fourth or twenty-fifth of Pharmuthi.[6]

---

[6] Clement of Alexandria, *The Stromata, or Miscellanies*, bk. 1, chap. 21, in *Ante-Nicene Fathers*, ed. Alexander Roberts, James Donaldson, vol. 2 (Peabody, Mass.: Hendrickson Pubs., 1995), 333.

Now the Egyptian calendar is an arcane science unto itself; in the second century, at any rate, in Clement's time, the twenty-fifth of Pachon fell on April 9 and the twenty-fourth or twenty-fifth of Pharmuthi fell on March 9–10.

Only since the second half of the fourth century was Christ's birth celebrated on December 25 in the West and on January 6 in the East. Incidentally, that did not result from a command of Constantine the Great, as is often maintained, nor did it have anything to do with the feast day of *sol invictus*, the Unvanquished Sun-god of the Romans, as was first claimed in the twelfth century by the Syrian Christian Dionysius Bar Salibi. Of course his hypothesis was gratefully taken up in the skeptical eighteenth century, which helped to spread it. In contrast, serious church historians today are of the opinion that the date of Christmas has a completely different origin.

Around the year 200, Tertullian maintained that 14 Nisan, the day of Jesus' death according to the Jewish lunar calendar, would correspond to March 25 of the Roman solar calendar. Because it was believed then that the Incarnation and death of the Lord fell on the same calendar day, March 25 was soon celebrated also as the day of the Annunciation to Mary—from which the birth date December 25 resulted by adding nine months. This convinced even important Fathers of the Church such as Saint Augustine, who broached the subject in his treatise *On the Trinity*. The poignant symbolism in identifying thus the milestones of Christ's Incarnation was recognized also by Bishop Epiphanius of Salamis (fourth century) when he wrote: "Enclosed within the spotless womb of the Blessed Virgin was the Lamb that in his eternal sacrifice has taken away the sins of the world." Other Christians in turn still knew (or had calculated) that Jesus was crucified on April 7, A.D. 30, and they equated this day with the day of the Annunciation and reckoned January 6–7 as the birthday. Thus even today the Armenians celebrate the Annunciation on April 7 and Christmas on January 6 of the Julian calendar.

However, the astronomical data, the time of the tax assessment (probably at the same time as the Temple tax), the local circumstances, as described in the Gospels (sheep on the meadows!), but above all the plausible date of the massacre of the children of Bethlehem (May 18) and of the murder of Zechariah (May 20), at earliest forty days after Mary's delivery (Luke mentions his Presentation in the Temple!), or, rather, more than fifty-three days afterward (for the magi's journey lasted that long), all point to the *birth of Jesus* and not to his *conception by Mary* in the month of Nisan (March/April). But Roman and Jewish thinking collided here—for among the Romans, as we say with Augustus, the day of the conception counted more than the birthday. And so knowledge about the *Jesus appearing in the flesh* in Nisan turned into belief in the *Annunciation to Mary* in that month. Later (from the fourth century on), there was an additional factor: people did not want to celebrate the two major feast days of Christianity, Christmas and Easter, at the same time. That is why December 25 was attractive on account of its symbolic power—as a sign of the victory of light over darkness.

Jesus, however, was no doubt born in Nisan, which in the Jewish year 3756 (5 B.C.) began on March 9, which also makes sense theologically. For the Jews were convinced, to cite Rabbi Eliezer: "In Nisan the world was created. In Nisan the patriarchs were born; at the Passover Isaac was born . . . and in Nisan they (our posterity) will be redeemed in the future." This month in spring is for the Jews the symbol par excellence for renewal: "This month shall be for you the beginning of months; it shall be the first month of the year for you", the Lord said to Moses and Aaron (Ex 12:2). It was the month in which the Paschal lambs were born, which then, when they were one year old, were brought into the houses on 10 Nisan and slaughtered in the Temple on 14 Nisan. What month would have been more fraught with symbolism for the birth of the Redeemer who became the sacrificial Lamb of God?

What about the year? It is generally known that our system of reckoning time goes back to the monk Dionysius Exiguus (470–540), a native Ukrainian, who was commissioned by the pope to devise a more exact calendar. In doing so, he calculated that A.D. 1 corresponds to the year 754 *ab urbe condita*, that is, since the founding of Rome in 753 B.C. He did not figure in a "zero year" because the arithmetical concept of zero was unknown in the West in his day.

Unfortunately, he never revealed how he arrived at that year. All that is known is that most of his sources were originally from Egypt, since in his reckoning of the date of Easter he used the so-called *Alexandrian Cycle* of the Egyptian monk Anianos. In Egypt, as we read in Clement of Alexandria, they dated the birth of Christ to the twenty-eighth year of Augustus. Since this honorary title was awarded by the senate to Octavian in 27 B.C., Dionysius seems in fact to have taken this year as the point of departure for his calculation. But the grant of the title was historically of secondary importance. Octavian's rule as monarch began *de facto* in 32 B.C., when he had himself proclaimed *dux Italiae* [ruler of Italy] and the entire West took an oath of loyalty to him, before he set out and conquered Mark Antony one year later at Actium. If we take this date as the point of departure, then the twenty-eighth year of Augustus was actually the year 5 B.C., the last year that can be considered as the year of Jesus' birth, since King Herod died in March of 4 B.C. Was it chance that precisely at that point in time, around 1 Nisan in the year 3756, according to the Jewish calendar (or March 9, 5 B.C., according to our way of reckoning time), the sign of the Messiah —a new, bright star, a supernova—appeared in the heavens?

9

The Flight into Egypt

The whole field is a wasteland of ruins. But upon closer inspection, one quickly notices that these are no ordinary ruins but, rather, fragments of a gigantic Egyptian temple complex: columns and inscriptions, wall paintings and statues. Which depict cats again and again. For the cat was considered here a "sacred animal", consecrated to the goddess Bastet, who was once revered in the temple of which this stone chaos is the only remaining evidence. The locality owes its name to her: *Baset*, in Old Egyptian; *Bubastis*, in Greek; *Tell Basta* ("Bastet's Hill"), in modern Arabic.

Founded already in the early dynastic period, around five thousand years ago, Bubastis in ancient Egypt was not only the capital of the *nome* of Am-Khent but also a beloved place of pilgrimage. Its heyday, however, was back in the time of the Libyan (22nd) Dynasty, when Pharaoh Shoshenq (946–924 B.C.) made it his capital for a short time. Under the name Shishak, we find him in the Bible, also; he attacked Jerusalem in 925 B.C., in the fifth year of the Jewish King Rehoboam, son of Solomon, and plundered the Temple (1 Kings 14:25–26). Out of the booty, which included Solomon's golden shields, he had the temple to his goddess thoroughly and monumentally extended. It lasted almost a millennium, until another "King of the Jews" caused it to collapse, as the story goes.

The flight of the Holy Family into Egypt is another disputed chapter in the narrative of Jesus' infancy; here, too, Matthew is accused of having invented it so as to make it appear that a prophecy about the Messiah was fulfilled.

After the magi left Bethlehem, it says in chapter 2 of his Gospel, an angel appeared to Joseph in a dream: "Rise, take the child and his mother, and flee to Egypt, and remain there till I tell you; for Herod is about to search for the child, to destroy him" (Mt 2:13). Then, although it was the middle of the night, Joseph arose, untied the donkey, and "took the child and his mother . . . , and departed to Egypt". That was nothing unusual in itself; persecuted Jews had always sought refuge along the Nile. Even King Herod had fled to Egypt when the henchmen of Antigonus were pursuing him. Alexandria, the capital of the Ptolemaic Kingdom, had the largest Jewish diaspora community in the ancient world, and its members included not a few political refugees, first from the Hasmoneans, then from Herod. In all of Egypt, we read in the works of Philo of Alexandria, there were over a million Jews and even a replica of the Jerusalem Temple. But after he related this completely plausible story, the zealous Matthew just had to show the Jews once again why Jesus was the long-awaited Messiah. Thus he wrote: "This was to fulfil what the Lord had spoken by the prophet, 'Out of Egypt have I called my son'" (Mt 2:15).

But anyone who looks up the quotation in the source, the Book of Hosea, finds that it is not all that cut and dried. For the passage there in its entirety reads: "When Israel was a child, I loved him, and out of Egypt I called my son. The more I called them, the more they went from me; they kept sacrificing to the Baals, and burning incense to idols" (Hos 11:1–2). Consequently, this Scripture passage refers instead to the Exodus and the falling away of many Jews in the Promised Land who suddenly worshipped the local deities. Once again, therefore, Matthew has tried at all costs to find a Scripture passage that somehow could be related to an event in the life of Jesus, in this case the flight of the Holy Family. To suppose the contrary is therefore absurd; previously, in fact, not one single Jew had any reason to suspect that Hosea's words contained an announcement of the Messiah.

But these admittedly somewhat vague words of the evangelist were not the whole story; on the contrary, again and again the faithful tried to reconstruct the route of the refugees from Bethlehem on the basis of apocryphal writings, local traditions, and mystical visions. But however dubious many sources may seem, ultimately even the skeptic must admit that the various testimonies, taken together, produce a rather plausible composite picture.

One of the first to follow the trail of the Holy Family in Egypt was a German, the Lutheran pastor, theologian, Coptic scholar, and archaeologist Otto Meinardus. Meinardus (1925–2005) was born into a family of Lutheran scholars and was a genuine Hanseatic world traveler, whose wanderlust led him first to study in England, and then to accept his first pastorate in the United States and to study at Harvard University. After a pastoral side trip to Australia and New Zealand, he managed to arrive in Egypt in 1956, even though he had married and fathered two children meanwhile. The land of the Pharaohs and its two-thousand-year-old Christian tradition became the love of his life. Finally, he found in the Coptic Church the rootedness in tradition and mysticism that he obviously missed in his own evangelical Lutheran faith, even though he remained loyal to it all his life. He studied Eastern Church art and early Christian archaeology while working as a Lutheran pastor in Maadi near Cairo and had enough time left over for activity as a researcher for the Deutsche Archäologische Institut, the Institute of Coptic Studies, and an ever-growing German readership. One of his main topics was the Egyptian tradition about the flight of the Holy Family, about which he finally wrote a book in 1963. Even though it was not very widely read in either the German or the English edition (which is too bad, for it is competently and charmingly written), it became a milestone in the rediscovery of these traditions. Forty years later, the American Paul Perry followed this up with his travel book *Jesus in Egypt* (with a foreword by the then seventy-eight-year-old Meinardus), which was well received, at least in the United States. But three years before that, on June 1, 2000, the Coptic Church in Egypt had reacted to the previous study by the German scholar. On that day the Coptic Patriarch (who as patriarch of all Africa traditionally has the title "pope" as well; incidentally, his Church was founded by Mark the evangelist at the behest of Saint Peter) Shenouda III, met with his Catholic counterpart, Stephanus II, Egypt's Prime Minister Atef Ebeid, Minister of Foreign Affairs Amr Moussa, and the Muslim Sheikh Mohammed Sayed al-Tantawi in the Coptic Orthodox Church of Maadi on the bank of the Nile to commemorate the most significant event in Egyptian history—the arrival of Jesus, Mary, and Joseph two thousand years before (officially, even though it was actually 2005 years ago). A large-format, lavishly illustrated 168-page volume in ten languages was presented to all the participants in this ecumenical meeting as well as to representatives of the world press, the results of an assessment of the still living traditions about the places involved in the flight. Moreover, the book contains a map, approved by Pope Shenouda III with his personal signature, of the route traveled by the Holy Family, as it could be reconstructed with the greatest possible exactitude.

Some of these places have been revered at least since the fourth century, even though the written sources concerning them come from a later period: for instance, the *Gospel of Pseudo-Matthew* (which some scholars date to the fourth century and others as late as the eighth), the *Arabic* and *Armenian Infancy Gospel* (fifth to eighth century), the vision attributed to the Patriarch Theophilus (385–412), as well as a sermon by Zechariah, Bishop of Sakha (seventh century). In the twelfth century, Yuhanna ibn Said al-Kulzumi drew up in his *History of the Patriarchs of the Egyptian Church* a list of nine places that were visited by the Holy Family, while a century later Abu el-Makarim in *Churches and Monasteries of Egypt* mentioned fourteen stations. The medieval *Synaxaria* (calendar of saints) of the Egyptian and Ethiopian Copts name nine cities that were blessed by the Child Jesus and his Mother.[1] With that, the tradition was canonized for the first time. But how authentic are these places and their legends; how plausible is their claim? In order to get some idea about it, I traveled in March 2010 to Egypt; and I, too, could hardly resist its magic and its holiness.

It was probably during the night of May 17–18, 5 B.C., that the Holy Family set out in the direction of the Nile region. According to Egyptian tradition, they were accompanied by two persons, the midwife Salome and Joseph's youngest son, Samuel, and also the family's donkey came along. Even though today, in the predominantly Muslim Near East, the "lord of creation" [head of the household] rides on the donkey, while his wife and child valiantly jog behind him, Christian iconography makes it clear that it was different back then: of course Mary rode, with the Child Jesus in her arms, while the youth went ahead and Joseph, leaning on his walking stick, followed after with Salome. In fact, this corresponded to Jewish custom; there was even a example of it in the Old Testament, where the Book of Exodus (4:20) says: "So Moses took his wife and his sons and set them on a donkey, and went back to the land of Egypt; and in his hand Moses took the rod of God." There is no doubt that Joseph, being a master builder, could afford a donkey, indeed, urgently needed one as a beast of burden. And to complete the picture: of course Mary and Joseph were not dressed in the medieval clothing with which we are familiar from art, or in the attire of present-day Arabs. In antiquity, men and women wore a

---

[1] The different numbers should not be surprising; sometimes people counted only the places where the Holy Family spent a few days, other times the cities and towns that were explicitly blessed by Jesus and Mary, but then also localities that they simply passed through or where they spent only one night.

1) The Advocata *icon in Rome, the oldest known Marian image*

2) The Altar of the Augustan Peace in Rome

3 and 4) The image on its frieze (left) *inspired the painter Raphael* (right) *and others*

5) Herod's Temple in Jerusalem. Mary grew up in its shadow.

6) The grotto monastery of Kosiba, an Essene foundation

7) Over the house where Mary was born the Church of Saint Anne stands today

8) The interior of the Holy House of Loreto, proofs of its authenticity:

9) Hebrew and Greek graffiti by pilgrims

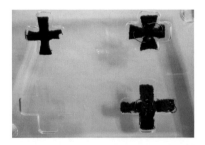

10) Cloth crosses of the Crusaders

11) "Nabataean" masonry

12) Altar of the Apostles with stones from Nazareth

13) The Church of the Well in Nazareth

14) Mary's well

15) The "royal" necropolis beneath the convent of the Sisters of Nazareth

16) The Grotto of the Annunciation in Nazareth: The Holy House stood here!

17) A Jewish residence, first century, in the shadow of the Basilica of the Annunciation in Nazareth

18) Ein Karem, the birthplace of John the Baptist

19) Mary's Well: the scene of the Magnificat!

20) Ruins of the Kathisma Church on the road to Bethlehem, stone "Mary's Rest"

21) The Milk Grotto of Bethlehem

22) Marian Grotto in Musturud   *23) Marian bowl in Samannud*

24) The ruined church in Sakha   *25) Stone with "Jesus' footprint"*

26) Mary's tree in Matariyah/Cairo

27 and 28) Staircase and ancient row houses in Maadi

29) The Marian well in Babylon / Cairo

30) The Marian Grotto of Gabal al-Tayr

31) Deir al-Muharraq: In this house the Holy Family lived for six months

32) Father Philoxenos shows us the altar "in the midst of the land of Egypt" from the prophecy of Isaiah

33) The Dormition Basilica in Jerusalem, built over the house where the Mother of God lived and died, photographed from the roof of the Cenacle

34) The large Essene mikveh on Zion

35) A small mikveh on the grounds of Dormition Abbey

36) "Meryemana", the Marian house in Ephesus

37) Pope Benedict XVI praying inside the Marian house

38) Mary's tomb in the Kidron Valley, right next to the grotto of Gethsemane

39) Interior of Mary's tomb; the burial bench, place of the Assumption

40 and 41) The oldest depictions of Mary in the Catacombs of Priscilla

*42) "Luke's painting" in Santa
Maria Nova in Rome (fifth century)*

*43) Luke's painting in Jerusalem,
Saint Mark's Monastery*

linea, an ankle-length robe, and over it a *tunica*, a knee-length garment with short sleeves, and finally a *planeta* or *casula*, a sort of poncho that offered warmth at night and protection against wind and rain. While working and traveling, "one girded oneself", that is, held these garments together with a belt at the waist; sandals were worn to protect the feet. In the liturgical vestments of the Catholic Church, this "style" has outlasted the centuries almost unchanged. Mary's *planeta* may very well have been the long *maphorion* or veil worn close around the head that two Byzantine noblemen named Galbius and Candidus acquired in the Holy Land in the fifth century and brought to Constantinople. As provisions for the journey they had, besides meat, fish, and bread, also broad beans, lupines, peas, cucumbers, onions, garlic, and leeks, along with grapes, dates, and figs.

First their flight went northeast past the Herodium, toward the rising sun. After nineteen miles as the crow files, or twenty-two miles by land, a day's journey, they arrived at the Jordan River. While driving today on Israeli Highway 90 from the Dead Sea toward Galilee, one unfailingly notices on the right, just before the exit to the place where Jesus was baptized, a silver dome. It belongs to the Greek Orthodox monastery of Saint Gerasimos, the "founding father and patron saint of the desert along the Jordan". In 455 he founded here a *laura*, a colony of hermits in the caves above the Wadi en-Nukheil, which attracted many pilgrims in the sixth century, because the sudarium, or face cloth, of Christ, one of the most important relics of his Passion, was venerated here. (Today it is in Oviedo, Spain.) This locality is also called Kalamonia, the "good place", because here "Mary, Joseph, the Christ Child, and James" (as the monks thought) rested for the first time on their flight to Egypt. How long they stayed there is not recorded; some monks think that it was only one night; others maintain that it was a few days. Here, in any case, Joseph must have understood that he could not follow the same route as Herod had taken on his flight. For the direct way leading south, along the Dead Sea, was guarded on both shores by mighty royal fortresses: Masada on the western side, Machaerus on the eastern side (where thirty-two years later John the Baptist was executed). A safer option was the western route, the old *Via Maris* [maritime road] along the Mediterranean. And so the Holy Family probably traveled by way of Hebron to the old Philistine city of Askalon. At least that is what the Armenian *Infancy Gospel* says; there is no local tradition. But the *Gospel of Pseudo-Matthew* also reports a

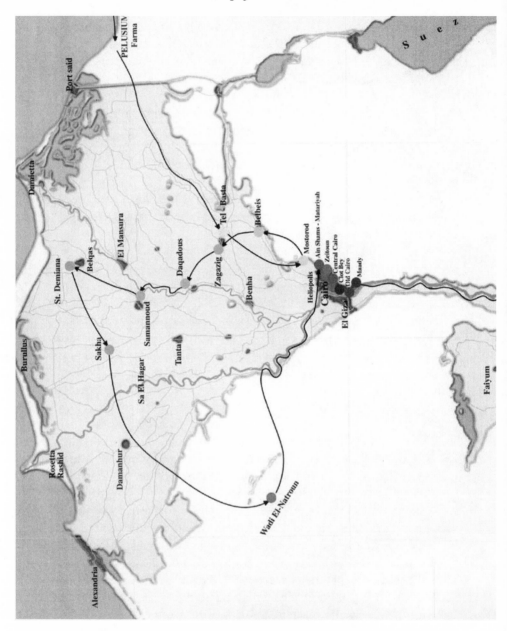

The Coptic Patriarch Shenouda III authorized in the year 2000 this reconstruction of the route traveled by the Holy Family through Egypt.

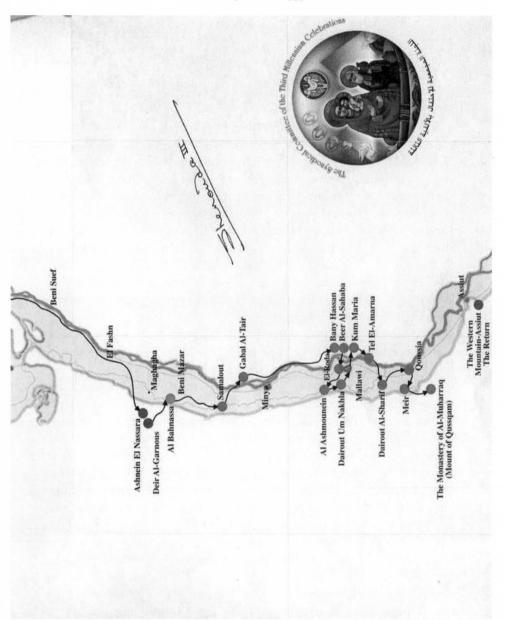

decision by Joseph not to take the road through the desert but to travel along the sea:

> While they were going on their journey, Joseph said to Jesus: "Lord, the heat is roasting us; if it please you, let us go by the seashore that we may be able to rest in the cities on the coast."

So they went from Askalon farther to Gaza, an old fortress of the Canaanites on the sea road. They crossed the Wadi Gaza and reached Han Yunes, which in the Hellenic period was called Jenysos and is even mentioned by Herodotus, then to Raphia, or Rafah. Today all these places are found in the Gaza Strip, ruled by the radical Islamist group Hamas, which makes visiting them extremely difficult. It took another day's journey, or twenty-seven miles, for the Holy Family to reach the Wadi el-Arish, "Egypt's brook", which had been the border to the Nile region since the days of Abraham. According to the Egyptian tradition, this happened on June 1—not a bad fit with our chronology, which has the flight during the night start before the massacre in Bethlehem (on May 18, 5 B.C.).

El-Arish, then as now a dusty Egyptian border city, did not have a good reputation in antiquity: it was called *Rhinocolura*, for the Ptolemies sent prisoners there after having their noses cut off to add to the punishment. Today the ruins of three churches testify to a former Christian presence, but we search in vain for a local tradition. This is true also of the next station, al-Zaraniq (also called al-Filussiyat), which lies twenty-three miles to the west. Tell el-Farama, or Farma, ancient Pelusium, is the first stop for which there is reliable evidence from sources. For example, the ninth-century Greek monk Epiphanius and Bernard the Wise (870) mentioned a tradition that the Holy Family visited the city, which is surrounded by marshes; the Islamic historian el-Maqrizi described it as one of the wonders of Egypt. According to Bernard, a Marian church stood then over the spot where the Child Jesus rested with his Mother and Saint Joseph, and it was visited by many pilgrims on the way to Jerusalem ("a six-day journey"). In 1118, the Crusader King Baldwin of Jerusalem occupied the city; but since he could not defend it, he had it destroyed. So today ruins are the only remaining evidence of Pelusium, whose only high ground once had so many houses of worship on it that it was called the "Hill of Churches".

The first destination of the Holy Family was obviously the Land of Goshen, where the Israelites lived during the time of their Egyptian slavery. It was located within the triangle formed by the cities of Zagazig, Bilbeis, and Tell el-Kebir, although some sources—including Flavius Josephus—consider the Wadi Tumilat with the cities of Pithom and Ramses as well as the city On (Heliopolis) as part of it, also. Probably they wanted to go to Leontopolis, which was well known not only for its large Jewish community but also because the second Jewish Temple stood there. It had been built around the year 170 B.C. by the high priest Onias, who had fled Jerusalem during the persecution by King Antiochus IV. The road to it led through Bubastis, situated two miles to the north, the city of the cat goddess. Here the Child Jesus came into contact for the first time with Egyptian paganism—an encounter with dramatic consequences, according to the legend.

Just before they reached Bubastis, the story goes, the Child felt hungry and thirsty. And so Mary set out on the road into the city, but she found no one who could provide her with what she needed; maybe she simply could not manage to make herself understood, since she spoke no Egyptian. Finally she ran into a Syrian by the name of Clum, who was just coming home from working in the fields and spoke Aramaic as she did. When Mary explained that she and her family were fleeing from Herod's soldiers, the man invited them all into his house. His wife was crippled, but the moment she saw the Child Jesus she was healed.

Out of gratitude, Clum wanted to do a favor for the Child. In Bubastis, the great feast of Bastet was held each year in June, also called the "Fine Feast of Drunkenness". The Greek Herodotus, known as the "father of historiography", describes it at length in book 2 of his *Histories*:

> The following are the proceedings on occasion of the assembly at Bubastis: men and women come sailing all together, vast numbers in each boat, many of the women with castanets, which they strike, while some of the men pipe during the whole time of the voyage; the remainder of the voyagers, male and female, sing the while and make a clapping with their hands. When they arrive opposite any of the towns upon the banks of the stream, they approach the shore, and, while some of the women continue to play and sing, others call aloud to the females of the place and load them with abuse, while a certain number dance, and some standing up uncover themselves [by holding their robes up high]. After proceeding in this way all along the river-course, they reach Bubastis, where they celebrate the feast

with abundant sacrifices. More grape-wine is consumed at this festival than in all the rest of the year besides. The number of those who attend, counting only the men and women and omitting the children, amounts, according to the native reports, to seven hundred thousand.

The feast, which was about fertility first and foremost, occasionally took on an orgiastic character; after being blessed by the goddess, no pilgrim wanted to spend the night alone. Nine months later, in March, the children of this wild celebration came into the world, without their mothers being able to remember even the names of their fathers; and since they had been begotten during the feast of Bastet, they invented a new word for them: bastards.

By day, in contrast, it was a colorful spectacle. Processions took place everywhere, flutes played, cymbals or drums were beaten to accompany singing, while magnificently outfitted cats, the sacred animals of Bastet, were carried in little sedan chairs and baskets through the temple grounds. The shrine was situated in a valley, on an island in a branch of the Nile River, so that hundreds of thousands of pilgrims could follow what was happening from the surrounding hills, too. The temple itself was made of red granite; in its inner court loomed the monumental image of a cat, surrounded by trees, which was unique for an Egyptian temple. "Other temples may be grander and may have cost more in the building, but there is none so pleasant to the eye as this of Bubastis", Herodotus wrote. Clum did not want the foreigners and their wonderworking child to miss that.

But no sooner did they set foot on the temple grounds, so the story goes, than the images of the cat goddess began to totter, then they collapsed, just as it says in the prophecy of Isaiah:

> Behold, the LORD is riding on a swift cloud and comes to Egypt; and the idols of Egypt will tremble at his presence, and the heart of the Egyptians will melt within them. (Is 19:1)

Not only did the Child Jesus destroy the idols; he also caused a spring to gush forth right beside the temple, and anyone who drank of its water was healed. But the inhabitants of Bubastis did not want to give up their old beliefs. They called soldiers to have the Holy Family arrested, and only with Clum's help were they able to escape. Before they continued their journey, the Holy Child blessed the Syrian, his family, and his home. On the site of his house, a church stood in the fourth century; on its ruins was built the present-day Mar Girgis Church in Zagazig not far from Tell Basta. And the spring still exists, too, right beside the aforementioned "field of the fallen idols". The wellspring was rediscovered only in 1991 during excavations on the temple grounds. Six years later, Professor Mahmud Umar, an archaeologist from the University of Zagazig, published the results of his investigation. Whereas Roman brick work surrounded the well, they found at the bottom of it the bones of animals that had fallen into the water hole that had originally been there. The oldest of them could be dated to A.D. 20–70; the wellspring must have come into existence shortly before then. And whereas no one knows precisely when the formerly magnificent Bastet temple was abandoned and its idols toppled, one thing is certain: no Roman author ever reported anything more about the orgiastic pilgrimage of Bubastis. Sometime around the turn of the eras, the cult must have come to an abrupt end.

According to Coptic tradition, the Holy Family fled south to Musturud, about thirty-three miles away; today it is a dirty suburb of the metropolis of Cairo. Its Coptic Church is scarcely to be found, for it is situated in a back yard on the street that runs along the canal bank, the Teraaet El Esmaiellah; house numbers in Egypt are as rare as street signs. Only after repeated questions does Muhammad, my Muslim driver, find the entrance. In front of the gate that leads into the churchyard sit two policemen with machine guns. They give me some inkling of how often there is harassment against the courageous, staunchly orthodox Coptic minority. Over the passageway, a tower juts into the sky; a mosaic showing the Holy Family taking a rest tells me that I am at the right place. I enter the church; a deacon notices me and is immediately ready to show me the crypt, which according to tradition was the shelter of the Holy Family. Here a pharaonic temple from the time of Ramses II once stood, he assures me. I descend a narrow staircase into the narrow passageway that is decorated with colored lights; in the center of it stands an altar with dozens of thin candles on its surface and a Marian icon. The walls are lined with stone; the dimensions of the original cave can only be surmised. On the opposite side, another narrow staircase leads back to the ground level, to a well. The friendly deacon removes from it a red cloth with an image of the Virgin embroidered on it, draws water, and in English invites me to drink: "Holy water. Many healings!" I am ready to believe him, and I drink. In the hotel I would never have touched the tap water; I use bottled mineral water. But it is in fact "holy water": I stay healthy. "Musturud was once called Al-Mahamma", the deacon tells me in broken English. "It means 'The Place of the Bath'." For here the Virgin Mary bathed the Child Jesus and washed his swaddling clothes. At almost every Marian station in Egypt, there is such a well with its very own legend. But that is not surprising at all, since the journey, of course, led from one well to the next, and they stopped where there was clean water. The next stop was Bilbeis, where the Holy Family is said to have rested under a tree as a funeral procession was passing by. The Child Jesus, according to the account by Bishop Zecharias of Sakha, had mercy on the mourners and awakened the dead man to life, who immediately praised "the true God, the Savior of the world". Of course, the whole village immediately believed in the Holy Child. In Daqadus, too, the Holy Family was kindly received; the well of the village, which the Child Jesus blessed, is located today on the grounds of the local Marian church. It dates back to the nineteenth century, but it was built over a church from the year 1239, which in turn stood on the ruins of a fourth-century church.

If we are to believe the Egyptian tradition, King Herod, upon learning about the flight of the Holy Family, sent soldiers to pursue them. We can assume that he had excellent contacts with the Roman governor in Egypt—from 7 to 4 B.C., a man by the name of Gaius Turranius—who had no objection to the persecution of a Jewish pretender to the throne. This persecution would explain why the Holy Family moved so restlessly from one place to another, even when they were welcomed hospitably by the local people, as is so often the case in the Nile delta.

In any case, their travels continued to Samannud, the former Sebennytos, or Zeb-nuter, an especially charming place. My trip to its Coptic church leads past a produce market that seems to offer for sale all the fruits and vegetables of the garden of Paradise. The church appears to be quite new; it, too, was built over much older predecessors. To my amazement, it is dedicated, not to the Virgin Mary, but to Saint Apanoub, a twelve-year-old youth who suffered martyrdom during the persecution of Christians by the Roman Emperor Diocletian (284–305). Together with eight thousand mostly young Christians, he is said to have been executed after long, cruel torture. Since then his relics, which are venerated in the church of Samannud, have worked miracles. Yet the history of the church goes back even farther. It stands, the story goes, over a house in which the Holy Family remained for between fourteen and seventeen days—their longest stay in Northern Egypt. This is attested even today by an old well with a heavy wooden cover, whose water is said to work miracles, and also by a very special relic. It stands right beside the well, in the churchyard, and no visitor can overlook it. The square concrete pedestal covered with black and white bathroom tiles makes sure of that, as does a large bilingual sign that announces in English and Arabic: "Virgin Mary used it when she was here." This refers to a large granite bowl that looks like the sacrificial bowl of an Egyptian temple and once was just that. The Blessed Virgin supposedly kneaded dough in it; now the pilgrims fill the bowl with well water, so as to decant it then into small bottles on account of its twofold *baraka*, or power, to bless.

We arrive at my next destination, Sakha, at dusk. Again I look for the church, and you can scarcely miss it—it stands on a hill, the highest point of the city. Its tower, visible from a great distance and surrounded by scaffolding, projects into the sky, and at its feet there are twelve clay domes, with a cross planted on the tallest. But as I approach, I have my doubts—all this seems more like a construction site than like one of the oldest, most important churches in Egypt. Ever since the fourth century, "Christ-loving" Sakha (earlier Sabakh) has been an episcopal see; in the seventh century, Saint Agathon Stylite, who lived atop a pillar, worked many miracles; here during that same period, Bishop Zecharias composed his famous sermon in which he recorded the Egyptian tradition about the flight of the Holy Family. As late as the fifteenth century, according to the Egyptian historian Al-Maqrizi, so many pilgrims streamed into Sakha that it was compared to Jerusalem. Since Marian apparitions occurred every year on June 1, this day was celebrated as the "Feast of the Apparition of the Virgin Mary". Yet only a few years ago was Sakha's greatest treasure rediscovered.

As Otto Meinardus was writing his book in 1963, he read in the Coptic and Ethiopic *Synaxarium* about a city called *Bikha Isus* [also spelled *Pekha-Issous*], which means "Jesus' footprint", in the province of Gharbiya on the Rosetta tributary of the Nile; there a stone with the imprint of the sole of the Holy Child was venerated. Bishop Zecharias, too, was acquainted with the story. He writes that the Child Jesus was thirsty, but his Mother could not find any water. Then, when Mary had set him down, the Child put his foot on a rock, and immediately a stream of pure water bubbled up from the ground. The stone was later doused with oil by the faithful, and many received blessings from it. Yet the place, which from then on was named after the miracle, could not be found. "Despite long searching and traveling back and forth, I found neither an ancient, a medieval, nor a modern place name in the Nile Delta that resembles the expression *Bikha Isus*", Meinardus noted with resignation. Nevertheless, one of the experts whom he had questioned, Dr. Murad Kamil, was convinced that *Bikha Isus* was the old name of Sakha; but he could not prove it, and in the church in Sakha no one knew anything about such a relic.

In April 1984, as construction workers were trying to lay a drainage pipe in front of the entrance to the church, at the depth of five feet they first hit a buried half of the capital of an ancient column. Slowly they hoisted the fragment, which weighed several tons, and then they noticed that a second, smaller stone lay beneath it, as though the capital was supposed to protect it and also point to it. It was rectangular, light gray, and about seven inches long. On one side, it displayed a brown-colored, heel-shaped hollow; on the other was an Arabic inscription: *i(bn) Allah*, "Son of God". The deacon who was supervising the construction workers, Halim Philippus Mikhail, knew about the old reports and immediately understood the importance of the discovery. Without hesitation he fell to his knees and drank the drainage water that had trickled into the excavation. It was now holy water, and to this day he swears that a sweet fragrance emanated from it. A man who had suffered for years from a serious eye disease washed with this water; he was healed. Since the Coptic Pope Shenouda III at that time was confined to a monastery in Bishoi by order of President Sadat, they brought this stone to him. Three times the patriarch celebrated the Divine Liturgy over it and prayed, and then he announced that the relic is genuine. Sakha was *Bikha Isus* [*Pekha-Issous*], there could be no more doubt about it! In the following years, the little town again became a place of pilgrimage for Christians from the north. A large, modern monastery was built, and on June 1 many thousands again streamed to the town in order to be present when the stone with Jesus' footprint was carried through the streets in solemn procession. But all that changed abruptly one fateful night, on June 16, 2008, when the church of the Virgin Mary burned down. "A short circuit", the Muslim governor had his spokesman announce after a rather superficial investigation; arson by radical Muslims, one Christian tells another with a hand in front of his mouth. As recently as May 31, the eve of the feast, the two groups had clashed; one Muslim was killed in the melee, and four Copts (two of the monks) were seriously injured. The church's precious Marian icon from the sixteenth century perished in the flames.

So the house of worship today is one big construction site. But right at the entrance, while conversing with the policeman on duty, I bump into the sacristan, who tells me about the fire. When I ask about the stone, he takes me into a locked closet in an adjoining building. I am relieved to see that it withstood the fire undamaged. It is kept in a wooden display case, surrounded by hundreds of slips of paper on which people have written their petitions. The sacristan opens it, reaches inside, and brings out the stone. Reverently I examine it from all sides. In fact, the heel-shaped depression cannot be missed, since the oil with which it was repeatedly anointed colored the stone at that spot. Whatever it is, it has become holy through the centuries of its veneration.

Sakha, in any case, became the turning point along the flight of the Holy Family. Whereas thus far it looked as though they were headed for Alexandria, here they turned aside so as to travel through the Wadi al-Natrun toward modern Cairo. Did someone warn them that Herod's henchmen were already waiting for them in Alexandria? Were their pursuers still at their heels? At any rate, we pick up their trail again only in Cairo, in the region of the ancient cities of On, Babylon on the Nile, and Maadi near Memphis.

First the refugees came to Heliopolis, which in ancient Egyptian was called On and in Hebrew Bet Shemesh, "House of the Sun". The Greek Strabo, who traveled to Egypt around 23 B.C., described the holy city of the ancient Egyptians as forsaken and depopulated. Here and there temple guards showed shrines with a historical rather than a religious value, but otherwise the city had only been a relic of its once so impressive past since the Persian attack in 525 B.C. As the story goes, its idols, too, crumbled as the Holy Family passed them, but there is no record of a stay there, for instance, at a well. Only in Matariyah, a northeastern suburb of Cairo, did the little group rest. This is one of the best attested places on their flight, since it is already mentioned in the *Arabic Infancy Gospel* from the fifth century:

> And they traveled farther to a city of idols [a reference to Heliopolis], which, as they approached, disintegrated into hills of sand. Next they found at the side of the road the sycamore fig tree that today is called

Matarea, and in Matarea the Lord Jesus caused a spring to well up, in which Mary washed his clothes. And in this region, balsam was produced from the sweat that the Lord Jesus poured out here.

To this day it is a place with a very special charm, indeed, an oasis in the stone and concrete wilderness of Cairo. A cement wall surrounds the garden, which is sacred to all religions; for a long time Muslims, too, used to make pilgrimages to the Virgin Mary Tree, and they wrote their petitions on scraps of fabric that they hung on the tree. Nowadays, of course, they just collect the admission fees, offer their services as guides, and gather the dried sycamore figs in order to give them to the visitors in exchange for a baksheesh.

From the many accounts of medieval and early modern pilgrims to the Holy Land, we know that Matariyah enjoyed great popularity early on. To the pilgrims who had set out from Jerusalem, crossed the Sinai, and prayed at the Mountain of Moses, the garden with its well and the shady tree seemed like Paradise. Already in the fifteenth century, the Mamluk Emir Yashbak invested in tourism and built an inn for pilgrims right beside the garden, to which he also demanded admission. In return, the visitor could even bathe in the pond that the water from the sacred spring now formed. Christians as well as Muslims were convinced that it was not just holy but also medicinal. In those days, they also used to show the pilgrims the trunk of the gigantic sycamore fig tree, of which only offshoots exist today; it was hollowed out, and the Holy Family is said to have taken refuge inside it when two bandits waylaid them. According to another legend, the Child Jesus broke pieces off Saint Joseph's walking stick and planted them in the ground at Matariyah. Out of them, they say, grew the balsam trees for which the garden was once famous. The Copts used the balsam that they made out of the fruits and by boiling the twigs to prepare the oil of anointing for their baptisms, but it was also applied as medicine in cases of poisoning and snakebite.

For the Holy Family, nevertheless, Matariyah was to be only a way station; their destination now was the Egyptian Babylon on the bank of the Nile, where there was another Jewish colony. The road to it led past Zeitoun, whose Marian church became well-known in 1968 because of a series of Marian apparitions, and via Haret Zuwaila, where they rested beside its well. Jesus, the story goes, blessed its water, and Mary drank of it. The church that has stood over the well for at

least a millennium is difficult to find; its entrance is located in a narrow alley right next to a Coptic convent. I pass the obligatory guard
and go in. Its interior is shrouded in a mystical semi-darkness; on the
walls of the side aisles, magnificently colored, archaic icons are held
by heavy, dark wooden frames. The central nave is lined by ancient
columns with Corinthian capitals. Rushing and splashing breaks the silence, and quickly I find out where it comes from. To the right of the
iconostasis, which screens off the sanctuary, there is an ancient spring
whose water is conducted into a channel that runs around the interior
of the church. Once a year, on June 28—according to tradition, the
day on which the Holy Family rested here—Ethiopian priests draw
water from this spring and bring it back home with them.

The only thing that Egyptian Babylon had in common with the city
on the Euphrates was its name. In this case, it is the Greek transcription
of the Egyptian *Per-hapi-n-on*, "House of On", or of the Semitic name
Bab ila On, "Gate to On", for here landed the boats of the pilgrims who
then continued their journey to the old, sacred city of On (Heliopolis)
on foot. The Greek Diodorus of Sicily, on the other hand, maintained
that real Babylonians, prisoners of war of the Pharaoh Sesostris from
the Twelfth Dynasty, had occupied a fortress here after a rebellion and
named it after their home. Later, around the year 100, Emperor Trajan
built a bastion on this spot in which he stationed a Roman cohort.
It was expanded again by Emperor Arcadius around A.D. 400, and its
ruins, including the mighty, round watchtowers, are well preserved.
Today, former Babylon is the Coptic district of Cairo (also called Misr
el-Qadima, or Old Cairo) and again something of a fortress. For fear
of attacks by radical Muslims, a large area of it is cordoned off by the
police, and it can be accessed only by pedestrians. Two places here
claim to have served as a shelter for the Holy Family, which is not
surprising: their return trip necessarily led by way of Babylon, too.

On the way to these sites, I walk past the Ben Ezra Synagogue, which
is especially sacred to the Jews. Here, they believe, the boy Moses was
found in his bulrush basket by Pharaoh's daughter, and to this place
Moses returned again and again, while he was living in Egypt, to pray
to God. As early as 605 B.C., a synagogue was built at this spot, they
say, which later bore the name of the prophet Jeremiah; the Romans
destroyed it, and the Christians built in its place a church, until the
Coptic patriarch in the twelfth century made the property over to
the Jewish Rabbi Ben Ezra. In the nineteenth century, this synagogue

became the scene of a scientific sensation. Two Scottish sisters, Agnes Lewis and Margaret Gibson, received permission then to do research in its *geniza*, its storeroom for old and damaged books. As they worked, they came across, a half century before Qumran, what were then the oldest known original Jewish writings, some of which went back to the second century B.C. (and thus were exactly as old as the oldest Dead Sea Scrolls). It is quite possible that one of them was being read when the Holy Family came to Babylon.

Only a few steps away from the synagogue stands the Church of Saint Sergius, in Arabic: *Abu-Sargah*. I turn to the left and come into a room from which a narrow staircase leads down to the crypt that developed out of the cave (which maybe served also as a basement vault?) where the Holy Family once stayed. The Christ Child allegedly lay in a niche in front of which the altar was later erected. This tradition, too, is quite ancient; the disputed point is whether or not this was on the return trip. In any case, the Coptic *Synaxarium* says that it was. The church was mentioned for the first time in a document in the early sixth century. After the construction of the Aswan Dam, its crypt was underwater for decades because the ground water table rose throughout Cairo; not until the year 2000 did the Coptic Church attend to it and begin an extensive, costly renovation. Since then, the ground water has been pumped out, and soon the crypt should be accessible again to visitors.

A second cave that likewise claims to have sheltered the Holy Family is in the possession of the Greek Orthodox Christians. Their church, dedicated to the Dormition of our Lady, is situated right in the middle of the Greek cemetery on the northern edge of the Coptic district. The ceiling fresco of its apse shows the flight of the Holy Family from Joseph's dream until their arrival in Babylon; the Greeks believe that that was their final stop. "For three years they stayed here, then they returned to Palestine", a Greek priest explains to me, while I walk past the sanctuary on the left and climb down the stairs into the crypt. There, in the middle of it, stands a large, circular well, topped with a ring of white marble. With a bucket fastened to a cord, I draw some of the blessed water. Then the priest shows me a niche in the rock. On a marble bench stands an icon with the image of the Holy Family; Mary is seated, and the Child Jesus gives a blessing while standing on her lap. It is quite possible, or even very likely, that the Holy Family spent the night here. But wherever there is a well, it has always been a public place; no one could have lived here undisturbed for three years.

At any rate, in Babylon someone must have given Saint Joseph a tip as to where Mary and the Child would be safe. Perhaps he spoke with a rabbi at the synagogue, or maybe the tradition that he met relatives here is true. In any case, the apparent wanderings of the Holy Family came to an end in Babylon; from then on, it seems, they headed for a very specific destination in the south. Probably it was too unsafe to board a boat in Babylon to take them upstream; Herod's men may still have been at their heels. In any case, the tradition says that they got on board four miles farther south in Maadi in order to set out on their journey to the interior of the country, to Upper Egypt.

Today Maadi is an elegant city district in which many foreigners live, most of them diplomats and merchants, along with members of the Egyptian upper class. Along the bank of the Nile, big-bellied restaurant ships are moored, and there is even a little yacht harbor and in between a well-tended, just renovated church with three domes made out of dried Nile mud. It is said to have been built over the ruins of a synagogue from the time of Jesus, a deacon tells me. I enter and say a prayer, then I step into the side room, the vault. There, beneath a slightly kitschy, gold-embroidered, plastic-covered Marian icon, the relic of a modern miracle is preserved. On March 12, 1976, the faithful who were just coming out of the early Divine Liturgy noticed an open book floating on the waters of the Nile, not far from the place where, according to tradition, the Holy Family boarded their boat. When the congregants fished it out of the river, it proved to be a Bible, opened precisely to the passage from the Book of Isaiah that deals with Egypt:

> In that day there will be an altar to the LORD in the midst of the land of Egypt, and a pillar to the LORD at its border. It will be a sign and a witness to the LORD of hosts in the land of Egypt; when they cry to the LORD because of oppressors he will send them a savior, and will defend and deliver them. And the LORD will make himself known to the Egyptians; and the Egyptians will know the LORD in that day. . . . In that day Israel will be the third with Egypt and Assyria, a blessing in the midst of the earth, whom the LORD of hosts has blessed, saying, "Blessed be Egypt my people." (19:19–25)

The fact that this thousand-page, large-format Bible, which was soaked and therefore twice as heavy, was open and floating on the Nile must have seemed to the pious Copts to be a miracle, a sign of God's blessing. It is understandable, therefore, that it is fervently venerated, almost as much if not more than the ancient steps to the riverbank on which the Holy Family once walked or the excavation revealing a now underground row of houses in which the refugees lived until they found a suitable ship; for ten whole days, as they assured me in Maadi.

Travelers used to land at several places, interrupting their voyage to spend the night on land or to buy provisions. Stops mentioned by tradition include al-Bahnasa, ancient Oxyrhynchus, which reportedly had 366 churches, and the village of Ishnin al-Nasara, where the Holy Family drank out of the local well and blessed it; every year on August 21, this event is commemorated with a major pilgrimage. In Dayr al-Ganus, which was once called Dayr b-Isus, "the House of Jesus", the travelers are said to have lived for four days before their voyage continued farther south.

The stop along their itinerary through Egypt with the most beautiful landscape is no doubt Gabal al-Tayr. Here the shrine is situated on the ridge of a steep rock face that looms high over the Nile Valley; in Jesus' day, the river ran directly past it. So the legend maintains that a gigantic piece of rock came loose and would have fallen onto the boat carrying the Holy Family had the Child Jesus not raised his hand and cast it into the river. The imprint of his hand was venerated until the nineteenth century, then the stone disappeared mysteriously; visitors claim to have seen it in the British Museum in London. Maybe to recover from the scare, the group of travelers landed here. Today 166 steps lead up to the church of the former Marian monastery, which is one of the oldest places of worship in Egypt. According to an inscription, it was dedicated in 44 A.M. (*Anno Martyro*, that is, after the commencement of the rule of Diocletian in A.D. 284, with which the Coptic reckoning of time begins), and therefore in A.D. 328; it goes back to a foundation by Saint Helena, the mother of Constantine the Great. Evidence that it is in fact quite ancient includes the early Coptic bas-relief (although it only dates back to the sixth century) over its entrance and the archaic columns that line the central nave; they were carved directly out of the stone of the cave that was originally located here. In one of them, you can still see a recess in which, the story goes, the Child Jesus was once laid. The altar is flanked by two unmistakably Roman columns with Corinthian capitals. Right beside it is the entrance to the part of the cave in which the Holy Family supposedly spent the night. According to the local tradition, this was August 22, which to this day is celebrated in Gabal al-Tayr as a major feast with a pilgrimage.

One and a quarter miles south of the height of Gabal al-Tayr, at the foot of a rock face and at one time right on the bank of the Nile, the Shagarat al-Abid, or "worshipping tree", stood until recently. Legend has it that the acacia once bowed as the Holy Family went past it and from then on continued to grow horizontally. As late as 1999, a brochure of the Egyptian Ministry of Tourism, which was just discovering the potential of tourism by pilgrims, mentioned this unique prodigy. Two years later, rumors circulated in that area to the effect that the government wanted to fence the tree in so as to demand admission from the visitors, as in Matariyah. Of course that displeased the local inhabitants: the Muslims must have been afraid that their properties would be confiscated and their houses torn down. So the tree disappeared overnight. It was abruptly felled, and even its roots were taken out of the ground so that no shoot could be cultivated. The man who did this also tried to sell the wood as "relics", but the Egyptian Ministry of Antiquities learned about the business and intervened.

At dusk we reach Al-Ashmunayn, the former Hermopolis, the city of the god Toth (or Hermes), whom the Egyptians depicted as a baboon or an ibis. Two mighty stone apes greet us at the entrance to the archaeological park that was established here on the grounds of one of the most important places of worship in ancient Egypt, and their backs are turned toward the setting sun. One of them is shattered and is missing its head; both of them were dug out of the ruins and set up again at the edge of the excavation site. Even today they attest to what is described in the *Gospel of Pseudo-Matthew* with a specific indication of the place:

> Rejoicing and exulting, they came into the regions of Hermopolis and entered into a certain city of Egypt that is called Sotinen; and because they knew no one there from whom they could ask hospitality, they went into a temple, which was called the Capitol of Egypt. And in this temple there had been set up three hundred sixty-five idols, to each of which on its own day divine honors and sacred rites were paid. And it came to pass that, when Mary went into the temple with the child, all the idols prostrated themselves on the ground, so that all of them were lying on their faces, shattered and broken to pieces; and thus they plainly showed that they were nothing.

At first Aphrodisius, the town major, wanted to have the perpetrators of this sacrilege arrested by his soldiers. But when he "saw all the gods lying prostrate on their faces, he went up to Mary, who was carrying the Lord in her bosom, and worshipped him." Then he said to his men: "Unless this were the God of our gods, our gods would not have fallen on their faces before him, nor would they be lying prostrate in his presence: therefore, they silently confess that he is their Lord."

In fact the most impressive testimonials of ancient Hermopolis are not Egyptian temples but, rather, the columns of a Christian basilica that was built in the early fifth century. It is certainly no accident that it stood in front of the main well of the city, as though it was an intentional reminder that the Holy Family drank its water, too.

There is no doubt that the refugees stayed here. The Greek geographer Strabo reports that special tolls were levied at Hermopolis, the border city between the Thebais and Middle Egypt. Thus everyone who passed by there had to pay two percent of the value of the wares that he was bringing with him. In the vision of Patriarch Theophilus, horse monuments stood at the four corners of the city gate; they fell down and broke to pieces when the Holy Child was carried past them. On the other hand, Sozomenus of Gaza, the author of a fifth-century Greek Church history, reports:

> At Hermopolis, in the Thebais, is a tree called Persis, of which the branches, the leaves, and the least portion of the bark, are said to heal diseases, when touched by the sick; for it is related by the Egyptians that when Joseph fled with Christ and Mary, the holy mother of God, from the wrath of Herod, they went to Hermopolis; when entering at the gate, this largest tree, as if not enduring the advent of Christ, inclined to the ground and worshiped Him. I relate precisely what I have heard from many sources concerning this tree. . . . The inhabitants of Egypt and of Palestine testify to the truth of these events, which took place among themselves.[2]

Even though at first glance one might think that Sozomenus meant here the Shagarat al-Abid of Gabal al-Tayr, this impression is wrong. For the Egyptian Abu el-Makarim (thirteenth century) also knows about this tree near Hermopolis, which bore red fruits that were called *sebastan*. When the Muslim governor tried to have it felled in the seventh century, the Coptic Patriarch Agatus (658–677) stood in front of this holy

---

[2] *The Ecclesiastical History of Salaminius Hermias Sozomenus*, bk. 4, chap. 21, in *Nicene and Post-Nicene Fathers*, second series, vol. 2, ed. Philip Schaff and Henry Wace (Peabody, Mass.: Hendrickson Pubs., 1995), 343.

tree to protect it, while such a strong wind blew up that the axes of the woodcutters flew into their faces.

After the rather brief episode in Hermopolis, the Holy Family continued traveling by the land route until they finally reached their destination.

Today the monastery of the Blessed Virgin of Deir al-Muharraq is considered the holiest place in Egypt. A pilgrimage to it, they say, has the same spiritual value as a pilgrimage to Jerusalem, which presently is not possible for reasons of church polity; in order to avoid suspicion of maintaining contacts in Israel, which are viewed with mistrust, the Coptic Church forbids its faithful to visit the Holy Land. And in fact the mighty walls, fortified with battlements, that surround the monastery are reminiscent of the walls of Jerusalem. Here, then, on the edge of the desert, the Holy Family is said to have found their final refuge, until news of Herod's death reached Joseph.

My driver stops on the expansive parking lot in front of the main gate of the monastery, and I walk in. Probably it is not difficult to spot me as a foreigner; in any case, while I am still looking for the shrine, a tall, thin, black-bearded monk with absolutely aristocratic dignity addresses me in perfect English and introduces himself as Father Philoxenos. I like him immediately, but I still have to smirk. In his right ear, beneath his *qalansuwa* (monastic cowl), which is embroidered with thirteen golden crosses, he is wearing an earpiece, which a cord connects with the cell phone in the breast pocket of his long, black cassock. So here, too, in the desert monastery, modern communications technology has made its appearance. When someone calls, I hear the ringtone and am enthusiastic: a recording of church bells playing the melody of a Coptic hymn to Christ the King. Father Philoxenos is willing to download it to my cell phone immediately via Bluetooth; since then with every call I am reminded of our meeting in the monastery of al-Muharraq.

He leads me through an avenue beneath a roof formed by the branches of thickly planted plane trees, past a villa in the colonial style that was once donated to the abbot of the monastery. "It serves today as a guest house. Our abbot lives as we do in a perfectly normal cell," Father Philoxenos confides to me, as though he were trying to apologize for this bit of monastic luxury. Then we reach the oldest part of the monastery complex, again surrounded by a high wall, guarded by a medieval tower, a place of refuge that is separated by a drawbridge from the ramp leading up to it. "We have never used it", the monk says, seeing my astonished expression. "Jesus blessed this monastery, and ever since then it has been protected by heaven. All the other monasteries were attacked by Berbers, but here we monks were always safe. The Lord prophesied to us that it would continue to exist until the Last Judgment."

In the middle of the courtyard stands the actual shrine, a two-story church covered with Nile mud, with thirteen domes looming over it: "They stand for Christ and the twelve apostles", Father Philoxenos explains. "That is of course a later addition. The core of this church is the house in which the Holy Family lived for exactly six months and five days. But naturally we had to extend it and expand it in order to accommodate all the faithful who wanted to celebrate the Divine Liturgy here."

We go in. A wooden partition wall with a splendid screen divides the addition from the original house, which serves today as the monastic choir. On a wooden ambo lies an old Coptic Bible, which the tall priest opens, in order to read aloud to me once more the prophecy of Isaiah: "Seven hundred years before Christ the prophet foretold the founding of this church when he wrote: 'In that day there will be an altar to the LORD in the midst of the land of Egypt.'" He assures me: "This place here is the geographical center of Egypt. And now I will show you the altar of which he spoke." He opens the door in the middle of the wooden iconostasis, and before me stands an altar covered with violet cloth. When he removes another covering made of red velvet, a monolithic limestone cube comes into view in which an ancient Egyptian altar stone is embedded. I bow down and kiss this altar, which Father Philoxenos describes as "the first Christian altar ever, established by Jesus himself, in the oldest Church of Christendom". "Here the Child Jesus slept", he claims. "After his Resurrection, the Lord came back to this place, together with his disciples and the Mother of God, and consecrated this altar. When Saint Mark became bishop of Alexandria, he made a pilgrimage to this house and had it rebuilt as a church. In the fourth century, monks settled here, and since then this monastery has existed. There were already more than three hundred monks when our (Coptic) Pope Theophilus came to al-Muharraq on pilgrimage in the year 385 and asked the Mother of God to reveal to him which places the Holy Family visited on their flight. Here, in this church, he had his famous vision. Actually he planned to tear down the small church and replace it with a new, splendid house of worship. But the

Mother of God asked him not to do that. It was always her favorite house, and she wanted it to remain as it is."

Despite all my Western skepticism, despite my astonishment at the certitude of Father Philoxenos' faith, modern as he is, the holiness of this place convinces me that until the end of days the Sacrifice of the Mass will be offered here and prayers will be answered. The monk also invites me to have a cup of tea in the monastery's modern guest house, which is so full of light and peace that I do want to believe in the prophecy. It is a place of rest in the midst of the turbulence of our times. A rather incidental remark by the priest then makes me prick up my ears: "Many Ethiopian Christians come here, too, to celebrate on November 15 the arrival of the Lord in al-Muharraq." If you add six months and five days to this date, you get May 20; we know that Herod the Great died in mid-March of 4 B.C., and two months of uprisings and unrest followed, until the Romans under Varus had restored order to the land and Herod's son Archelaus could ascend the throne. Matthew's Gospel speaks about him, too: "But when (Joseph) heard that Archelaus reigned over Judea in place of his father Herod, he was afraid to go there, and being warned in a dream he withdrew to the district of Galilee" (2:22). Therefore, the date fits perfectly into our chronology, which makes me believe that we are dealing here with an authentic tradition.

Now the Copts like to claim that the Holy Family spent three and a half years in Egypt, but this number is derived from the Revelation of John, where it says about the apocalyptic Woman:

> And the woman fled into the wilderness, where she has a place prepared by God, in which to be nourished for one thousand two hundred and sixty days. (Rev 12:6)

This is too reminiscent of the 1,290 days of the prophet Daniel (Dan 12:11) to be interpreted in any other way than in an eschatological context, and it may reflect the three and a half years between the flight of the original Christian community to Pella in the Jordanian desert and the destruction of the Temple. Thus the apocalyptic Woman is indeed Mary but, at the same time, the personification of the Church, so that we cannot expect any biographical information in this passage. To describe fertile Egypt, the breadbasket of the Roman Empire, as a "wilderness" would probably never have occurred to John.

In fact, when you add up all the Egyptian local traditions, the result
is at most a stay of one year:

> Pelusium (Farma): 1 night
> Bubastis (Tell Basta): 3 days
> Musturud: 1 night (June 14/15)
> Daqadus: 1 night
> Samannud: 14–17 days
> Dimyana: 1 night
> Bikha Isus (Sakha): 1 night
> Nikiou: 7 days
> Matariyah: 1 night
> Harat Zuwaila: 1 night (June 28)
> Babylon: 1 night
> Maadi: 10 days
> Dayr al-Garnus: 4 days
> Oxyrhynchus (Al-Bahnasa): 1 night
> Ishnin al-Nasara: 1 night (August 21)
> Gabal al-Tayr: 1 night (August 22)
> Hermopolis Magna (Al-Ashmunayn): 1 night
> Bir al-Sahaba: 1 night
> Abu Sarabam (Dayrut al Sharif): a few days
> Al-Qusiya: 1 night
> Al-Muharraq: 6 months, 5 days (November 15–May 20)

Therefore, it was practically on the anniversary of the flight from
Bethlehem, on May 20, 4 B.C., when the events described by Matthew
came to pass here in al-Muharraq:

> When Herod died, behold, an angel of the Lord appeared in a dream
> to Joseph in Egypt, saying, "Rise, take the child and his mother, and
> go to the land of Israel, for those who sought the child's life are dead."
> And he rose and took the child and his mother, and went to the land
> of Israel. (Mt 2:19–21)

With a heavy heart I take leave of Father Philoxenos, look one last
time into his warm, intelligent eyes, which reflect something of the
holiness and venerable tradition of this place. I would have liked to stay
even longer, but I hope one day to be able to return to the Egyptian
Jerusalem.

Since there was no Nile harbor in al-Muharraq, the Holy Family had to travel a little farther south, to the region of Asyut, which today has the strongest Christian presence of any city in Egypt—and furthermore is clean, modern, and peaceful, aside from occasional attacks by Islamist fanatics. Right past Asyut lies Durunka, which in recent years has become the most popular destination for pilgrims in Upper Egypt.

The local police provide us with an escort, allegedly for security reasons; we gladly accept it, because we will find the way that much faster. No sooner have we left the city than I recognize in the morning haze something that at first glance looks like a modern, colorful, and architecturally varied hotel complex built on terraces and clinging to a rocky incline. The high wall that surrounds the "complex" and the security measures and guards at the entrance would confirm this impression were it not for a gigantic concrete cross towering over it. Only a second look reveals that the several-story houses are part of the largest, most modern monastery in the country. Granted, many of them are occupied only once a year, between August 7 and 22, when the largest *mulid*, or pilgrimage, in Egypt takes place and as many as 500,000 believers flock to Durunka. After all, the monastery is the status symbol of Bishop Mikhail of Asyut, who is revered by the local Christians as a saint. Now ninety-nine years old, he himself works miracles. So says a young, dainty nun from the monastery, dressed in an intense bright blue, Sister Martyra, who addresses me in English and asks whether I might need a guide. Right afterward, she resolutely refuses the *baksheesh*, or tip, that is otherwise customary in this country. She does allow herself to be persuaded, however, to show me where the poorboxes are. "Whenever he comes here to celebrate Mary's Assumption with us, heavenly lights appear, indeed, even doves made of light", she assures me. The Marian apparitions, at least, that took place in the year 2000 in Durunka in the presence of thousands of witnesses guaranteed headlines worldwide.

Although Durunka is not mentioned in any source concerning the flight of the Holy Family, it is certain that hermits lived in its former tombs and caves from the fourth century on. It is also a fact that Asyut, which then was called Lycopolis, was the only Nile harbor in the region. Travelers, therefore, had no other choice but to look here for a boat that could bring them downstream toward the north. In any case, Sister Martyra shows me a large cave that in the days of the Pharaohs served as a quarry and today is a church. "Here all foreigners stayed, the Holy Family, too", the little nun assures me, pointing to a narrow side room, on the walls of which modern Marian images are hanging: "This is where Saint Joseph stayed." Separated from his family, evidently, because only on the opposite side of the cavern hall, in front of a second, more spacious niche, does she say: "and that is where the Blessed Virgin slept with our Lord and God."

In the adjoining cave, three baptismal fonts stand right next to each other. "Here there are mass baptisms during the *mulid*. People from all over Egypt bring their newborns, in order to receive the blessing of the Mother of God", Sister Martyra explains, not without some pride. I then enjoy the view from the monastery terrace overlooking the Nile Valley, see Asyut with its churches, and sense the Holy Land in the distance. Mary, too, must have been very homesick when she once stood here. The flight was over, but not her concern about her Son. Decisive years lay ahead of her: thirty, until her Son's public ministry began, and then three more in which he proclaimed the Gospel. But he needed only three days to conquer death forever.

∽

10

Beneath the Cross

As Maria stood on Mount Golgotha outside the gates of Jerusalem on April 7, A.D. 30, beneath the Cross of Jesus, the years probably passed before her mind's eye like a film in fast motion. There could be no greater contrast than the one between that time of new beginnings and hope and the hour of supreme sorrow and complete despair that she had just endured.

She probably remembered the prophecy of the aged Simeon, who once awaited the coming of the Messiah in the Temple. At that time, in mid-April, 5 B.C., when Mary dedicated her firstborn Son to the Lord according to the Law, he praised the Child as "a light for revelation to the Gentiles, and for glory to your people Israel". But he also warned the Mother of God: "This child is set for the fall and rising of many in Israel, and for a sign that is spoken against (and a sword will pierce through your own soul also), that the thoughts out of many hearts may be revealed" (Lk 2:32–35). Both statements exhibit Essene terminology—so clearly that a whole series of exegetes identified Simeon as a member of that community immediately after the publication of the Dead Sea Scrolls. In a way that fits chronologically, Flavius Josephus, too, reports that there was an Essene prophet by the name of Simon, who prophesied against Herod's successor, Archelaus. No doubt he was inspired by the Holy Spirit when he characterized Mary's Son so accurately, while also intuiting her sorrows beneath the Cross.

We can only conjecture to what extent the Son of God had an ordinary childhood and youth in Nazareth, to what extent rural life shaped him, but also the Hellenic influence of the district capital Sepphoris, which was only four miles away, and how frequently the divine nature and supernatural power in him came to light. The apocryphal childhood gospels tell of a whole series of mysterious signs, healings, and miracles in those early years. Luke, in contrast, is the only one of the four evangelists to mention one unusual incident that occurred at Passover in the year A.D. 8 (which on that year was celebrated from April 9 to 17). Mary and Joseph had made the pilgrimage to the Temple in Jerusalem for the feast, as they did every year (which Luke explicitly emphasizes), and they had brought their only Son along, probably for the first time. In fact, the Jewish Law commanded adult men to visit the Temple on the three major feasts, while the current rabbinical teaching declared it a duty to make only one pilgrimage a year, if a man lived farther than one day's journey from Jerusalem. The fact that Mary came along testifies, on the other hand, to the Jews' close attachment to their holy place and a well-defined "Temple piety". Children, too, were exempt from the duty to make a pilgrimage, but pious parents probably took their sons with them on the trip starting at an early age so as to familiarize them with this religious practice. Thus the Talmud treatise *Soferim* records that in Jerusalem during the Temple Period, teachers of the Law used to bless growing boys who at the age of eleven or twelve had fasted for the first time. At that time, Jesus was already twelve years old, and in a year he would celebrate his *bar mitzvah*, his admission to the covenant of Abraham and religious maturity. Then he would be allowed to read from the Torah during worship at the synagogue.

After the conclusion of the eight-day festival, the caravan of pilgrims (*synodia*) from Galilee set out again on their journey back. It was customary for the women and smaller children to go on ahead, and the men and youths followed; not until evening did they meet up again. So Mary and Joseph did not notice until the first resting place, as everyone set up encampment for the night, that Jesus had not come along. None of his relatives, no one from the village had seen him. With their nerves completely frayed, they went back to Jerusalem, which was around twenty-two miles distant, to continue their search for the youth there. They could not believe their eyes when "on the third day" (the reference to Easter is obvious) they saw what had happened. As calm as can be, Jesus was sitting in the midst of the scribes and the rabbis on the broad flight of Temple steps that led up to the Huldah Gates of the Temple from the south. We can imagine this rather vividly, because this ascent to the Temple is still preserved today. A Jewish book, the *Tosefta Sanhedrin*, corroborates that here the great teachers of Israel, for instance, "the Rabbi Gamaliel", the later teacher of the apostle Paul, "and the elders sat on the steps to the Temple Mount".

Although he was still a "minor" with regard to religious observances, he was "sitting among the teachers, listening to them and asking them questions; and all who heard him were amazed at his understanding and his answers." Mary and Joseph could not comprehend it, and so his mother remonstrated with him, whereupon he replied in utter amazement: "Did you not know that I must be in my Father's house?" (Lk 2:46–49).

Luke leaves the anecdote at that. On the other hand, to our surprise, he adds another sentence that sounds exactly as though the Child's parents had long since forgotten what had been revealed to them by the angel: "And they did not understand the saying which he spoke to them" (Lk 2:50). The evangelist goes on to emphasize that from then on Jesus was "obedient" to them, which can only mean that it really was a rather uneventful childhood. Jesus did not want and was not allowed to reveal himself yet, and so it is surprising only at first glance that the inhabitants of Nazareth rejected him because they had experienced him as a completely average youth and not at all as a "child prodigy". If there had already been signs of his power, then they were inconspicuous and subtle. Luke summarizes: "His mother kept all these things in her heart. And Jesus increased in wisdom and in stature, and in favor with God and man" (Lk 2:51–52).

We have to pause at this passage and realize what it would mean for Mary to spend three decades in the immediate presence of God, all the while carefully keeping the greatest of all secrets. In the words of Blessed John Henry Newman:

> He was nursed and tended by her; He was suckled by her; He lay in her arms. As time went on He ministered to her, and obeyed her. He lived with her for thirty years, in one house, with an uninterrupted intercourse, and with only the saintly Joseph to share it with Him. She was the witness of His growth, of His joys, of His sorrows, of His prayers; she was blest with His smile, with the touch of His hand, with the whisper of His affection, with the expression of His thoughts and His feelings.[1]

Meanwhile, the world, indeed, all of creation yearned for his coming and awaited their redemption by him. Not until he had returned from

---

[1] John Henry Cardinal Newman, "On the Fitness of the Glories of Mary", discourse 18 in *Discourses Addressed to Mixed Congregations* (London: Longman, Brown, Green, and Longmans, 1849), 383.

his baptism in the Jordan could Mary ask him to reveal his secret to everyone. She knew that the waiting was now ended, that the time of salvation had begun.

Thus the Gospel of John puts her right at the beginning of the public ministry of Jesus. With him is the Mother of God, who gave the decisive "nudge" to her Son, who may still have been hesitating or perhaps was waiting for the suitable opportunity to reveal himself. Furthermore, she also spoke the words that caused her to become forever the *Hodegetria*, the Woman who shows the way to salvation: "Do whatever he tells you" (Jn 2:5). What followed, the sign that Jesus then performed, was like a mission statement, because it stands more clearly for the New Covenant than any other miracle.

The location of the incident is a village by the name of Cana in Galilee, where "on the third day" (Tuesday was the Jews' favorite day for weddings, but again it is a reference to Easter as well!) a wedding was being celebrated. Unfortunately, it is not the same as the modern Arab village of Kefr Kenna ("Village of the Daughter-in-law") right beyond Nazareth, even though there are two "wedding churches" there—one Catholic and one Greek Orthodox—and they have an especially sweet wedding wine that they like to serve to the many pilgrims. Historical Cana, as I show in my book *Jesus von Nazareth*, was located eight miles north of Jesus' hometown, on a pyramid-shaped hill that still towers over the Beit Netofa Valley today. In recent years, archaeologists have thoroughly investigated this excavation site, which unfortunately is difficult to reach, and in doing so they uncovered not only the first-century village but also a Byzantine shrine that had been built in the fifth century on the site of the biblical wedding. Many pilgrims visited and described it. The first to publish a detailed report was an Italian from Piacenza, who claimed to have seen here two of the six water jars and the dining couch on which Jesus and Mary once reclined. Between the seventh and the ninth century, one of the water jars ended up among the relics housed in the Cathedral of Oviedo in Northern Spain (see my book *Das Bluttuch Christi*). And so Saint Willibald, who went to Cana between 724 and 726, saw only "one of the six water jars" left. As the artifacts unearthed there prove, Cana was a wealthy village that relied for its livelihood not only on farming and the production of olive oil but also on raising doves and handicrafts. Thus, they found workshops belonging to cloth dyers and leather tanners as well as the remains of a small glass factory. Its synagogue, built on a hilltop, must have been an imposing structure. The prosperity of the town explains the arrogant reaction of Nathanael, who would later become a disciple, when he heard that Jesus was from Nazareth: "Can anything good come out of Nazareth?" (Jn 1:46). Cana is well attested in other ways as well. Not only is it mentioned in the writings of the Jewish historian Flavius Josephus, unlike the insignificant Nazareth, but its strategically favorable location from time to time made it the headquarters of the Jewish troops in their rebellion against Rome.

Obviously, relatives of Mary lived in Cana, which is not surprising, since her mother, Anne, came from nearby Sepphoris. In any case, the evangelist expressly notes that the "mother of Jesus" was actually a guest at the wedding ("there was a marriage at Cana in Galilee, and the mother of Jesus was there" Jn 2:1), while Jesus had "also" been invited —and then he brought his first disciples along, too—but apparently because he was Mary's only son. Indeed, at that time no one would have expected a woman to travel the eight miles from Nazareth to Cana alone, and since the whole village was invited anyway, a few more guests made no difference. But as it often happens when there is no set guest list, it appears that more guests had come than were expected. And so what had to happen happened, and every host's worst nightmare came true: the wine ran out, just as the festive mood reached its peak! Very soon the guests would be standing there with empty cups, and a happy celebration, the most beautiful day in the life of a young couple, would end abruptly in collective frustration.

Mary, who clearly was always remarkably conscientious about social matters and quite sensitive to all-too-human cares and needs, appeared at that early date, without even being asked, as a mediatrix and advocate. In doing so, she was outspoken and resolute; quite different from what clichés about the silent, passive, and aloof Oriental woman would have us believe. In any case, she was the one who pointed out the imminent predicament to her son: "They have no wine." His answer sounds at first rather brusque: "O woman, what have you to do with me? My hour has not yet come."

Actually, Mary did not even ask but only pointed out a problem. But even that, combined with a demanding tone that is second nature to mothers, seems on closer consideration to be rather daring. What, if I may ask, did her Son as a mere guest have to do with the host's supply problems? Quite obviously Mary was hoping for a miracle, because the host could also have sent his servants to the nearest wine market, perhaps in Sepphoris, which of course would have taken several hours. The problem, at any rate, is that in the previous chapter John said not a word about Jesus' miraculous power. We learn only about his baptism in the Jordan and the call of his first disciples. Even the Gospel of Luke tells about the wisdom with which the twelve-year-old boy Jesus impressed the scribes in the Temple, but not about any miracles that he worked. Nevertheless, there must have been some, for that alone would explain Mary's indirect demand that he do something. In light of this, the apocryphal childhood gospels and the traditions about the miracles that were worked already in Egypt through the presence of the holy Infant no longer seem quite so incredible. In that case, though, Mary in fact became the first "witness of his glory".

Jesus hesitated. Yet in that moment he was not only fully man but, above all, fully God. He could not be won over for the sake of something trivial. He did not want to work miracles in order to prove his power or amaze others; certainly not to keep a drinking party going. At any rate, his reply sounds harsher in translation than in the Aramaic original, which the Greek Gospel renders laboriously. "What is that to me and to thee?"—as it reads literally—is an idiom that certainly has parallels in the Old Testament, for instance, in Judges 11:12, 2 Chronicles 35:21, and 1 Kings 17:18, where it means approximately: "That is your concern; what does that have to do with me?" Of course, like his answer when they were looking for him in the Temple, this implies a certain distance: Jesus took a stand beyond all familial ties and obligations so as to subject himself solely to the will of his Heavenly Father. The term of address *Woman* sounds harsh only in Western languages; in Hebrew, it was a very polite title, respectful albeit aloof, comparable to the English expression *My Lady*. We find it in all the Gospels; this was how Jesus usually addressed women. Therefore, this is no longer about a personal or familial matter but, rather, about something of more general significance. Mary was also addressed once again as "Woman" in another passage, when her Son, hanging on the Cross, entrusted her to his beloved disciple John. This was the explanation given by Pope Benedict XVI when he spoke about this Gospel passage during his trip to Germany in 2006, appropriately enough in Altötting, a place of pilgrimage:

> [T]his title really expresses Mary's place in salvation history. It points to the future, to the hour of the crucifixion, when Jesus will say to

her: "Woman, behold your son—Son, behold your mother" (cf. Jn 19:26–27). It anticipates the hour when he will make the woman, his Mother, the Mother of all his disciples. On the other hand, the title "Woman" recalls the account of the creation of Eve: Adam, surrounded by creation in all its magnificence, experiences loneliness as a human being. Then Eve is created, and in her Adam finds the companion whom he longed for; and he gives her the name "woman". In the Gospel of John, then, Mary represents the new, the definitive Woman, the companion of the Redeemer, our Mother: the name, which seemed so lacking in affection, actually expresses the grandeur of Mary's enduring mission.

Not only the name *Woman* alludes to Golgotha but also Jesus' reference to *his hour*, which has not yet come; it had come at the time of his sacrifice. It began when he himself hosted the meal, consecrated the wine, and gave it to his disciples, whereby he instituted the Sacrament of the Eucharist. Now, though, Jesus used the plight of the host in Cana to refer already to his own banquet at the beginning of his public ministry.

What did he do, then? "Now six stone jars were standing there, for the Jewish rites of purification, each holding twenty or thirty gallons", John relates. Such water jars have been found by archaeologists throughout Israel; fragments in Nazareth, too, right across from the plot of land belonging to the Holy Family. They were used only during one short phase of Judaism, namely, at the time of the Herodian Temple, between 19 B.C. and A.D. 70. The new construction of God's House, which indicated that the coming of the Messiah was imminent, along with the fear of foreign influences, created at that time throughout Judea a veritable obsession of the faithful with the laws of the *Halakha* and questions of ritual purity. It served both to set Jews apart and also as a way of preparing for the end times. The *Tosefta* sums up the situation then in five words: "Purity broke out in Israel." This also affected the Jewish art of making vessels. Since they were afraid of impurities in porous vessels made of clay, and silver was used for coins with images of pagan gods, only stone was considered *kosher*, ritually pure.

Indeed, the *Halakha* lists countless possible sources of ritual impurity: every time someone touched bodily fluids, a newborn, a corpse, objects and symbols belonging to the cult of pagan idols (including non-Jewish coins), or skin diseases or had contact with creeping animals or an animal cadaver, immediate countermeasures were required. The believer had to bathe in "living" (flowing) water, and for this purpose many Jewish houses had their own *mikveh*, a purification bath. But household items that had become "unclean" also had to be purified by washing. So that it would remain pure, water used in the ritual cleansing of objects was stored only in (kosher) stone jars and was drawn with stone cups. There are still numerous well-preserved examples of these mighty stone jars, called *krater* or *kallal*, for instance, in the Jewish quarter of the Old City of Jerusalem. Some modern translations of the Bible exaggerate in calculating their capacity. In the original Greek text, John speaks about "two or three *metretas*". One *metretes* ("measure") was the equivalent of exactly 5.75 gallons, so that we can calculate that a jar held 11.5–17.5 gallons, which apparently was the norm and was only a little less than the capacity of the stone jars in Jerusalem.

When Jesus changed this water, which was used in ritual purification, into wine, he was indeed speaking to the people of his time and of ours by means of a "sign". For wine, in turn, became in the Eucharist the truly cleansing Blood of Christ, which removes from the soul the impurities of all guilt and sin. So Saint Jerome, when asked what ultimately happened to the approximately seventy-nine gallons of wine, replied with wise, subtle irony: "We are drinking of it to this day." It is, figuratively speaking, still being used today in every church in the world for the Consecration. With Christ's sacrificial death, the cultic purifications of the *Halakha* became superfluous in the New Covenant, and the water that cleansed externally has been replaced by the sacrament of the altar, which cleanses interiorly. Mary, however, was the one in both scenes, in the initial revelation and in the ultimate confirmation on the Cross, who stood by her Son, who pointed to him from the start and still leads us to Jesus today.

After the wedding, John goes on to write, "(Jesus) went down to Capernaum, with his mother and his brethren" (Jn 2:12). His *brethren* (cousins) must have accompanied Mary, because now Jesus could no longer take care of her. He himself lived apart from her in the spacious house of Saint Peter's mother-in-law, which was excavated and thoroughly studied between 1968 and 1991 by the two Italian Franciscan archaeologists Virgilio Corbo and Stanislao Loffreda. Towering over its ruins today is a modern concrete church with a glass floor, the last in a series of shrines that recalled Jesus' ministry here. For as early as the second half of the first century, they discovered in the dig to their astonishment, the house of a large family that made a living by fishing, as the numerous fishhooks prove, had been turned into a place of worship. They found also in the oldest inhabited level cooking vessels and jars, but these abruptly disappeared, and in the next stratum only the remains of oil lamps and supply containers were to be found. At the same time, the walls and the floor of a special room were plastered, which was a unique phenomenon in all Capernaum. Everything indicates that it was very soon made into a so-called *house church*, exactly as a nun named Egeria, on a pilgrimage from Northern Spain or Southern France around the year 383, recorded in her diary: "And in Capernaum, what is more, the house of the prince of the apostles has been transformed into a church, with its original walls still standing. Here the Lord healed the paralytic."

In this special room, where early pilgrims scratched invocations to Jesus and Saint Peter in the wall plaster, Jesus must have taught and worked his miracles. It was not all that big, around twenty-three feet on each side, but it was the largest room in a residential complex made up of eight stone cottages with thatched roofs that were arranged around two interior courtyards. It was situated right on the north-south axis of Capernaum, on the street that led also to the nearby synagogue, right next to the entrance gate to the first courtyard. Because the gate and the first cottage of the complex were set back somewhat from the street, there was a little square in front of it, the only one of this sort in all Capernaum. This circumstance alone would have sufficed to identify the house as the scene of the Gospels. For when the Gospel of Mark says: "And the whole city was gathered together about the door" (Mk 1:33), that is difficult to imagine in the narrow streets and alleys of this fishing town, except for this one house with its sufficiently large front patio. What Matthew describes in the following passage must have taken place here:

> While [Jesus] was still speaking to the people, behold, his mother and his brethren stood outside, asking to speak to him. But he replied to the man who told him, "Who is my mother, and who are my brethren?" And stretching out his hand toward his disciples, he said, "Here are my mother and my brethren! For whoever does the will of my Father in heaven is my brother, and sister, and mother." (Mt 12:46–50; parallel passages: Mk 3:31–35; Lk 8:19–21)

With this answer, Peter's house became the first church; the people
gathered in it, however, became not only its congregation but also the
new, eschatological family of Jesus. In it there were no privileges, no
birthright, no precedence based on one's relatives; anyone who wanted
to belong to it first had to prove himself. There is no doubt about the
fact that Mary had long since passed this test. Yet neither Matthew
nor Luke tells us the occasion for this visit. What was so urgent that
Jesus' relatives absolutely had to speak to him, although he was obviously busy at that moment? Only Mark reveals the answer. Apparently
scribes who had heard about Jesus' miracles had come to Capernaum
in order to collect evidence against him. The evangelist quotes them as
saying: "He is possessed by Beelzebul, and by the prince of demons he
casts out the demons" (Mk 3:22). Now Jesus always knew what to say
to them, but the situation was still cause for concern. The authority of
the scribes was too great; their word could easily have upset the mood.
They would be quick to accuse Jesus of blasphemy, which after all was
punishable by stoning. That is why, or at least this is the most likely
explanation, when his relatives and neighbors heard about it, "they
went out to seize him, for they said, 'He is beside himself.'" "Beside
himself" perhaps because he was setting himself up for a confrontation. But "beside himself" also because his *brethren* did not understand
him. The fact that Mary "kept . . . in her heart" the circumstances of
his birth, as Luke writes, testifies to her reticence; her Son should be
able to grow up undisturbed and decide for himself when he would
reveal himself. Probably she broke her silence for the first time on
her deathbed. But even if his *brethren* already suspected then that he
was the Messiah, we do not know for what sort of Messiah they were
hoping. A warrior Messiah-king who would drive out the Romans,
as most Jews expected? Or a "fundamentalist" Essene-Messiah who
would emerge from the elite of the Qumran sect? Whatever the case,
Jesus went his own way and made no effort to fulfill existing expectations. That must have led to misunderstandings and doubts. A passage
from John's Gospel suggests that the cousins were in fact close to the
Essene order: "Now the Jews' feast of Tabernacles was at hand. So
his brethren said to him, 'Leave here and go to Judea. . . . If you do
these things, show yourself to the world.'" Jesus replied that his time
had not yet come, and he remained in Galilee. But in the very next
sentence we read: "But after his brethren had gone up to the feast, then
he also went up" (Jn 7:2–10). The next sections describe his ministry

in Jerusalem during that same weeklong feast. Maybe in fact he was only avoiding the large caravan of pilgrims from Galilee and preferred to travel alone a day or two later with his disciples. It is also possible, though, that he decided to celebrate the feast according to a different calendar than the one used by his *brethren*. For the "official" Jerusalem of the Temple hierarchy observed a lunar calendar, whereas documents discovered in Qumran prove that the Essenes reckoned their feast days according to the solar calendar. As a result, the Essene feasts as a rule fell a few days before the "official" feast days, which could explain the "early" departure of the *brethren of the Lord*. Jesus' decision would then have expressed something about his mission: he intended to be the Messiah of all Israel, not the figure hoped for by a sect, however close his family may have been to it.

Of course the cousins tried to win Jesus' mother over to their side; she was perhaps the only authority that Jesus heeded. But even if they temporarily believed that he was "beside himself", not one word in the passage gives us reason to assume that Mary, too, doubted him. Certainly she was worried; but she had to trust him unconditionally, for she knew who he was. He, for his part, knew his destiny. For him the accomplishment of his mission was more important than the petty fears of his relatives.

A similar situation developed once again when Jesus, accompanied by his disciples, returned to Nazareth. That may have been sometime around early March of the year 29, a full year after the beginning of his public ministry, at any rate, though on a Sabbath, when the Jews gathered to pray in the synagogue of the village. It is part of the Jewish worship service for a grown man over thirty years old to read aloud and interpret a passage from Scripture. So this time Jesus went to the front, and the synagogue attendant handed him the scroll containing the Book of the Prophet Isaiah.

> He opened the book and found the place where it was written, "The Spirit of the Lord is upon me, because he has anointed me to preach good news [in Greek, *evangelísasthai*!] to the poor. He has sent me to proclaim release to the captives and recovering of sight to the blind, to set at liberty those who are oppressed, to proclaim the acceptable year of the Lord." And he closed the book. (Lk 4:17–20)

All eyes were on him as he gave back the scroll and slowly sat down on the Throne of Moses, the "professorial chair" that stood and still stands today in every synagogue. The homily that he gave immediately afterward was short, and Luke gets right to the point of it: "Today this Scripture has been fulfilled in your hearing" (Lk 4:21).

In Nazareth they had heard a lot about him, especially about the miracles that he worked in Capernaum and elsewhere around the Sea of Gennesaret. But the inhabitants of the town could not imagine that the Messiah had grown up in their midst. At first glance, that may be surprising, and not only because rumors about the early pregnancy of his mother must have circulated through the town. And there was talk about the miracles that Jesus worked as a child, at least in the various apocryphal childhood gospels. Since most people who lived in Nazareth were in fact of the house of David, as indicated by the place name "Shootsville" and the "royal" necropolis in the town, they must have had high hopes that the Messiah would emerge from their clan. But here, too, the question arises: What sort of Messiah? Quite obviously, in the years before his public ministry, Jesus had not made the slightest attempt to reveal his power and majesty. Envy, grudges, and rivalry are still very common in families today. "Is not this the carpenter?" the inhabitants of the town asked one another, since until then he had appeared on the scene only as the apprentice of his foster father. Evidently they knew that Joseph was not his natural father; after all, they called him the "son of Mary" (Mk 6:3). And they did so even though in the next breath they mentioned his *brethren* "James and Joses and Judas and Simon" as well as "his sisters" who, long since married, lived "here with us". His former neighbors demanded at least that Jesus work a few miracles right before their eyes so as to correct their misconception. Yet the Son of God, who never bothered to satisfy human expectations, refused to perform any healing for show. This angered the townspeople of Nazareth, and they drove him out of the city and tried to throw him off a cliff, which to this day is known as the Mount of Precipice, and probably to stone him. Luke ends his description of the incident: "But passing through the midst of them he went away" (Lk 4:20–30). Mark (6:4) quotes him as saying, "A prophet is not without honor, except in his own country, and among his own kin, and in his own house." His "kin" were all inhabitants of Nazareth, the village of the House of David. Nevertheless, the quotation might also have applied to his *brethren*. Nothing indicates that they followed him already during his lifetime; only beneath the Cross, it seems, was there a reconciliation between the group of disciples and the family of Jesus, before the Easter event, the Resurrection, made it clear to his cousins, too, that he is truly the Messiah, the Son of God.

And Mary? We do not even know whether she was present during this visit to Nazareth; only the disciples are mentioned in the Gospels. She may therefore have remained in Capernaum. Nevertheless, the local tradition maintains that she ran after the homicidal mob, until she broke down in tears on the ridge of a hill. To this day a chapel on the site commemorates "Mary's Fear". We can be certain at least that, from that day on, the Blessed Virgin never again returned to Nazareth.

If the local tradition is true, she must already have had some idea then of how everything would end. Again and again in Capernaum she had witnessed the hostilities to which her beloved Son was exposed. The fact that she alone knew his secret made the whole situation that much more difficult for her. "They have eyes to see but do not see; they have ears to hear but do not hear", she must have exclaimed again and again in despair.

She suffered all the more on that day when the mob in Jerusalem, incited and paid by representatives of the Temple aristocracy, assembled unlawfully in the praetorium of Pilate to demand nothing less than the death of God. Of course, Jesus' family, like all believing Jews, had made the pilgrimage to Jerusalem for the Passover. Certainly Mary was present at Jesus' trial, since one of the disciples had told her that her Son had been arrested the night before in the Garden of Gethsemane. So she watched it all up close: Pilate's hesitation, his attempt to satisfy the bloodthirsty rabble by the sadistic spectacle of the scourging of Jesus, the blows with the lead-weighted whips that tore his flesh and covered the noblest of all men with bleeding wounds. She saw how his ashen, sweat-covered, trembling, and tottering body was hauled before the tribunal again and presented to the crowd, while his blood still glistened on the pavement of the inner courtyard. Legend has it that she thereupon wiped it up with her veil—we can be certain that she did not refuse him this loving service, which was in keeping with Jewish custom. In humbling herself this way, she took part in his suffering. But then the heartrending cry of the mob, "*Crucifige! Crucifige!*" rang out and echoed in the courtyard, where it elicited only a sarcastic grin from Pilate's brutal Legionaries. Mary must have nearly swooned at that moment; as the crowd roared, she felt a piercing pain, like a sword, boring ever deeper into her heart. The prophecy of the aged Simeon had been fulfilled. Yet, in the distance, the angel's words still reechoed: "Be not afraid, Mary!"

Christian tradition has assigned to Mary a fixed place along the *Via Crucis*, the Way of the Cross. Usually it is the Fourth Station: "Jesus meets his Mother." Not one word is said about such an encounter in the Gospels. But how could we doubt that a mother would want, indeed, would have to be as close as possible to her son in his most difficult hour? His disciples may have fled and were hiding somewhere, anxious and desperate; only she had nothing more to lose, for the one dearest to her was about to be sacrificed. At some point, she must have managed to walk the 660 yards from the praetorium to Mount Calvary so as to be close enough to console him one last time in that darkest hour of world history.

And then she stood beneath the Cross. Of the Twelve, only John, the beloved disciple of Jesus, had ventured to draw near in order to support the Mother of God now. We do not know whether Jesus suffered on the gibbet for only three hours (as John says) or for six (as in the Synoptic Gospels); in either case, his Passion must have seemed endless to Mary. Yet in the midst of what was apparently utter hopelessness, when the soldiers had just cast lots for Jesus' last earthly possessions and the dark clouds of a sandstorm were approaching, the Son of God accomplished his salvific work on earth:

> When Jesus saw his mother, and the disciple whom he loved standing near, he said to his mother, "Woman, behold, your son!" Then he said to the disciple, "Behold, your mother!" And from that hour the disciple took her to his own home. (Jn 19:26–27)

John, who did not die until the year 100 at an advanced age in Ephesus, was the "Benjamin" of the disciples; he was perhaps fifteen years old when he ran into Jesus and at most eighteen when he stood beneath the Cross. He was the only one of the Twelve who was unmarried, which likewise is evidence of his youth. Although all the other apostles were around Jesus' age, there was a real master-pupil rapport between Jesus and John, which had some qualities of a father-son relationship. He allowed him to have the most profound insight into his mystery, as the high Christology of the Fourth Gospel testifies. Actually it is also the Marian Gospel, which depicts the Mother of God at the beginning and the end of Jesus' ministry. John was so closely united to Christ that later in Christian communities the belief circulated that he would not die before the Second Coming of the Lord. The compiler of the Fourth Gospel, probably a disciple of John, mentions this notion in his appendix (which was probably added posthumously): "The saying spread abroad among the brethren that this disciple was not to die" (Jn 21:23), so as to reject it explicitly.

But it was not only practical considerations that caused Jesus in his last hour to entrust Mary to his youngest disciple, who could readily care for her because he had no family of his own to look after. As one of the Twelve, John also represented the young Church, now sealed with the Blood of the New Covenant. The Church herself was entrusted then by Christ to his Mother; at the Savior's command, she received Mary into her midst.

Since then the Church and the Mother of God have been inseparably united to each other, and she is the Mother of the Church.

As his human life, this phase of his salvific work, reached its completion, he sealed it with the words: " 'It is finished'; and he bowed his head and gave up his spirit" (Jn 19:29–30). Jesus knew that with his Mother, his Church was in the best hands.

∼

11

Daughter of Zion

Just two lines in the New Testament report about the subsequent life of the Mother of God. We gather from John's Gospel that the beloved disciple took her to his own home from then on, which should be understood quite concretely but not only in that sense. She now lived with him, he cared for her; through him she entered into the company of the apostles and became the praying, loving heart of the Twelve. As such we find her again at the Ascension of Jesus and the Pentecost event that followed it:

> When they had entered [Jerusalem], they went up to the upper room, where they were staying, Peter and John and James and Andrew, Philip and Thomas, Bartholomew and Matthew, James the son of Alphaeus and Simon the Zealot and Judas the son of James. All these with one accord devoted themselves to prayer, together with the women and Mary the mother of Jesus, and with his brethren. (Acts 1:13-14)

Thus we learn at least indirectly that Mary, too, was a witness of the Risen Christ and of his Ascension into heaven; the Gospels are silent about this, and even Paul, who provides us with an almost complete list of the (male) witnesses of the Resurrection in the First Letter to the Corinthians (15:4-8), refrains from mentioning her. The reason was that in Judaism women were considered unreliable witnesses; their statements had no relevance in court. This so astonished the Byzantine Christians, with their fervent love of Mary, that they decided to correct the record on their own. Ephrem the Syrian, for instance, the poet of the Mariologists (d. 373), did not hesitate to turn Jesus' meeting with Mary Magdalen at the empty tomb (Jn 20:15-16) into a dialogue with his Mother. And the Greek *Acts of Thaddeus* from the sixth century categorically state: "And he appeared first to his Mother and to the other women."

That may very well be true, for other Easter events have come down to us without details, for instance, the appearance "to more than five hundred brethren at one time" (1 Cor 15:6) that Paul mentions and the one to James from the same list. From the Gospel of Luke, we know about only the meeting with the disciples on the road to Emmaus (in Matthew, this is at least hinted at), which is perhaps representative of other self-revelations of the Risen Lord to members of his hitherto skeptical family—at any rate, Cleopas and Simeon were his uncle and one of the *brothers of the Lord*, or cousins of Jesus. Whatever else happened, we find the consequences documented in the first chapter of the Acts of the Apostles: Jesus' family had converted and now professed faith in him; together with the Twelve, they formed the core of the original Christian community. What Jesus had begun on the Cross, when he entrusted Mary to his beloved disciple and thus made her Mother of the Church, was therefore perfected by the Risen Lord: now the Church and the family of Jesus were one.

But all this meant even more. Mary, as a descendant of the royal and priestly line of Israel and as an orthodox Jewess with ties to the Essene community, stood uniquely for the Old Covenant, while John, as the beloved disciple, stood for the New Covenant. As Jesus on the Cross placed the Church into Zion's womb and then entrusted Zion to her protection, he actually intended to prevent what later became the most heinous sin of Christendom: fatal anti-Semitism. It became the utter betrayal of the faith of Jesus, Mary, and the apostles, the violent separation of the Church from her roots, with the most disastrous consequences, as we know. For nothing in the Acts of the Apostles suggests that the original Christians were anything other than faith-filled Jews who were different from their fellow believers at first only inasmuch as they acknowledged Jesus of Nazareth as the Messiah. Again and again the Gospels, the Acts of the Apostles, and the Apostolic Letters emphasize the continuity of the divine plan for salvation. The disciples of Jesus lived out the faith of the Old and the New Covenant harmoniously, as demonstrated by how often the Acts of the Apostles mention that they went "up to the temple" to pray (Acts 3:1), now as before. Luke describes their parallel religious practices as follows: "Day by day, attending the temple together and breaking bread in their homes, they partook of food with glad and generous hearts" (Acts 2:46).

But where were "their homes" located; most importantly, where was the "upper room where they were staying" and where Mary lived with

John during the Pentecost event and in the following years? Christian
tradition has an unequivocal answer to this question: on Mount Zion
on the southwest edge of Jerusalem, where according to tradition the
Last Supper also took place.

This Holy Mountain of the old as well as of the New Israel is still
immense today. Regardless of the direction from which one approaches
Jerusalem, Zion looms over the Old City and dominates the skyline; it is
one of the four major landmarks of the Holy City, besides the Dome of
the Rock, the Church of the Holy Sepulcher, and the Tower of David.
We owe this to none other than the German Emperor Wilhelm II,
who had the most beautiful church in Jerusalem built on Mount Zion,
the neo-Romanesque Basilica of the Dormition. It owes its name to
the circumstance that tradition locates the "Dormition" of Mary, the
death of the Mother of God (in Latin: *dormitio Beatae Mariae Virginis*),
here also; but that is the topic for our final chapter.

It was probably no accident that the journey of the Hohenzollern
ruler to the Holy Land took place exactly eight hundred years after the
First Crusade. In any case, he did not hesitate to indulge in the most
bizarre anachronism in order to latch on to the former glory of the
Crusaders. In billing himself as the "Protector of the Holy Places", he
alluded at any rate to a tradition of the German Empire that had its
beginning with Charlemagne and reached its tragic climax with Frederick Barbarossa, who of course was never to reach the Holy Land (he
drowned in 1190 while bathing in an ice-cold Turkish mountain stream,
the Saleph). Thus Wilhelm II, as the distant heir of Barbarossa, so to
speak, rode through the Jaffa Gate on October 29, 1898, into the city
of Jerusalem, which was decorated with flags and garlands. Mounted
on his steed, accompanied by the empress, followed by a host of officers riding white horses and wearing handlebar mustaches, spiked hel-
mets ornamented with tufts, and broad white capes, he appeared like
a phantom from a long-lost era. However, he had not come to liberate
Jerusalem but, rather, as the guest of the Sultan of Constantinople, his
most loyal ally. The latter had spared no cost or expense to make the
pompous pageant possible in the first place. He even had a breach made
in the walls of Jerusalem so that the imperial retinue could ride into
the Holy City without problems. For one week, Wilhelm II resided
in the Holy City as the "last Crusader in history". There he not only
dedicated the Protestant Church of the Redeemer, the first Lutheran
house of worship in that locality, he also met with German Catholics

who represented the German Association for the Holy Land [Deutsche Verein vom Heiligen Lande] headquartered in Cologne. In order to demonstrate that he did not discriminate against his Catholic subjects, he granted them a tract of land on Mount Zion and entrusted it to the Archbishopric of Cologne. Back in Germany, the imperial pilgrim had the people hail him as though he were returning home victorious from an Eighth Crusade. The building project was then financed by donations.

At that time, the site of the present-day Dormition Abbey was just a vegetable garden in the shadow of the upper room, which was still a mosque. But scarcely had it changed its owner than Ethiopian and Syrian Christians of Jerusalem declared their misgivings: "What will happen to the stones from Mary's house?" they anxiously asked the Germans. Then they showed them two large, roughhewn blocks of stone that had been revered there for centuries.

Of course they were salvaged. When the cornerstone of the Basilica of the Dormition was laid in 1900, its architect, Heinrich Renard of Cologne, made sure that they were incorporated into the base of the wall of its bell tower. To this day, African and Arab Christians come to the spot to caress or kiss the "holy stones", which are easy to recognize because of a sign of the cross carved into them. And rightly so, because their tradition is quite ancient; it was mentioned for the first time in A.D. 635 by Sophronius, the patriarch of Jerusalem at the time.

The basilica itself cannot deny that it was designed in Cologne; its blueprint is too plainly inspired by the Romanesque Church of Saint Gereon in the German Cathedral city, with allusions in any case to the Palatine chapel of Charlemagne in Aachen. Thus, its neo-Romanesque central dome, flanked by four small towers, is visible from a distance in the sky over Jerusalem, to testify for all eternity to the fact that the noblest Daughter of Zion once fell asleep here.

The basilica, which was consecrated in 1910, does in fact stand on historic ground, indeed, the original ground of Christianity. However, the designation of the southwest hill as Zion is based on a misunderstanding. For the original Zion, the castle of King David, stood on the southeast hill, which adjoined the Temple Mount Moriah. Today this is the site of the predominantly Arab quarter of Silwan, named after the Pool of Siloam, which from ancient times provided water for the city. It is a powder keg. Ever since the Israelis, in search of their roots, started to confiscate tracts of land one after the other, in order

to uncover further remains of David's city and of its Canaanite predecessor, there have been disturbances at regular intervals. Politics aside,
the excavations are actually extremely interesting, since they bring Old
Testament scenes to light. The most important of them is a pyramid-
like set of staircases, five stories high, the tallest building from the Iron
Age that has ever been found in Israel. Archaeologists are certain that
this discovery is the Jebusites' legendary stronghold of Zion, which
King David conquered in 1000 B.C. (2 Sam 5:7).

Not until their return from the Babylonian Captivity did the Jews
consider the higher southwestern hill to be Zion, and this nomencla-
ture has been definitive since the time of the Maccabees. It made no
difference that it did not have its own source of water and, thus, was
unsuitable as a fortress; the inhabitants of Jerusalem simply could not
imagine that the magnificent palace of their greatest kings had been
on the low, utterly unspectacular eastern hill. Thus even Flavius Josephus, the most important Jewish historiographer, in the first century
A.D. identified the southwestern hill as the site of the City of David.
Since the biblical kings were "buried in the City of David" according
to 1 Kings 2:10 (a custom that was extremely unusual for Jews), they
also searched for their tomb there. Probably, though, they were laid
to rest in one of the three beautiful horizontal gallery tombs that the
French archaeologist R. Weill discovered in 1913 on the southeastern
hill, not far from the Pool of Siloam, which would be consistent with
the biblical evidence (for example, Neh 3:15–16). In late antiquity, on
the other hand, everyone suspected that the tombs of the kings were in
David's birthplace, Bethlehem, until the Crusaders recalled the eastern
hill.

For the first Christians, in any case, Mount Zion was on the southwestern hill from the start. About this place the prophet Isaiah had
prophesied: "Out of Zion shall go forth the law" (or "instruction";
2:3). Eusebius in the fourth century was not the first to apply this
to the proclamation of the Gospel; even earlier, Bishop Melito from
Sardis in Asia Minor, while visiting Jerusalem around the year 140,
had declared in his Easter Homily: "The Law became the Logos and
the Old became New. Both came forth from Zion and Jerusalem." So
it is not surprising that the early Christian community took possession
of this hill early on. They left it only when rebellion was imminent in
Jerusalem and their bishop, Simeon *the brother of the Lord*, led them to
Pella east of the Jordan. Right after the fall of Masada, the end of the

seven-year Jewish War, they returned to Jerusalem, which meanwhile had been completely destroyed by Titus. As the usually well informed Patriarch Eutychius of Alexandria wrote on the basis of older sources, "in the fourth year of Vespasian", that is, in A.D. 72/73, "the Christians (*Nasara*) . . . returned to the ruins of the holy city and inhabited it. They built a church (there)."

The Roman Emperor Hadrian found this church, too, when he visited Jerusalem in 160 on his second reconnaissance mission through the Near East. We read about this in the writings of Epiphanius of Salamis (315–403), a Cypriot bishop, who relied on older (and often Jewish-Christian) sources:

> And he found the Temple of God trodden down and the whole city devastated save for a few houses and the church of God, which was small, where the disciples, when they had returned after the Savior had ascended from the Mount of Olives, went to the upper room. For there it had been built, that is, in that portion of Zion which escaped destruction, together with blocks of houses in the neighborhood of Zion.

This account would be far less astonishing were it not for the fact that a part of this small "church of God" is still standing. Traces of it can be found right beside the Basilica of the Dormition, in the inner courtyard of a house that today has a synagogue on the ground floor and is revered by orthodox Jews as the tomb of King David, while its upper story is considered by Christians to be the place of the Last Supper. The Cenacle itself, in which Pope John Paul II had the privilege of celebrating the Holy Sacrifice of the Mass with only a few assistants during his journey to the Holy Land in 2000, is a medieval construction; the gothic style of architecture is unmistakable. The east and south walls of the building, however, consist partly of stone blocks that are plainly from the Herodian era, as they were used in constructing the platform on the Temple mount. Corners knocked off some of them are evidence of recycling. It seems as though its builders, at a time when all Jerusalem was a desolate landscape of ruins, deliberately chose stones from the Temple in order to latch on to its tradition. They wanted to show everyone that now the new Temple stood on Zion.

But who were these master builders? Not until 1948, when a Palestinian mortar shell exploded inside the synagogue during fighting on

Mount Zion, was this secret revealed. Three years later, the Israeli archaeologist J. Pinkerfield was commissioned to repair the damage, and he took the opportunity to make a thorough investigation. What is revered as King David's sarcophagus proved to be a *cenotaph* (a memorial for someone whose remains are elsewhere) that the Crusaders had erected. It was supposed to refer to the continuity of the tradition, to Jesus' descent "from the House of David". Behind it there was a niche that obviously belonged to the north wall of the original building. Finally, the masonry extended down to its former floor, a simple stone pavement, which lay four inches beneath a mosaic floor from the fourth century and twenty-three inches beneath the floor of the building from the time of the Crusades. Similar niches at a comparable height over the floor were found in the ancient synagogue; in them the scrolls of the Torah were once stored. So Pinkerfield thought at first that he was dealing with a synagogue from Roman times. But there was a hitch to this interpretation of the discovery. In every Jewish house of worship, the Torah niche points toward Jerusalem, toward the Temple. But here, of all places, where the Temple Mount was within sight, the niche was oriented, not toward the east, but rather to the north. It pointed straight to a hill on which only one sacrifice took place, one that made all other sacrifices superfluous: to Golgotha. Consequently, it was clear that this could not have been a conventional synagogue. Then Pinkerfield found on the lowest stratum of the floor fragments of plaster originally from the walls of the building in Roman times. Words were scratched on them in Greek characters, which proved to be Christian invocations: "Triumph, O Redeemer, have mercy!" we can read on them, and: "O Jesus, I wish to live, Lord of Lords!" Now there was no longer any doubt: it was a synagogue of Jewish Christians, the very same "small church of God" on Zion of which Bishop Epiphanius spoke, built over the site of the Pentecost miracle and of the Last Supper.

Additional evidence that the Church originated on Mount Zion is found in the Letter to the Hebrews, which some exegetes ascribe to James, "the brother of the Lord", whom Peter appointed the first bishop of Jerusalem. Its author compares Zion with Mount Sinai of the Old Covenant when he writes: "But you have come to Mount Zion and to the city of the living God" (Heb 12:22). Even clearer, however, is the reference in a Jewish-Christian document about the life of Jeremiah, which was composed in the late first century; in it the prophet says: "The Lord went from Sinai into heaven; but he comes again as lawgiver on Zion with power, and this will be the sign for you: All nations revere one wood", meaning, of course, the wood of the Cross. By this point in time, the term *Zion* therefore already has unambiguously Christian connotations. So it is that at the time of the first rebellion against the Romans (A.D. 66–70), the Jews still stamped "Freedom of Zion" and "Redemption of Zion" on their coins; during the second rebellion (132–135), these slogans were no longer used; they were replaced by "Freedom of Jerusalem" and "Redemption of Israel".

Apparently this "small church of God" that was considered the "church of the apostles" remained in the possession of the Jewish Christians until the fourth century. A pilgrim from Bordeaux (A.D. 333) and Bishop Epiphanius write in almost the same words that it was surrounded by seven synagogues, "which had stood alone on Zion like huts. Of these one remained until the time of Bishop Maximonas and Emperor Constantine, like a booth in the vineyard, as Scripture says (Is 1:8)." The fact that Constantine the Great did not build here and the fact that Zion is not mentioned in the fourth century as the scene of ecclesiastical memorial ceremonies suggest that at that time it was still entirely in the possession of a Jewish-Christian community. "The high ground on Zion once had precedence, but now it has been cut off", Epiphanius commented quite impertinently. As for the synagogue that is expressly distinguished from the small church, it might, at least in the opinion of the Benedictine archaeologist Bargil Pixner, be the former "house of the apostle John and (the) site of Mary's death".

Not until Emperor Theodosius declared (orthodox) Christianity the state religion and all heterodox currents were persecuted did the history of Jewish-Christian Zion end. Bishop John managed to incorporate it into his flock around 390, while on the hill, right next to the "church of the apostles", he built at first an octagonal monument. As a nod to the Jewish-Christians, it was dedicated on the Jewish Feast of Atonement, of all days, on September 15, A.D. 394. It is quite possible that the octagon stood over the former house of Mary.

Apparently the new shrine attracted pilgrims so swiftly that it was soon bursting at the seams. At any rate, Bishop John replaced the eight-sided monument after only twenty-one years with a large basilica having several aisles, which directly adjoined the church of the apostles, the former "upper room". Now it bore the name of *Hagia*

Sion, "Holy Zion". When the Gallic Bishop Arculf visited it around 670, he sketched its floor plan: To the southeast lay "the place of the Lord's Supper", in other words, the Cenacle, and in the northwest it says, "Here Blessed Mary died", and in the southwest: "Here the Holy Spirit descended upon the apostles." As if that were not enough to lend importance to the "mother of all churches", they also set up in the middle of it the pillar from Pilate's praetorium where Jesus was scourged.

Bishop Arculf's plan of the Basilica on Zion in the seventh century; it encompassed the Cenacle ("locus hic caenae domini") and the house where Mary died ("hic sancta maria obiit").

Twice the Hagia Sion was almost completely destroyed, first in 614 by the Persians, who carried out a veritable massacre, and then in 1009, by the fanatical Muslim caliph al-Hakim. When the Crusaders conquered Jerusalem in 1099, they found nothing but ruins at the spot. So they built over them a new church, in which the Cenacle was now incorporated, and called it Sancta Maria in Monte Sion. It was to last only a short time. After their defeat at the Battle of Hattin in Galilee, the Crusaders entrusted it in 1187 to the Syrian Christians. The Syrians had no other alternative but to transfer the tradition about the "church of the apostles" to another shrine that was in their possession now as before: the Church of Saint Mark, built over the place where the original Christian community took refuge while they were being persecuted by King Herod Agrippa.

The Cenacle, in contrast, must have been in a sorry state at that time, if we are to believe the reports of pilgrims from the thirteenth and early fourteenth century. Not until the Franciscans were allowed to buy the tract of land between 1335 and 1337 and to build a monastery there did it assume its present-day form. Yet the friars did not remain "protectors of the holy Mount Zion" for long. As early as the sixteenth century, they were violently driven out by the Turks, who transformed the tomb of David and the Cenacle into a mosque. Only with the founding of the State of Israel did the complex come into Jewish hands, and presently the Vatican is endeavoring to regain at least the upper story for the Church. Remains of the Byzantine Hagia Sion Basilica and of the Crusaders' church were brought to light during the construction of the Basilica of the Dormition and also during later archaeological excavations.

Since 1906, the neo-Romanesque Basilica of the Dormition has been staffed by German Benedictines from the monastery in Beuron, who at that time were leaders in liturgical art and found here a rewarding field in which to work. During World War II, the American Benedictines replaced them, but soon after the end of the war, the Germans returned. In 1974, they were joined by a then fifty-one-year-old man from South Tirol who already had an eventful life behind him. Virgil Pixner had started his theology studies in 1940 and joined a Catholic mission society. When he was forcibly recruited by the German *Wehrmacht*, he refused to take an oath of loyalty to Adolf Hitler and barely escaped execution by firing squad. After his priestly ordination in 1946, he worked in the Philippines, in Europe, and in the United States as a missionary and acquired American citizenship. Then he was drawn to the Holy Land, where at first he founded the peace village Neve Shalom near Anwas. Upon his arrival, an Israeli border official mistakenly wrote his name *Bargil*, which in Hebrew means "son of joy"; Pixner saw this as a providential sign and accepted the new name. In Anwas, which some researchers take to be the biblical Emmaus, he came into contact with the Benedictine Order, which he joined in 1972; two years later, he took his perpetual vows on Zion. But whereas other monks put off their old name like a worn-out coat, he wanted to keep the name

Bargil. Fascinated by the history of his new field of activity, he immediately began to devote himself entirely to archaeology. His profound
knowledge of ancient Judaism and especially of the Essene community
soon made him one of the most important experts for New Testament
archaeology. He coined the expression "the Fifth Gospel", meaning
the topography and archaeology of the Holy Land, through which the
four canonical Gospels can be understood so much more profoundly.
Through his discovery of the biblical Bethsaida, the birthplace of Saint
Peter, he gained worldwide recognition. At the same time, he was
a genuine bridge builder in the Christian-Jewish dialogue. On April
5, 2002, precisely one day before the 1972nd anniversary of the Last
Supper, he passed away peacefully in the Abbey of the Dormition in
Jerusalem.

When Father Bargil Pixner moved into this monastery in 1974, its
ancient tradition became his greatest challenge. It was clear to him
that its credibility depended on whether it could stand the test of an
archaeological investigation. But before he could begin excavating, he
had to learn as much as possible about the history of the southwestern
hill.

As so often happens when someone tries to learn about the Jerusalem
of the time of Jesus and Mary, his search, too, began with the study of
what are perhaps the most important contemporary sources, the writings of the Jewish historiographer Flavius Josephus. The latter, however, relates little about Mount Zion, with one exception that is all the
more astonishing. In the fourth chapter of book 5 of his account of
the *Wars of the Jews*, he describes the course followed by the city wall
of Jerusalem in the first century:

> But if we go the other way westward, it began at the same place [that
> is, at the tower called "Hippicus"] and extended through a place called
> "Bethso", to the gate of the Essenes; and after that it went southward,
> having its bending above the fountain Siloam.

Pixner reasoned that this gate at the southwest corner of ancient
Jerusalem, and thus at the foot of Mount Zion, was not so named
by accident. For the fact that it was called "the Gate of the Essenes"
must have meant that it led to a settlement of that sect. This could not
have been located outside the gate, because beyond the wide Hinnom
Valley there was nothing but the road to Bethlehem. Therefore, the
Essenes must have settled on Zion when Herod the Great invited them

into the Holy City of Jerusalem upon taking office. That was in 37 B.C., and meanwhile the monastery in Qumran on the Dead Sea was abandoned for almost exactly one generation—that is, until the death of Herod in 4 B.C. In fact, Zion plays an important role in the writings of the community; the hill is praised again and again: "Great is your hope, O Zion: peace will come and the salvation for which you long. Generation after generation shall dwell in you, generations of the devout shall be your splendor", we read in one psalm-like hymn from Qumran (11Q5). In the *Visions of the Patriarch Henoch*, too, one of the Essenes' sacred writings, the author begs for the "presence of the Just One" on the "holy mountain". A whole series of Essene hiding places listed on the Copper Scroll were located on the southwest hill.

But could Pixner's hypothesis about an Essene quarter on Mount Zion be proved archaeologically as well? In 1977, the Benedictine monk finally had permission to dig at the place where two English researchers a century earlier had already run into traces of an ancient gate. The site in question was located on the southeastern edge of the Lutheran Cemetery, the burial place of Oskar Schindler, who saved so many Jews, and of several other great men. During the excavation, Pixner in fact came across the remains of the ancient city wall from the Hasmonean period, in which a gate had been added subsequently, specifically at the time of Herod (as pottery shards confirm). That in itself fits the hypothesis: when the Essenes were brought by Herod to Jerusalem, their strict purity laws required that they have their own entrance to the city. But the last doubts were removed by the discovery of a double pool outside the city wall and forty-four yards northwest of the gate, right on the path that led to it.[1] It was a Jewish ritual bath, a *mikveh*. Of course in Jerusalem there were any number of *mikvehs* (in Hebrew: *mikvaoth*) that were used in ritual purification; but they were all located around the Temple Mount. A *mikveh* in front of a city gate, on the other hand, is evidence that the people who lived on the other side of it attached great importance to ritual purity. The *Community Rule* of Qumran proves that this was true of the Essenes. It required of the inhabitants of every Essene settlement, of every so-called "camp" (in Hebrew: *machanoth*), painstaking compliance with all the regulations concerning purity in the Book of Deuteronomy. There it says: "When you . . . are in camp, then you shall keep yourself from every

---

[1] Today on the grounds of the "Greek Garden", roofed over with an ugly metal shed.

evil thing. If there is among you any man who is not clean by reason of a nocturnal emission, then he shall go outside the camp, he shall not come within the camp; but when evening comes on, he shall bathe himself in water, and when the sun is down, he may come within the camp" (Deut 23:9–11). Thus in Qumran, too, there is an almost identical ritual bath facility outside the settlement. It, too, has two parts, which evidently was a characteristic of the Essene *mikvehs*. Someone who stepped down into it unclean on the left side was supposed to be able to climb out clean on the right side, without his feet coming into contact again with the former impurities. A water pipe that was supplied from within the residential district provided supervised kosher running water ("living water"), as the Essene purity laws required.

Yet the "place called Bethso" that Flavius Josephus mentions also points to the Essenes. The name in Hebrew means much the same as "House of Dung" (*beth-zo'a*), and it designates a toilet facility. "You shall have a place outside the camp and you shall go out to it", we read in the Book of Deuteronomy (23:12). Whereas in Qumran excrement was buried in the wilderness with a pickaxe, the *Temple Scroll* of the Essenes prescribed stricter rules for Jerusalem: "You shall make latrines for them outside the city, where they are obliged to go, outside, to the northeast of the city, houses (*bathim*) with beams and wells within them, to which the excrement (*zo'a*) shall drop." In fact, around forty-four yards northwest of the *mikveh*, on the grounds of the present-day Bishop Gobat School, they discovered a vat almost ten feet wide carved out of the rock, which may well have been a cesspool for the Essene outhouses. In 1998, the Israeli archaeologist Boaz Zissu came across a group of tombs right next to it that were all facing north, just like the tombs in Qumran; the Essenes supposed that Paradise was in that direction.

But if Zion was the Essene quarter at the time of Mary and Jesus, then it is no accident that the oldest tradition identifies it as the cradle of the original Christian community, and there must have been very close contacts between the eschatological sect and the Messianic movement. Of course, Jesus was not an Essene; after all, he consistently broke with all Jewish purity precepts and taught that what makes a man unclean is not something external but rather what is within him. Yet precisely his radical claims, his demonstrative embrace of sinners and outcasts, and, consequently, his break with so many regulations of the Mosaic laws might also have impressed many Essenes. For the prophecies in their scriptures, too, said that the Messiah would proclaim his own Torah. Still, Jesus united in himself the royal line of David and the priestly line of Aaron, which made him at least potentially a legitimate candidate for the title of Messiah. Had not Isaiah and the other prophets fore-told so much of what he was doing? And according to the prophecy of Daniel, was not the time for his coming long overdue?

The sect, after all, was very close to Jesus' family, and so it is quite possible that at least some of its members followed his ministry benev-olently and finally professed faith in him after his Resurrection. But how close this contact really was is demonstrated in particular by a very special episode in the Gospels, the search for the room of the Last Supper.

Jesus died on the Cross at the same hour as the lambs were being slaughtered in the Temple for the Passover (1 Cor 5:7). Scarcely had his body been taken down from the Cross and buried in a nearby tomb when all Jerusalem gathered for the Seder supper that commenced the feast. Yet at least in the Synoptic Gospels (Matthew, Mark, and Luke), the day before the Last Supper is described as "the first day of Unleavened Bread, when they sacrificed the Passover lamb" (Mk 14:12; see also Mt 26:17; Lk 22:7). Obviously, therefore, the disciples of Jesus followed a different calendar from that of the Temple hierar-chy, which still deliberately avoided Pilate's praetorium on Good Fri-day "so that they might not be defiled, but might eat the Passover" (Jn 18:28). As was already mentioned, there was such a second calendar. It was the solar calendar that the Essenes used, according to which every first of the month automatically fell on a Wednesday. Accord-ingly, the fifteenth of Nisan, the first day of the Passover, was like-wise a Wednesday, just as the Gospels indicate. Official Jerusalem, in other words, the Sadducees, reckoned dates by the moon; for them the fifteenth of Nisan always corresponded to the first full moon in spring. In the year A.D. 30, this fell on April 8, a Sabbath. And so the Paschal lambs were slaughtered on Friday afternoon in the Temple, and that evening the Seder celebrations took place, just as the Gospel of John describes. Jesus, who never intended to be the Messiah of a sect, therefore decided on a compromise when he scheduled his Seder meal for Thursday evening, knowing of course that he would no longer be alive on Friday evening. But there was only one place in all Jerusalem where an "early" celebration was possible—the Essene quarter!

Therefore, he gave his disciples very specific instructions. He told them to go into the city. Since they were staying then in Bethany, the most direct way led through the Water Gate in the southeast, right next to the Pool of Siloam. There they were to pay attention to "a man carrying a jar of water" (Mk 14:13). That was not particularly difficult; throughout the Near East, then as today, fetching water was women's work. The only exception might be a celibate order like the Essenes. The *Rule of the Community* of Qumran explicitly prescribed celibacy for the inhabitants of the Essene quarter in Jerusalem: "No man shall lie with a woman in the city of the Temple, so as not to stain the city of the Temple with her impurity."

In any case, they were supposed to follow the man carrying the water "wherever he enters" a house. That was not difficult, either, if the house was located in the Essene quarter, because from the Pool of Siloam a staircase led directly up Mount Zion; to a great extent it is still preserved today. There they were to ask "the householder" on behalf of their Master for a room where he might eat the Paschal lamb with his disciples: "And [the householder] will show you a large upper room furnished and ready" (Mk 14:15). Did this room of the Last Supper, which apparently was located in an inn of the Essenes, become the "upper room" where the original Christian community gathered after the Resurrection? This is maintained, at any rate, by the oldest Christian tradition, as recorded, for example, in the Syriac *Doctrina Addai* from the fourth century. Spatially too, therefore, the "church of the apostles" was the direct successor of this birthplace of the Eucharist.

Did the original Christian community settle here, too, in the Essene quarter, until gradually it took possession of Zion entirely? Luke's account of Pentecost seems to suggest this, when it says: "Now there were dwelling in Jerusalem Jews, devout men" (Acts 2:5). What sounds at first like a trivial observation—of course Jews lived in Jerusalem, who else?—becomes significant on further reflection. For at the place where we read about "devout men", the original Greek text has *eulabeis*, a word that is used already in the Septuagint for the Hebrew *chassidim*, "the devout". From the Aramaic version of it, *chassayya*, the word "Essene" is derived (a more indicative transliteration would be "Essaiyan"). Then the Pentecost event also took place in the Essene quarter. At Pentecost, the Jewish Feast of Weeks, the Essenes celebrated the renewal of the Old (Mosaic) Covenant and admitted novices to their community. That may explain the large number of pilgrims mentioned in the Acts of the Apostles. Another clue suggesting that Zion was the scene is the fact that in his sermon Peter quotes the prophet Joel, a passage that goes on to say: "For in Mount Zion and in Jerusalem there shall be those who escape, as the LORD has said" (Joel 2:32). The final evidence of proximity to the Essene settlement is the fact that the original Christian community followed their example and shared all their possessions.

> Now the company of those who believed were of one heart and soul, and no one said that any of the things which he possessed was his own, but they had everything in common. . . . There was not any one needy among them, for as many as were possessors of lands or houses sold them, and brought the proceeds of what was sold and laid it at the apostles' feet; and distribution was made to each as any had need. (Acts 4:32–35)

There is a similar-sounding passage in the Essene *Community Rule*. When a man is permitted to "join the foundations of the Community according to the priests and the majority of the men of the covenant, his wealth and his belongings will also be included at the hands of the Inspector of the belongings." There was just one difference: Among the Christians, the sharing of goods was voluntary, while for the Essenes it was an obligation. Yet the procedure of drawing lots that the Twelve used to replace the betrayer Judas in their number (Acts 1:15–26) is also found in the Qumran regulations for filling important offices. And the Essene role of community overseer (*mebakker*) seems to have been the pattern for the Christian ministry of the bishop, since the Greek term *episkopos* has the same meaning etymologically.

But are there archaeological traces, too, of this early Christian commune? That proved to be the case in 1983 when the Benedictines bought from the Franciscans a little garden right beside the Abbey of the Dormition, so as to enlarge their monastery with a porch. According to Israeli law, they were obliged to have the site investigated by an archaeologist of the Israeli Antiquities Authority before beginning the construction work. The excavations unearthed not only the foundations of the former Crusaders' church but also, deep beneath them, ruins from the first century. At a depth of thirteen feet, a narrow street hewn out of the rocks ran from north to south. On either side there were houses "that were built in the simplest manner out of unfinished stones and made a very poor impression as to their style and

Ausgrabung 1983

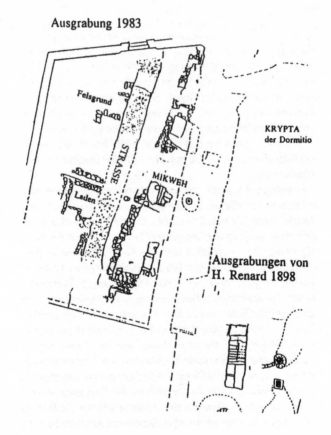

KRYPTA
der Dormitio

Felsgrund

STRASSE

MIKWEH

Laden

Ausgrabungen von
H. Renard 1898

LEGEND: Ausgrabung 1983 > 1983 Excavation. Felsgrund > bedrock. KRYPTA der Dormitio > CRYPT of Dormition Abbey. STRASSE > STREET. MIKWEH > MIKVEH. Laden > shop. Ausgrabungen von H. Renard 1898 > 1898 excavations by H. Renard.

Remains of simple residential buildings from the first century beneath the Abbey of the Dormition, which Father Bargil Pixner identified as the settlement of the original Christian community.

appearance", as Father Pixner reports. Moreover, they made a striking contrast with the opulent villas of the wealthy, whose districts bordered Mount Zion on the north and the east. Actually, the poverty of the original Christian community is a theme of the Acts of the Apostles again and again; Paul, too, collected donations in the communities that he founded, which he personally brought to "the poor among the saints at Jerusalem" (Rom 15:26). The fact that each house had its own *mikveh*, despite its poverty, is evidence that their inhabitants were extremely devout Jews. Sketches of the abbey's construction site and of excavations on neighboring parcels of land even prove that there was an unusually "large concentration of ritual baths" (as the archaeologist and scholar in Judaic studies Rainer Riesner put it) in this quarter. These modest houses remained standing until they were destroyed by the Romans in A.D. 70.

Over the course of the excavations, various coins were found, the oldest of which was from the time of the Procurator Valerius Gratus, the immediate predecessor of Pilate. The most recent coins had been minted in the second year of the Jewish Revolt, A.D. 67. At that time, it seems, these houses had already been abandoned by their inhabitants. That would be in keeping with the tradition that the Christians, led by their Bishop Simeon, fled to Pella across the Jordan before the beginning of the battle of Jerusalem. And Mary? Everything indicates that she once lived with John in this very same first Christian settlement on Mount Zion.

It is well known that from her earliest childhood she had been familiar with the Essene milieu and with the special spirituality of this monastic sect, whose monastery was located right next to the Christian settlement. Like no other woman, therefore, she represented the continuity of the divine plan of salvation, and she became, so to speak, both the embodiment of Israel and the archetype of the young Church, which soon understood herself to be the "New Israel". Since Divine Providence speaks to us in signs, it was no accident that the Mother of God from then on "found a home in Zion", as the prophet Jesus Sirach had foretold (24:10; the RSV-2CE reads "I was established in Zion"). She thereby revealed herself, for all to see, as the true "Daughter of Zion" from the Old Testament prophecy.

The great Mariologist Father René Laurentin, at least, sees the greeting of the angel, *chaire* ("rejoice"), to be an allusion to Zephaniah 3:14 ("Sing aloud, O daughter of Zion; shout, O Israel! Rejoice and exult with all your heart"), in which Mary is introduced as Daughter of Zion. In the Old Testament, the Daughter of Zion is described as the spotless bride of God, the mother of the people of God, and the virgin Israel. She is, therefore, the personification of the Messianic people with its eschatological commission, both Bride and Daughter,

Virgin and Mother, just like Mary in the New Testament. Nowhere else is that as clear as in the *Magnificat*. Here the Incarnation of the Son of God is the crowning glory of a series of miracles that he had already performed for his people Israel. The Litany of Loreto rightly calls Mary "Queen of patriarchs and prophets", for in her Yes to God's plan of salvation were gathered all the Yeses to all the great vocations of the Old Covenant, from Abraham to Esther. In Mary, the whole history of Israel culminates, so to speak, in its most mature fruit, when through God's mercy the Redeemer of all mankind is born of her.[2] Or, as Joseph Ratzinger puts it in his book *Daughter Zion*: Mary "is the true Israel, in whom Old and New Covenant, Israel and Church, are indivisibly one. She is the 'people of God' bearing fruit through God's gracious power."[3] On Pentecost, therefore, Zechariah's vision was fulfilled: "Sing and rejoice, O daughter of Zion; for behold, I come and I will dwell in the midst of you, says the LORD. And many nations shall join themselves to the LORD in that day, and shall be my people; and I will dwell in the midst of you" (2:10–11). But just as the Gospel had to be carried into the world from Zion, perhaps Mary, too, had to be a sign for the Gentiles and leave Zion again for a time.

The stone from Mary's house, now embedded in the base of the tower of Dormition Abbey.

---

[2] I heartily recommend, to those interested in the theology of this topic, the important work by Gerhard Lohfink and Ludwig Weimer, *Maria—nicht ohne Israel* (2008).

[3] Joseph Cardinal Ratzinger, *Daughter Zion: Meditations on the Church's Marian Belief*, trans. John M. McDermott, S.J. (San Francisco: Ignatius Press, 1983), 43.

12

Mary in Ephesus

A light morning mist lay over the smooth knolls of Mount Nightingale, while the mild autumn sun made its way through the multicolored foliage of its dense forests. Its rays became ever warmer and stronger, longingly awaited by the chilled crowd of people who had gathered here. But soon their waiting came to an end. It turned into a peaceful, pleasant day, that sun-drenched November 29, 2006, when Pope Benedict XVI, during his historic journey to Turkey, came to Ephesus also to pray in the house that may have become the Temple of God's new Ark of the Covenant. Here, surrounded by the luxuriant woods of a mythical landscape, Mary perhaps found refuge once when she had been driven away from Zion.

Since then, little has changed on Mount Nightingale. The road up to it has been improved and widened, and Mary's House—Meryem Ana Evi, as the Turks call it—has a spacious parking lot and now a papal altar with a roof had been built especially for this day. Most striking, however, was the profusion of flowers with which a few Turkish nuns had lovingly decorated the site for this very special occasion. For security reasons, the grounds, which are difficult to survey, had been cordoned off to form a perimeter. Thus only a few invited guests were present, most of them active members of the Christian communities of the Archdiocese of Smyrna (Izmir) and their priests, when around eleven o'clock the chugging of the papal helicopter interrupted the songs and prayers of the waiting crowd. But before Benedict XVI celebrated Mass with them, he himself, accompanied only by his secretary, Msgr. Georg Gänswein, and the local ordinary, Bishop Ruggero Franceschini, O.F.M., entered Mary's House. For several minutes he prayed fervently before the altar of the holy domicile, which has been transformed into a chapel, which he then left, deeply moved.

He was not the first pope to be attracted to "this place, which is so dear to the Christian community" (as Benedict XVI said in his homily on the occasion). Angelo Roncalli, who later became Pope John XXIII, had come to visit while he was still serving as apostolic nuncio in Turkey, and after him almost every one of his successors: Paul VI in July 1967, John Paul II in November 1979. Although the house even today is palpably "blessed by the presence of Mary Most Holy" (Benedict XVI), its history is mysterious, and for a long time it was forgotten.

The series of events that led to its rediscovery began in Germany, of all places, specifically in the town of Dülmen in Westphalia. Living there, at the beginning of the nineteenth century, was a consecrated religious by the name of Anne Catherine Emmerich, who not only bore the stigmata of Christ but also had visions of the lives of Jesus, Mary, and the biblical prophets and saints. After her convent had been secularized, this Augustinian nun found refuge in the house of a priest who had fled from revolutionary France, who became the first witness of her stigmata. Neither the doctors whom he called in nor the members of a public commission of examiners, made up of skeptical Freemasons and Protestants, could explain the appearance of the bleeding wounds, accompanied by detailed visions of biblical events. (I discuss her case in detail in my book *Stigmata: Sie trugen die Wundmale Christi*.) [1]

When the Romantic poet Clemens Brentano learned about the stigmatist, he had just returned to the Catholic Church. The news from Dülmen seemed to him to be God's answer to his deepest yearning, his quest for a mission in life. Now he would find his destiny in recording the visions of the bleeding nun. "A whole world is opening up to me here; now I glimpse what the Church is", he wrote with deep emotion in his diary. He spent the next five years, until her death in 1824, beside her bed of suffering. His book with the transcription of her visions of the Passion, *The Dolorous Passion of Our Lord Jesus Christ*, published in 1833, became a best seller; the German edition alone went through seventy-seven editions by 1926 and thus was more widely read than the works of Goethe and Schiller. Nevertheless, another volume, *The Life of the Blessed Virgin Mary*, did not appear until 1852, a decade after Brentano's death, followed by the three-volume *The Life of Our Lord and Savior* (1858–1860). These books, too, were translated into numerous foreign languages and sold briskly throughout Europe. In

[1] Michael Hesemann, *Stigmata: Sie trugen die Wundmale* Christi (Güllesheim: Silberschnur Verlag, 2006).

1858, the process for the beatification of Anne Catherine Emmerich was officially opened, but not until October 3, 2004, was she solemnly beatified by Pope John Paul II in Rome. It was the last but also the most moving beatification of the Wojtyła papacy.

In her visions, Emmerich maintained that the Mother of God spent the final years of her life in Ephesus. She described the house where she lived in all its detail:

> Mary's dwelling was on a hill to the left of the road from Jerusalem some three and a half hours from Ephesus. This hill slopes steeply toward Ephesus; the city as one approaches it from the southeast seems to lie on rising ground immediately before one, but it seems to change its place as one draws nearer. Great avenues lead up to the city, and the ground under the trees is covered with yellow fruit. Narrow paths lead southward to a hill near the top of which is an uneven plateau, some half-hour's journey in circumference, overgrown, like the hill itself, with wild trees and bushes. . . . A little way behind [the house] was the summit of the rocky hill from which one could see over the trees and hills to Ephesus and the sea with its many islands. The place is nearer the sea than Ephesus. . . . The district is lonely and unfrequented. . . . Between the Blessed Virgin's dwelling and Ephesus runs a little stream that winds about in a very singular way.

These were, to put it mildly, very precise specifications, which Brentano of course could not verify; during his lifetime he had never visited Asia Minor, nor had Anne Catherine Emmerich herself, who was of very humble origins; she was the daughter of a farm laborer. So it took a few decades until someone set out to investigate her visions.

The first to start a search for the house was a French priest from Paris by the name of Father Julien Goyet, who had been fascinated by a translation of Emmerich's *Life of the Blessed Virgin Mary* that he had read. When he came to modern-day Turkey in 1881, he incurred no risk. First he introduced himself to the Roman Catholic archbishop of Smyrna and asked him for a guide familiar with the locality. Then he set out accompanied by that guide. On his briefcase was a sticker with a note in Greek: "Please be considerate to a harmless traveler with no financial resources." Even so, his journey was not without incident, but obviously it was successful, too. Finally he was able to announce proudly to the archbishop as well as to his superiors in Paris and Rome: "I have found the house. It exists." But since at that time

no one seemed to be interested in his discovery, he unfortunately refrained from writing a report.

Ten years later, the mother superior of the Sisters of Charity in
Smyrna brought the visions of Anne Catherine Emmerich to the attention of the Vincentian priest Father Eugène Poulin. As a scholar
and director of the French College in Smyrna, he was more than skeptical, especially when he read about the alleged life and death of the
Mother of God in Ephesus. Nevertheless, he mentioned the book in his
conversation with his priest-confrères. Father M. H. Jung, who taught
natural sciences at the college and also was the father confessor of the
nuns, was especially skeptical, saying that he considered the visions
to have been "childish daydreams". But the sisters were not so easily
dismissed, and finally the Vincentians decided to send an expedition
to Ephesus headed by the skeptical Father Jung, in order to investigate
on the spot the claims of the nun from Westphalia.

On the morning of July 27, 1891, Father Jung, his confrère Father
Benjamin Vervault, the Greek guide Pelacas, who had worked as a
railroad manager in Ayasoluk (today Selçuk), and the Persian servant
Thomaso as their porter set out on their journey. First they boarded
the train to Ayasoluk, where they hired the Turk Mustafa as a mountain guide and bodyguard. Then, after a visit to the ruins of ancient
Ephesus, they could begin their search.

They spent a day and a half roaming through the wooded hill country of Ephesus. The first clue they pursued, which came from a Me-
chitarist Father (an Armenian Benedictine monk), led them to a Greek
monastery. No one there knew anything about a house belonging to
Mary, but they did offer them generous hospitality and the delicious
wine made by the monastery. The next morning, with a dull headache,
Father Jung decided to proceed like a general staff officer and to follow the descriptions of the stigmatist nun to the last detail. First the
men determined the ancient Roman road to Syria and Jerusalem. After
passing the ruins of Ephesus while walking along it, they watched for
a road branching off from it that might lead into the hill country. After
an hour, when they had finally found one, the sun was already high
in the sky. In the baking heat, the men fought their way through the
narrow footpath, which was overgrown with thorn bushes. The sweat
streamed out of all their pores, made their soaked clothing stick to
their skin, trickled down their foreheads and irritated their eyes, which
were dazzled by the sun. The path led up a steep hill, and the more

vigorously the men breathed, the more their parched throats burned. The water they had brought with them in flasks had long since been used up when the exhausted wanderers, almost dead of thirst, finally reached a plateau on which women were working in a tobacco field. "Nero!" Pelacas called to them in Greek: "Water!" "We have none left!" the farmers replied, "but back there, at the *monastiri*, there is a spring!"

Ten torturous minutes later they were standing in front of an old, ramshackle house, surrounded by ruins, beside which fresh water was in fact welling up from a spring. But only after they had been thoroughly refreshed did the men pay closer attention to the ruin. It seemed to be quite ancient—and inhabited. Two Greek farmers, Andreas and Yorgy, eyed the strangers at first with some skepticism, until they were sure that they were not dealing with Turkish officials. Only then did they become friendlier and offer the men something to eat. While his companions were resting, Father Jung took the opportunity to inspect the ruin more closely. It did not take long for him to realize that the dimensions of the dilapidated house corresponded fairly exactly to Anne Catherine Emmerich's description: "Mary's house was built of rectangular stones, rounded or pointed at the back. The windows were high up near the flat roof", it said in her book. Was it possible to see the sea and the city at the same time, as the stigmatist nun maintained? Yes, you can, Yorgy assured him. "Here on the Bülbüldagi is the one and only place where that is possible. Shall I show it to you?" The Vincentian priest did not wait to be asked a second time. Together with his confrère and the porter Thomaso, he climbed up to the nearby peak. And in fact: if you looked north, you saw the plain of Ephesus, whereas in the west lay the sea and, in the distance, the island of Samos —exactly as Anne Catherine Emmerich had described it. "We searched and we found it", Father Jung noted that same evening in his diary, after Andreas had brought him and his companions down safely again to Ephesus.

For two more days, the men inspected the area, in order to learn as much as possible about the history of the ruin. Andreas told them that it had once belonged to a monastery and from time immemorial had been known by the name of Panagia Kapuli—"Gate of the All-Holy Virgin". People had always come there from his village to pray to the Mother of God. In recent decades, there had been such frequent attacks by bands of robbers that only a few people still ventured into the area. He had leased the tobacco field, however, and lived here every summer. With the help of the native, the team discovered the remains of an old cistern and a baptismal font, but also stones that, as Father Jung believed, bore Hebrew characters.

Back in Smyrna, he reported his discovery to Father Poulin. But the superior did not want to believe him. Only when he himself set out on the journey and was convinced on the spot that everything was just as Emmerich had described it did he take the initiative. Once again he sent Father Jung to Ephesus—but this time at the head of a group of laymen, among them scientists and a photographer, who were commissioned to investigate the site thoroughly. After a week on Mount Nightingale, they discovered two additional proofs corroborating the visions of Anne Catherine Emmerich. The one involved the ruins of a small ancient fortress located three-fourths of a mile from the house; the stigmatist spoke also about a "castle" right nearby Mary's house. Moreover, she mentioned that on the crest of the hill Mary had arranged a sort of Way of the Cross, the high point of which represented Golgotha. Father Jung's team thought that they had discovered a series of markers, one of them on an elevation, but it was impossible to determine the date of their origin. But there was a bitter disappointment, too. According to Emmerich, the tomb of the Mother of God was supposed to be not far from the hill; despite all their efforts, however, the men did not succeed in finding the alleged burial place of Mary.

But that did not detract at all from their enthusiasm about their discovery. So the religious congregation finally decided to purchase the plot of land with the ruin. Fortunately, it happened that one of the nuns who from the start had believed in the visions, Marie de Mandat Grancey, had just inherited a considerable fortune. She was immediately willing to make the money available for this purpose. Finally, they were introduced to the Turkish landowner, who after tough, wearisome negotiations finally affixed his signature to the bill of sale. Only then did Father Poulin dare to inform Archbishop Timoni as well. His hesitation was completely groundless; His Excellency had already heard of Emmerich's visions and "always believed that Mary lived and died in Ephesus". Together with twelve dignitaries—seven clerics and five laymen—he immediately set out for Ayasoluk so as to reach Mount Nightingale on horseback. Upon his return to Smyrna, he wrote a report that compared the findings with the descriptions of the stigmatist and, signed by all twelve members of his commission, determined at last that "the ruins of Panagia Kapuli are truly the remains of the house in which the Virgin Mary once lived."

In the years that followed, the house that had been discovered as a ruin was lovingly reconstructed and built up again. A channel was built for the spring, better access paths were planned, a statue of Mary and an altar were set up in the house. No one seemed to be bothered by the fact that the oldest coins found on the site were from the fifth century; indeed, there was not the slightest proof that the house was actually two thousand years old. In any case, the findings indicate that a monastery stood there in the early Byzantine era; even in old Ottoman land registers it was still listed as "The triple-gated monastery of the *Panagia*" (the Most Holy Virgin). Was the monastery church built over an older shrine? That is quite possible. At any rate, Emmerich's visions proved to be correct in one further detail. When workers uncovered the floor of Mary's House on August 24, 1898, at a depth of twenty inches they hit a surface of black, burned stone. An archaeologist hurriedly summoned from Smyrna, Professor Weber, confirmed that the stones must have come from a fireplace. "(The house) was divided into two parts by the fireplace situated in the middle", we read in the writings of the stigmatist.

Pope Pius X congratulated the Vincentians in 1905 on their discovery and blessed their work; in 1914, he also granted to pilgrims who visited the shrine a plenary indulgence remitting all temporal punishment for their sins. But then the First World War broke out, and the whole region became a military blockade zone. As enemies in the war, the French had to leave the Ottoman Empire. When the Vincentians returned to Bülbüldagi in 1920, they found the altar demolished and the plane trees that used to provide cool shade in front of the house felled. The bronze statue of Mary had disappeared; the Turkish treasury officials had confiscated the tract of land, and the Greeks who used to live there had been forcibly exiled.

The battle for the site lasted thirty years. Not until 1951 were the circumstances of ownership recognized by the Turkish state. Since then the shrine has been called Meryem Ana Evi ("House of Mother Mary") or Meryemana ("Mother Mary") for short, and it belongs to a private association. It cost the association some trouble before it convinced the Turkish officials, too, that Mary's House could be the potential destination for foreign tourism. The Turks, too, have long since discovered the shrine for themselves, since Mary, after all, is revered by Muslims, too, as "Mother of the Prophet Jesus". Today French nuns staff Mary's House, to which Muslim women from the vicinity come also to ask Mary for help in their needs. It is a place of peace and unadorned simplicity, an oasis of tolerance in a land of martyrs. On long lines stretched between the trees hang notes with written prayers. Muslims and Christians alike drink from the same sacred spring. Here Mother Mary brings together brothers who had become enemies.

Against this background, the question as to the authenticity of Mary's House quickly loses significance. It is unquestionably holy, because Mary is at work in it today. But was she really in Ephesus? And did she also die there, as Anne Catherine Emmerich maintains?

One thing is certain: Anne Catherine Emmerich could not have known about the ruins of the Panagia Kapuli from reading, for instance, from the very well-stocked library of her convent. It is mentioned at all only once in Christian literature, specifically in the books by Gregory of Tours, a sixth-century Frankish cleric and historian, who writes: "On a mountaintop near Ephesus four walls without a roof are preserved. John lived within those walls."

Now there is no doubt that the evangelist and beloved disciple of Jesus actually lived and ministered in Ephesus. It is unclear, however, when he did that. When Saint Paul came to Ephesus for the first time in the year 52, there seems to have been no Christian community to speak of yet. Instead of John, we read in the Acts of the Apostles about an Alexandrian Jew by the name of Apollos, who was "instructed in the way of the Lord" (Acts 18:25) and "fervent in spirit" as he expounded the teaching of Jesus. He was, moreover, primarily a disciple of John the Baptist; Paul, it says, baptized the recent converts "in the name of the Lord Jesus". Thus Ephesus, the capital of the Roman province of Asia with its famous Temple of Artemis, one of the Seven Wonders of the World, became the mission territory of the apostle to the Gentiles. In 56/57, an uprising of the local silversmiths, who were anxious about the future prospects of their trade in silver statues of the pagan goddess of fertility, compelled him to flee, and he appointed his disciple Timothy as the first bishop of Ephesus. Only later is there evidence of missionary work by John, who, according to Irenaeus of Lyon, "stayed there until the days of Trajan" and died in Ephesus around A.D. 100. In the Syrian version of the legendary *Acts of John*, he lives and dies in a "hut" on a mountain near the city, from which he was able to look down on the Temple of Artemis.

Since the second century, the tomb of the apostle has logically been revered in Ephesus. Bishop Polycrates confirmed this in a letter to Pope Victor (ca. 186–197), who cited John in the controversy over the date of Easter: in Asia Minor the Resurrection of Christ was celebrated on 14 Nisan according to the Jewish calendar. Saint Jerome, too, in the fourth century had no doubt that the apostle came to Ephesus during the reign of Nero (54–88), was banished by Domitian (81–96) to Patmos, and returned after the emperor's death so as to live in the provincial capital again until the days of Trajan (98–117). Moreover, he "founded and governed all the Churches of Asia, until finally, at an extreme old age, in the sixty-eighth year after our Lord's Passion (A.D. 98 or 101), he died and was buried in the same city." In the fourth century, pilgrims reported that a church had been built over his tomb. In the early twentieth century, members of the Austrian Archaeological Institute unearthed the remains of that church, which being in the immediate vicinity of the wretched ruins of the Temple of Artemis are all the more impressive. Emperor Justinian had replaced the original cruciform house of worship in the sixth century with a basilica 426 feet long and 213 feet wide. The heart of the whole building was the apostle's tomb beneath the central dome, which was emphasized architecturally, too, by a two-tiered podium. The belief that the dust from a little hole in the burial chamber had healing powers made Ephesus an important place of pilgrimage well into the Middle Ages. On the other hand, not one single ancient source is able to report about a tomb of Mary.

Not until the ninth century did the Syrian bishop of Beth Ramman, Moshe Bar Kepha, maintain that Mary, too, died and was buried in Ephesus. Two twelfth-century Antiochene patriarchs, Dionysius Bar Salibi and Michael the Great, agreed with him. Yet Michael also maintained that Mary accompanied the apostle to the Island of Patmos and died only after their return; in that case, she would have been a remarkable 114 years old. The Syrian theologian Gregorius Abu-Farag Bar Hebraeus (thirteenth century) explained the absence of any local tradition by saying that John had deliberately kept Mary's tomb a secret.

Actually, though, it is extremely unlikely that Mary died in Ephesus, as Anne Catherine Emmerich maintained. But could she have lived at least for a time in the city of the mother-goddess Artemis, perhaps even in the above-mentioned House of Mary? That is quite possible.

The oldest tradition along these lines comes, of all places, from the acts of the Council of Ephesus, which conferred on Mary for all ages the title of *Theotokos*, or "God-bearer", in other words, Mother of God. The occasion for this third ecumenical council of the Church, which Emperor Theodosius II convoked, was a weighty controversy. Nestorius, the new patriarch of Constantinople, had claimed that Christ's humanity was only morally united with his divinity. Therefore Mary, his mother, could not be termed "God-bearer"; she was at most "Christ-bearer". This was contradicted quite vehemently by Cyril, the patriarch of Alexandria, who cited tradition. Since two natures, divine and human, had been inseparably united in Christ, Mary had been rightly called "Mother of God" from the earliest times. After six weeks and three summons for Nestorius to justify himself before the 250 Council Fathers, which went unheeded, the ecclesiastical assembly ended with the condemnation of the patriarch. He was relieved of his office and was thereafter considered a heretic, while the first Marian dogma was defined as binding in faith for all believers.

The council met, appropriately enough, in the Marian church of Ephesus, which had been built in the early fourth century over the foundations of a huge ancient complex of buildings; probably the former Museion, which had been destroyed during the attack of the Ostrogoths in 263. As the bishop's church, it was located in the center of the city; yet there was no tradition linking it with any activity of Mary in Ephesus. Nevertheless, the conciliar decision reads verbatim: "Wherefore also Nestorius, . . . when he had come to the city of the Ephesians, where John the Theologian and the Virgin Mother of God, the Holy Mary . . . , was condemned by the assembly of the Holy Fathers and bishops." Unfortunately the all-important verb is missing in this sentence after the mention of John and the Mother of God, both in the Greek original and in the English translation. So we can only surmise that it was supposed to read "lived"; if both had "died" in Ephesus, the Council Fathers certainly would have mentioned Mary in first place.

But when could Mary have come to Ephesus? When Anne Catherine Emmerich says, "After Christ's Ascension, Mary lived for three years on Zion, three years in Bethany, and nine years in Ephesus", that is absolutely out of the question. After all, the Acts of the Apostles state explicitly that during the first severe persecution of the original Christian community, after the stoning of Stephen in December 33, they "all scattered throughout the region of Judea and Samaria", although in the same sentence the text emphasizes: "except the apostles" (Acts 8:1). They remained in Jerusalem and merely sent Peter and John to make a visitation in the north, so as to baptize the new converts. Peter undertook his next journey to Lydda and Joppa alone; John probably remained in Jerusalem. Lastly, at that time there was no reason, either, to leave Zion, since Luke emphasizes: "The Church throughout all Judea and Galilee and Samaria had peace and was built up; and walking in the fear of the Lord and in the comfort of the Holy Spirit it was multiplied" (Acts 9:31). At that point, there was no talk yet about a mission extending beyond Israel. Of course, there were Christians in Damascus. But not even the first significant diaspora community, Antioch, had been founded by the apostles. It consisted of the "scattered" Christians who had fled after Stephen's martyrdom and had "traveled as far as Phoenicia and Cyprus and Antioch" (Acts 11:19). To them the Mother Church in Jerusalem first sent Barnabas, who was not one of the Twelve; they, it appears, were not yet making any preparations to go on major missionary journeys. So it was until the next wave of persecution in early 42, when King Herod Agrippa after his enthronement "laid violent hands upon some who belonged to the Church". James, the brother of John, was then executed by the sword, and Peter was arrested; he miraculously managed to escape. Luke writes that he was freed from prison by an angel. Only then, apparently, did the world mission begin. Peter, in any case, "went to another place" (Acts 12:17), and tradition tells us that it was Rome, where his ministry began "in the second year of the reign of Emperor Claudius" (41–54, therefore in A.D. 42). And what about John? After his brother's death, it is almost certain that he, too, fled. If she was still alive at that point in time, the Mother of God probably went along with him. In any case, by then she was certainly no longer in Jerusalem.

The hypothesis that the major missionary journeys of the apostles actually began in the year 42 is consistent with an old (albeit noncanonical) tradition. As early as the second century, Clement of Alexandria quotes from the apocryphal *Preaching of Peter*, which was composed before 150: "Therefore, Peter said, the Lord commanded the apostles, after twelve years to go out into the world, so that no one (of the Jews) could say: We have not heard the gospel." The same twelve years are mentioned in the apocryphal *Acts of Peter*, which likewise were composed in the second century; there it says about the prince of the apostles: "After the twelve years that the Lord had prescribed were completed, Christ showed him the following vision", telling him to travel to Italy. The Church historian Eusebius, in turn, cites a certain Apollonius, likewise from the second century: "He relates as being handed down by tradition that the Lord commissioned his apostles not to go forth from Jerusalem for twelve years." As we saw, this tradition is completely in conformity with the data from the Acts of the Apostles. About Mary, too, Hippolytus of Thebes (tenth century) declared on the basis of older traditions that she lived with John in Jerusalem for eleven years. Other sources in the first millennium speak about eleven and a half or twelve years. Assuming that figures were rounded up or down, this presents a rather consistent picture.

But where did John go in the year 42? Tradition speaks of no other field of ministry of the beloved disciple except the Roman province in the western part of modern Turkey. He is considered the real apostle of Asia, despite all the missionary accomplishments of Paul. While Paul may have founded the community in Ephesus, the communities in Smyrna, Pergamon, Thyatira, Sardis, Philadelphia, and Laodicea traced their origins back to John; moreover, he addressed the seven letters at the beginning of his Book of Revelation to them (and to Ephesus). Actually Paul deliberately avoided this province during his second missionary journey in the year 49, probably because he knew that they had been allotted to another apostle (Acts 16:6). That can only have been John.

John must have had his reasons for living in Ephesus at that time but doing missionary work elsewhere. First of all, his young age may have played a role: in 42, he was at most thirty years old, and his Master himself had not commenced his teaching ministry until the age of thirty-one. Perhaps, too, he did not want to leave Mary alone or put her in danger. We can credit the mystic among the four evangelists with relying at first on the power of prayer, so as to prepare the ground for a later mission. But maybe, too, there had been an early confrontation with the Jewish community in the city, which made further ministry in Ephesus seem too difficult for him. Had not Jesus himself taught: "If any one will not receive you or listen to your words, shake off the dust from your feet as you leave that house or town" (Mt 10:14)?

On the other hand, Anne Catherine Emmerich mentioned in her visions that at the time of Mary's arrival on the Bülbüldagi, "several Christian families and holy women had already settled here, some in caves in the earth or in the rocks, fitted out with light woodwork to make dwellings, and some in fragile huts or tents. They had come here to escape violent persecution." That is consistent, moreover, with a remark by Saint Jerome (fourth century) that the apostle John had in Ephesus "a little guest room and very dear friends" (*hospitiolum et amicos amantissimos*). If we assign even the slightest historical value to these statements, we have to ask who these devout Jews were. Had they received baptism already on Pentecost, when pilgrims from the province of Asia were on record as being present (Acts 2:9)? Were they perhaps originally from a milieu influenced by the Essenes? In fact, one of the largest Jewish diaspora communities had lived in Asia ever since King Antiochus in the third century B.C. settled two thousand Jewish families from Mesopotamia in the region of what is today western Turkey. A series of decrees by the Roman senate from the time of Caesar refer explicitly to the Jews in the province of Asia and confer the greatest possible privileges on them. They even had a tribunal of their own and were exempt from Roman jurisdiction. In any case, a colony of devout Jewish immigrants could have been the real reason why Mary and John ended up in Ephesus rather than somewhere else.

If the Mother of God did in fact come to Asia Minor, then one or another legend of the Greek Orthodox world could have a kernel of truth to it. For instance, the legend that on her journey she first arrived in Cyprus, where she visited Lazarus and his sisters in Larnaca. Or that she was driven by a storm to the shore of the peninsula of Chalkidiki and there blessed Mount Athos, because she saw in a vision that one day many holy men would live there. At any rate the monastic republic is still referred to today as *to perivóli tis Panagías* (garden of the Most Holy Virgin).

But how are we to explain the mixture of possibly true and quite obviously false information in the visions of Anne Catherine Emmerich? The best explanation of mystical visions per se is found in Joseph Cardinal Ratzinger's commentary on the most famous of all Marian apparitions, the *Third Secret of Fatima*:

"Interior vision" is not fantasy but, as we have said, a true and valid means of verification. But it also has its limitations. Even in exterior vision the subjective element is always present. We do not see the pure object, but it comes to us through the filter of our senses, which carry out a work of translation. This is still more evident in the case of interior vision, especially when it involves realities which in themselves transcend our horizon. The subject, the visionary, is still more powerfully involved. He sees insofar as he is able, in the modes of representation and consciousness available to him. In the case of interior vision, the process of translation is even more extensive than in exterior vision, for the subject shares in an essential way in the formation of the image of what appears. He can arrive at the image only within the bounds of his capacities and possibilities. . . .

The images described by [the saints] are [therefore] by no means a simple expression of their fantasy, but the result of a real perception of a higher and interior origin. But neither should they be thought of as if for a moment the veil of the other world [or of space and time, *Author's note*] were drawn back. . . . Rather the images are, in a manner of speaking, a synthesis of the impulse coming from on high and the capacity to receive this impulse in the visionaries.[2]

In Anne Catherine Emmerich's case, too, supernatural visions may have been mixed with fantasies and images from the visionary's subconscious. The Augustinian nun may therefore have received perfectly authentic impressions of Mary's House but, at the same time, interpreted them incorrectly. Thus the stigmatist saw images of the death of the Mother of God in Jerusalem, at the time of a council of the apostles, in an antechamber to the Cenacle. But she thought that Mary was cured again after a passing attack of faintness and died one and a half years later in Ephesus. On another occasion, she categorically declared: "The year 48 A.D. is the year of the Blessed Virgin's death." That is a reasonable date, which we find in a Latin translation of the Chronicle of Eusebius (fourth century), and since the time of Gregory of Tours (sixth century) many Church historians have tended to agree with it. But in the year 48, it is quite clear from Saint Paul's Letter to the Galatians (2:9), John was no longer in Ephesus; he was staying in Jerusalem again and participating in a council of the apostles.

~

[2] Joseph Cardinal Ratzinger, "Theological Commentary" for the Congregation for the Doctrine of the Faith, *The Message of Fatima*, June 26, 2000.

13

Body and Soul

Once again I travel to Jerusalem in order to get to the bottom of the greatest mystery concerning the Mother of God: the circumstances of her death. For when Pope Pius XII declared it an article of faith for all Catholics sixty years ago, on November 1, 1950, that Mary was assumed into heaven "body and soul",[1] he did not specify the place, the time, or the manner of this divine miracle. Thus the argumentation in the papal bull proclaiming the doctrine was exclusively theological and not historical. The new dogma was based on Mary's Immaculate Conception, a truth of the faith proclaimed just one hundred years earlier, which Pope Blessed Pius IX defined infallibly in 1854. That in turn was ultimately derived from one of the earliest theological descriptions of Mary's role in salvation history, the definition of her as the "new Eve". Since Eve had been created sinless, Mary, too, must have been conceived and born free of original sin. Moreover, how could the Son of God have chosen a sinner as his mother at his Incarnation? But if Mary was conceived immaculate, Pius XII argued along the lines of the Doctor of the Church Thomas Aquinas, then her body was sanctified from the very beginning, and then it cannot have fallen victim to the destruction by death and corruption that is caused by original sin. If God had already taken up great patriarchs and prophets like Enoch, Moses, and Elijah[2] bodily into heaven, as reported in the Old

---

[1] From the Apostolic Constitution *Munificentissimus Deus*: "After We directed Our prayers in supplication to God again and again, and invoked the light of the Spirit of Truth, . . . We pronounce, declare, and define that the dogma was revealed by God, that the Immaculate Mother of God, the ever Virgin Mary, after completing her course of life upon earth, was assumed to the glory of heaven both in body and soul.—Pius PP XII."

[2] They had one thing in common: They were allowed to look upon God in all his glory. But in Mary for the first time he made his appearance and became man. She is truly the Queen of the Patriarchs and Prophets!

Testament, how could he have withheld this privilege from his most faithful handmaid, the All-Holy Mother of God? This corresponded to the classic formula developed by the Marian Scholastic Duns Scotus in the thirteenth century: *potuit, decuit, fecit*: "It was possible [for God], it was fitting, he did it." Thus the proclamation of the new Marian dogma became the high point of the first Holy Year after the end of the most terrible of all wars. For Pius XII, however, it was far more than that: it was his challenge to the materialism that had brought so much disaster on mankind and his personal thanksgiving to the Mother of God, who had led the Church so reliably during the darkest phase of her history.

Yet, however plausibly Pius XII explained the dogma in his bull of proclamation, the resistance to the new dogma was just as intense, especially from Protestants, but also from advocates of a modernist theology. Their main argument was that not one single Scripture passage suggests the bodily assumption of Mary into heaven. There is no reliable information about the circumstances of the death of the Mother of God, not even from the early period of Christianity.

For three centuries, the Fathers of the Church remained silent about the end of her life. As late as the fourth century, Bishop Epiphanius of Salamis (315–403) noted in 377 in his *Panarion* that those who "search through the scriptures" will "neither find Mary's death, nor whether or not she died, nor whether or not she was buried". Resigned to this lack of evidence, he concludes his discussion: "God is not incapable of doing whatever he wills. No one knows her end."

Not until the fifth century was there widespread diffusion of several versions of a Christian apocryphal work describing the miraculous "falling asleep" of the Mother of God. Thus in the year 489, Bishop Jacob of Sarug (451–521) presented at a synod in Nisibis on the modern border between Turkey and Syria a poem that he himself had composed about the end of Mary's life, which was obviously based on a Jerusalem tradition. According to this account, Mary's burial took place "on the mountain of the Galileans", as the Mount of Olives was called; Jesus himself led her away, "surrounded by bright clouds". John, "as the true head of the house" in which she had lived with him until then, lay her body "in a grotto, a grave, a stone chamber". Since Jacob of Sarug compares this with the burial of Moses "carried out by God", he seems to be the first to hint at her *Assumptio*, her being taken up into heaven.

At around the same time, people in Jerusalem began to venerate her tomb at the foot of the Mount of Olives. No fourth-century pilgrim, no pilgrimage guide in the early fifth century seems to have known anything about it. A Coptic text that is attributed to the Alexandrian Patriarch Dioscorus (444–451) contains the first mention of the "Church of Holy Mary in Josaphat's Field", the Kidron Valley at the foot of the Mount of Olives. Bishop Juvenal of Jerusalem (425–458) is said to have dispersed a gathering of heretical Monophysites with the help of soldiers and thus caused a bloodbath. Insisting that Christ possessed only a divine nature and no human nature, they had opposed the condemnation of their belief at the Council of Chalcedon in 451. According to John of Damascus (d. 754), Juvenal had been received in an audience at that council by Empress Pulcheria, who asked him for a relic of the Mother of God. Thereupon the bishop told her that according to the tradition in Jerusalem, Mary's body had been buried in Gethsemane in the presence of all the apostles, except that Thomas, who had the longest journey, arrived two days too late. When he asked to see the Mother of God once more, they opened the tomb for him on the third day. But it was empty; only Mary's winding sheets and burial cloths were still there. This, he said, is why there were no relics of Mary's body, no bones. So the empress asked instead for the burial cloth and Mary's last garment, which were later sent to her by Bishop Juvenal.

But the authenticity of both of these stories is disputed; they could also have originated later. Scholars agree only that it is no accident that these accounts bring Bishop Juvenal into the picture, since he is generally considered the builder of the first Marian church in the Kidron Valley. Yet the first records that speak about this shrine are rather unspecific. Thus the North African Archdeacon Theodosius, who in 520 composed a book about the topography of the Holy Land, merely says that "in the Valley of Josaphat . . . the Church of Lady Mary, the Mother of God" stood. Even the pilgrim from Piacenza who in 570 reported rather thoroughly from the Holy Land and apparently left out no halfway plausible legend, knew only that "in this valley is the Church of Holy Mary, which, as they say, was her domicile, in which she was also carried away from the body." The only more precise record was the pilgrimage guide *Breviarius de Hierosolyma*, composed between 510 and 530. At the foot of the Mount of Olives, it states, "is the Church of Holy Mary, and her tomb is there. And that is where Judas betrayed Our Lord Jesus Christ."

This reference to the nearby Grotto of Gethsemane leaves no doubt that this Marian church stood on the spot where the tomb of Mary is revered in Jerusalem to this day.

The visitor gets to it by leaving the Old City of Jerusalem through Stephen's Gate (formerly Mary's Gate, see above, chapter 3) in the direction of the Mount of Olives. Right on the other side of the heavily traveled bypass, two outside staircases lead down to the open plaza in front of an old church from the Crusader era. Its plain Gothic portal and flat roof are in striking contrast to the importance of this shrine. Yet this restrained simplicity befits Mary, her silence and profound peace. Only when you go in do you notice that this church is entirely different from all the others. First a wide staircase with forty-seven steps leads down into the depths. In the tombs on either side, queens of the Crusaders are buried; folklore transformed one of them into the tomb of Joachim and Anne, Mary's parents. The crypt to which these steps lead is partly carved from the rock, partly built of stone; its vaulted ceilings are medieval. It has the form of a Latin cross with the longer beam pointing to the east. The actual tomb of Mary is located in the middle of it; a rock chamber with a burial bench is chiseled into a block and thus isolated from the bedrock. Is this merely a *cenotaph*, a memorial from the Byzantine era, a makeshift solution, so to speak, because no one really knew what had become of Mary after the last time she was mentioned in the Acts of the Apostles? Or was the Mother of God in fact buried here? And finally: What is the value of the apocryphal accounts about the "falling asleep" (*dormitio*) or the "passage" (*transitus*) of Mary? Are they Christian tales, at best pious legends? Or do they perhaps contain a historical kernel of truth? Archaeology was to offer the only way to answer these questions.

I begin my search for clues at the place where the Acts of the Apostles last situated Mary: on Zion. After all, the church and the abbey are dedicated to the memory of Mary's Dormition, her "falling asleep". In the center of her circular crypt, directly beneath the hexagonal dome construction, there is a life-size statue of the dying Mother of God, modeled after Byzantine iconography. Her gaze is directed toward the mosaic in the dome, which depicts Christ, who welcomes his Mother with the words of the Song of Solomon (2:13): "Arise, my love, my fair one, and come away." The tradition that Mary died on this very spot, we recall, goes back to the seventh century. "Torrents of healings / from the rock / where Mary, the Child of God, lay / sprang up for everyone", Patriarch Sophronius of Jerusalem wrote poetically around

630 for the dedication of the new building after the destruction of the old basilica on Zion by the Persians. Around 670, Bishop Arculf noted the exact location of the former House of Mary in his floor plan of the Hagia Sion Church. At about the same time, around 650, Hippolytus of Thebes recorded its ancient tradition: Saint John "took Holy Mary into his house on Zion until her assumption into heaven"; this house had been bought by his older brother, the apostle James, "with the inheritance of his father, Zebedee". It could very well have been one of the small houses that were discovered in 1983 by Father Bargil Pixner and Israeli archaeologists beneath the modern wing of the monastery. I wanted to see them, and so I met with a monk from the abbey. For its most valuable treasure is not open to the public. This may be because it cannot be presented appropriately, since the construction plans were already finalized long before its discovery. So the monk, a dyed-in-the-wool Düsseldorfer named Brother Josef, whom I meet at the monastery door behind the souvenir shop, leads me downstairs to the public restrooms. With a key he opens a side door, and then I am standing in front of the shelves of the abbey's seminary library. In a corner, beneath a heavy iron grill, is their treasure: a tiny *mikveh*. It belonged to a rather miserable house, whose inhabitants must have been as humble as they were devout. One of the earliest versions of the *Transitus Mariae* says that when the day of her death was revealed to her, the Mother of God first took a bath. Was it here, at this place? Suddenly the text, which is so difficult to understand, begins to take concrete form.

There are several versions of the *Transitus*, set in different locations. One presents itself as the report of the apostle John, another is attributed to his disciple Melito of Sardis, and a third to a fictional Pope Evodius (or does it mean Pope Evaristus, ca. 99–108, who is said to have been from Palestine?), while most of them do not indicate the author. In one, Mary lives on Zion; in another, "in her house in Bethlehem"; and in a third version, in her parents' house "near the Mount of Olives". Some of the texts testify that John was with her, while in many he is already in Ephesus and returns miraculously to Jerusalem, followed by the other apostles. They in turn travel to the Holy City either "according to a prompting by the Holy Spirit" or else brought to the Mother of God by angels on clouds. However much the versions may differ from one another, the same basic motifs run through them all.

Mary is consumed by the desire to see her Son again. Finally an angel (who is often identified with Christ) appears to her, brings her a palm branch from Paradise, and announces to her that in three days she will be taken away to heaven. The palm branch is to be carried before her at the burial. Now she summons her friends and relatives to bid them farewell. While the apostles are arriving in a mysterious manner in Jerusalem, Mary takes a bath, puts on new clothes, and lies down on a couch. The beloved disciple John, the first to arrive at her house, asks her for permission to prepare her burial. When all the apostles still living are gathered around her, praying and singing psalms, Jesus appears in radiant light, surrounded by a host of angels, and takes Mary's soul into heaven. Three virgins, companions of the Mother of God, wash and dress her body, and then the disciples carry it to the tomb. They process "to the right side of the city toward the east" to a "new tomb" at the foot of the Mount of Olives. John, the only one of the disciples who is still a "virgin" and consequently the purest, carries the palm branch in the lead. Many people who see the funeral procession and hear the singing of the apostles stop and follow it. This enrages a Jewish priest, who intervenes and even tries to throw the body down, but his hands are stricken with paralysis and remain stuck to the bier. In a panic, he begs the apostles to help him, and their prayer does in fact free him. He kisses the feet of the Mother of God and converts. In the Valley of Josaphat, "in the farthest chamber of a three-level tomb complex", the apostles lay her body on an "elevated bench". Then they close the tomb and sit down in front of it praying, while for three days they hear the heavenly singing of the angels. In some versions, they are witnesses to another apparition of Jesus with a host of angels: he commands one angel to remove the stone in front of the entrance to the tomb and other angels to carry Mary's body into Paradise. In other texts, the apostle Thomas later makes sure that the body has in fact disappeared from the tomb. In any case, the apostles finally return to their mission lands, giving thanks to God.

As was mentioned, records of this legend go back only to the fifth century. Or so everyone thought until 1971, when the great Franciscan archaeologist Father Bellarmino Bagatti published his groundbreaking study *The Church from the Circumcision: History and Archaeology of the Judaeo-Christians*. Until then, Father Bagatti had spent his life studying the belief system of those early Christians who had remained anchored in their Judaism—often influenced by the Essene community—and

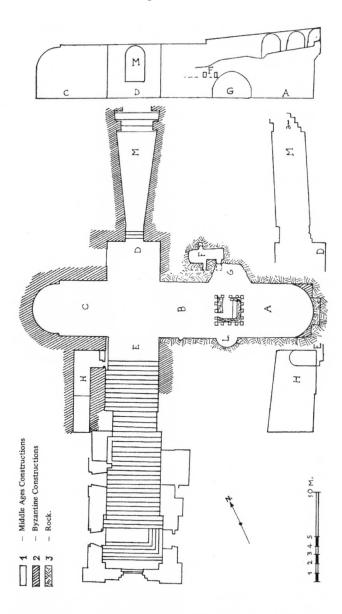

Plan of Mary's tomb. M was the original entrance to the "tripartite" Jewish-Christian tomb complex; E-D, its former rectangular antechamber, from which corridors led to the burial chambers, of which only F and Mary's "new tomb" (A) are preserved.

yet acknowledged Jesus of Nazareth as the Messiah and the Son of God. They could still rely directly on the traditions of the *brethren of the Lord*, who were their first bishops.

When Father Bagatti studied one of the oldest known versions of the *Transitus*, which is preserved in the Vatican Library under the catalogue number Codex 1982, it was as though the scales fell from his eyes. The whole theology on which this text was based was so unorthodox that it simply did not fit any more into the fifth century: it must have been from the time before the Council of Nicaea in the year 325! In it there were images—such as the apparition of Jesus as an angel, the palm branch from Paradise, the "cosmic ladder", the "seven heavens", and the revelation of "heavenly books" and "secrets"—that had been opposed forcefully by the Church Fathers of the fourth century because at that time they were already considered heretical. These were images and symbols of the Jewish Christians. Thus, Bagatti determined, "in light of the theological terminology used by the Jewish-Christians", that the *Transitus* must have originated in the milieu "of this sect, specifically in the second or third century".

When Father Bagatti published his study in 1971, he had no idea that it would be corroborated impressively only one year later. On February 7, 1972, a storm of truly biblical proportions raged over Jerusalem. A cloudburst caused the otherwise dried-up Kidron to swell into a rapid river, creating a waterfall that left Mary's tomb submerged. As the torrents cascaded down the steps, they swept massive amounts of sediment along with them and caused serious devastation. Two Greek priests almost lost their lives in the waves. Finally, the entire church was flooded. When the storm had died down, it was time to repair the damage and renovate thoroughly. After the dirty water had been pumped out of the crypt, lengths of fabric, pictures, and icons had to be taken down and cleaned, plastering removed, and altar stones carried away. Thus, for the first time in centuries, the bare rock of Mary's tomb came to light. Although the shrine was in the custody of the Greeks and Armenians, they allowed the Franciscans to conduct an archaeological investigation. It was discovered that the cruciform church had been built into an already existing grotto complex. This complex consisted of a trapezoidal entrance ramp, which had steps at the beginning and end. At a later point in time, it had been walled up, and now it serves as a sacristy. Once, though, it led to a rectangular antechamber and a complex of tunnels, of which only one side chamber is preserved today. Mary's tomb must have been part of that complex; it had been carved out of the rock by the Byzantines in the form of a block, so as to put it in the center of the crypt and thus to make it possible to venerate it. The architects of Constantine the Great had already done something similar with the empty tomb of Jesus, of which they left standing only a stone block with the two chambers, over which they constructed the massive dome of the Basilica of the Resurrection (today the Church of the Holy Sepulcher). Since the still extant side chamber proved to be a typical Jewish tunnel tomb from the first century, the original complex was easy to date: it went back to the time of Christ! The church had therefore been built into a Jewish tomb complex in the Byzantine period. There were undoubtedly good reasons for doing so.

What impressed Bagatti even more than the unquestionably Jewish origin of the complex, however, were the striking parallels to the descriptions of the *Transitus*. Where it speaks about a "three-level tomb complex", so this Jewish tomb did in fact consist of three parts, namely, entrance, antechamber, and the chambers. Where it said that our Lady's body had been laid in the "farthest chamber", this seemed right, also: the side chamber was much closer to the entrance. It was a "new tomb", for usually a chamber with a burial bench had three shafts proceeding from it in which to store ossuaries, stone urns containing the bones of those who had been buried previously; here that was clearly not the case. The tomb complex was described most precisely, however, in a manuscript of the *Transitus* that the British scholar Agnes Smith Lewis had discovered in the library of Saint Catherine's Monastery on Mount Sinai and published in 1902. In it the angel is quoted as follows:

> Take Lady Mary on that morning and go forth from Jerusalem on the road that leads to the end of the valley on this side of the Mount of Olives, where there are caves: a large exterior grotto, another cave inside, and a very small cave farther inside with a raised bench on the eastern side. Go in and lay the Blessed [Virgin] on this bench.

The bench on the eastern side of the burial chamber, which was only three feet wide and six feet eight inches long, had at first been taken for an altar that had been erected later. When the marble tabletop was removed, however, an entirely different picture came to light. For the bench, too, had been chiseled out of the rock and thus was obviously part of the original structure. It was slightly asymmetrical, be-

tween twenty-eight and thirty inches wide and between seventy-two
and eighty inches long and thus large enough to serve as a burial bench
on which to lay out a dead woman. Today it is possible to observe its
surface through a pane of glass. It is quite pockmarked, since generations of pilgrims scratched and scraped and chiseled at it in order to
get stone "relics". So today it cannot be said with certainty whether
it was once smooth or was a so-called "trough tomb" with a hollow
to receive the corpse. According to one version of the *Transitus*, the
apostles found it covered with roses when the body of the Mother of
God had disappeared.

In any case, the exact description of this tomb in some versions
of the legend about the Dormition is evidence that it has at least a
kernel of truth and is based on authentic traditions. But how can we
explain the fact that no attention was paid to it or to the tomb itself
until the early fifth century? Perhaps the answer lies in the old rivalry
between Jewish Christians and Gentile Christians. After all, even the
center of the original Christian community, the "church of the apostles", fell victim to a similar "conspiracy of silence". Like several early
legends, for instance, the story about the discovery of the Cross of
Christ by the Roman Empress Helena, they all have the same motif: the "Jews" of Jerusalem, which probably means the Jewish Christians, jealously guarded the holy places and relics of the early Church
and often were willing to reveal their location and their hiding places
only under threat of violence and torture. In fact, however, an early
anti-Semitism and the Gentile Christians' fears of coming into contact
with alleged "heretics" must have played a part. So it was logical for
fourth-century pilgrims to ignore Mount Zion also, whereas the ecclesiastical ceremonies on Holy Thursday or Pentecost took place at
the most unsuitable place imaginable, namely, in the Church of the
Holy Sepulcher. Only the Edict of the Roman Emperor Theodosius in
the year 391, which declared orthodox Christianity the state religion
and led to the persecution of heterodox Christians, changed all that.
Now the Jewish Christians were forcibly integrated into the orthodox
community of the Gentile bishop of Jerusalem, and their shrines were
taken over and expanded. This was the case on Zion, and this was the
case with Mary's tomb.

If we believe the usually well-informed Alexandrian Patriarch Eutychius, it was "King Theodosius who built the Church of Gethsemane
in Jerusalem, in which Mary's tomb is located". Unfortunately, it is

unclear whether he meant Theodosius I (379–395) or Theodosius II (408–450); the only certain thing is that the church already existed at the time of the Council of Chalcedon in 431. The Georgian calendar of feasts from the seventh century reveals even more. For August 15, it mentions a "Memorial for the Holy Mother of God" in the "Emperor Mauritius Building in Gethsemane". For October 24, it notes "in Gethsemane Dedication of the Altar at the Tomb of the Mother of God". Emperor Mauritius ruled the Eastern Roman Empire from 582 to 602. During his reign, the church of Mary's tomb was rebuilt and expanded. Probably not until then was the burial chamber isolated, as had been done with the Holy Sepulcher, and set in the middle of a gigantic crypt. At least that would explain the late date at which Mary's tomb began to be mentioned in the accounts of pilgrims. Whereas the upper church of Theodosius was destroyed in the attack of the Persians in 612, the crypt has been preserved to this day.

With the incorporation of the Jewish Christian community and the "discovery" of Mary's tomb, the account of the *Transitus* apparently came to the attention of the Gentile Christians, too. Evidence of this are widely differing versions of an originally oral tradition—just as in the case of the *Proto-Gospel*—and the variety of attempts to reconstruct the event that had long since been embellished with legends. The only thing everyone agreed on was its antiquity. Thus one version attributed the odd, heterodox elements to a certain Leucius, who was commonly considered to be the author of heretically tinged stories about the apostles from the second century, and cited Bishop Melito of Sardis, a disciple of the apostle John, as the guarantor of the veracity of its own tradition. In fact, Professor F. Manns of the Franciscan Academy for Biblical Studies in Jerusalem testified that at least the version recorded in the *Codex 1982* shows a striking resemblance to the Johannine school of theology in the first and second centuries. Moreover, one passage at the beginning of the *Acts of John*, which is now quite generally dated to the second century, seems to hint at Mary's Dormition. This fabulous text, which is attributed to Deacon Prochorus (who is mentioned in Acts 6:5), begins with a gathering of the apostles in Gethsemane. At it the Twelve decide to go out to all the world and proclaim the gospel, as the Lord had commended them. For now, says Peter, the hour has come to do this, "especially because the Mother of us all has departed from this life". With that the author seems to date the Dormition of the Mother of God to A.D. 42. Moreover, this is consistent with a ver-

sion of the *Transitus* that at least the Viennese Church historian Hans
Förster considers to be the oldest. The Coptic parchment preserved
in Vienna with the catalogue number P. Vindob. K 7.589 dates from
the ninth century, but it is probably a copy of a much older text, perhaps even the fragment of a "primitive Marian Apocalypse" from the
second century, as Förster at least thinks. Evidence for this hypothesis
are the simplicity of the text, its elementary theology, but above all
the consistent references to Mary as "Virgin" (*parthenos*) instead of
as "Mother of God" (*theotokos*), which became customary from the
fourth century on and after the Council of Ephesus would have been
absolutely imperative. The text is made even more convincing by the
historically accurate dating of the milestones in Mary's life:

> The Virgin bore Emmanuel, the living God. And when she had given
> birth to him, she was approximately thirteen years old. He lived for
> thirty-three years, namely, Jesus, the Christ, before his crucifixion.
> When they crucified the Lord Jesus, the Virgin was in her forty-
> eighth year.

Since, according to our dating, Mary was born in September 8, 19 B.C.,
in March of 5 B.C., at the birth of Christ she was in fact thirteen years
old, and at his crucifixion in April of A.D. 30 (when Jesus had just
turned thirty-four), she was in her forty-eighth year. It goes on to say:

> And she lived for eleven and a half years after the Resurrection of
> Our Lord Jesus Christ. Altogether, therefore, this makes sixty years
> [approximately—*Author's note*]. Furthermore: After the Ascension of
> our Redeemer, the Virgin Mary went with the apostles to proclaim
> the gospel. Afterward, the Holy Spirit led her on the way back up
> to Jerusalem. For the time had come for the Virgin to die. . . . This
> occurred, however, on the evening of the twentieth day of the month
> of Tybi, as the sun was setting.

That would have been January 16, A.D. 42, according to the Julian calendar (Gregorian: January 29), the day on which the Coptic Church
today still commemorates Mary's Dormition, whereas it celebrates her
Assumption into heaven 206 days later, on August 22.[3] Although the

---

[3] Records of the Feast of the Assumption of the Blessed Virgin Mary into Heaven
(August 15) go back only to the fifth century; before the construction of the Church
of St. Josaphat, it was celebrated in the Kathisma Basilica on the way to Bethlehem,
which obviously was a makeshift solution. In the sixth century, Emperor Mauritius in-

text indicates that the Mother of God went on a missionary journey "with the apostles", which surely means "with John" (to Ephesus then?), this dating rules out the Ephesian tradition. According to it, Mary had died before the execution of James the son of Zebedee, just as the *Acts of John* maintain. Indeed, the *Transitus* sermon of the alleged Pope "Evodius" (Evaristus?) maintains that Mary had already fallen asleep by the time the apostles went out into the world to proclaim God's word. We are dealing therefore with two traditions: one, for which there is a series of testimonies, maintains that Mary died in A.D. 42 at the age of almost sixty, whereas the other has her falling asleep at a later point in time, in any case, after the beginning of the mission to the world. In the latter version, which is represented too frequently to be ignored, the apostles return first from their distant journeys, and then Mary bids them farewell. The chronological indications prove, however, to be sheer speculation—sometimes sixteen years after the apostles' first missionary activity (as in one Syriac text), and other times at the age of seventy-two (thus a Latin translation of the *Transitus* according to John), not until twenty-two years after the Resurrection of Jesus (thus in Pseudo-Melito), or even at the hale age of eighty (thus in the *Life of Mary* by Maximus the Confessor), and so on. If there is a kernel of truth to this tradition, then it can refer only to the year 48, the time immediately before the council of the apostles.[4] In that case, the historical basis of the legend could be reconstructed as follows:

Apparently, when the apostles set out on their missionary journeys in the year 42, they decided to meet again in Jerusalem "in the seventh year". That was no accident, for the year 47/48 was a so-called Sabbatical Year. In the Torah, it was prescribed (Ex 23:10–11; Lev 25:1–7) that the Jews should let the land lie fallow, cancel debts, and free slaves, for this year belonged to the Lord, like the seventh day of the week. It is not surprising, then, that in that year the apostles returned home again in order to offer up their prayers in the Temple. John would have brought Mary along. The Mother of God was at

---

troduced this feast as obligatory for the entire Eastern Roman Empire and, thus, for Egypt, also. This probably explains the absurdly long interval between the Dormition and the "Assumption".

[4] Additional evidence that 48 was the year of Mary's death is the reticence of the Gospel of Mark about her; according to the most recent estimates, it was composed as early as the year 44–45; certainly Mary decisively forbade any personality cult during her lifetime.

that time sixty-five years old, an old woman according to the standards of the time. It is conceivable that the long journey from Ephesus to Jerusalem wore her down, but it is more likely that she was consumed by the longing to be with her Son. In any case, she and the beloved disciple arrived in the Holy City shortly before the others. The only plausible place for her death is the settlement of the original Christian community next to the Essene quarter, Mount Zion. There is no reason why she could not have been buried in a tomb at the Mount of Olives, where in fact some of the oldest Jewish-Christian tombs were found, for instance at the Church of *Dominus Flevit*. Probably the same family that allowed Jesus and his disciples to rest in the grotto of Gethsemane on the night of his arrest later placed the tract of land at the disposal of the original Christian community. Quite possibly it was the family of the evangelist Mark; he is the only one to mention a youth who fled naked when Jesus was arrested, which some exegetes consider to be an autobiographical interpolation. In any case, a tomb complex had developed at this very spot, in which the apostles buried Mary. Then her body must have disappeared under mysterious circumstances from the face of the earth. Nothing would have been revered more fervently than her holy body. As it happened, Christians over the next two millennia were acquainted with all possible and impossible relics, just not of Mary's bones. In churches throughout the world there are countless stones from the Holy House and the tomb of the Mother of God, scraps of material from her mantle and her cincture, her tunic and outer garment, her veil and burial cloth, indeed, bushels of her hair—but not the tiniest bone allegedly from the Mother of God. Such relics, which would have been the pride of any church and would have drawn countless pilgrims, did not exist, and no one even took the trouble to counterfeit them, for they could not exist. In every age Christians knew or sensed that.

The exact circumstances of her death and her Assumption,[5] on the other hand, remain a mystery forever. It is not possible for us to prove it by the methods of historiography or archaeology. The aforementioned Bishop Epiphanius of Salamis seems to have had similar difficulty; he, too, was not sure what he should make of the literally incomprehensible reports. Thus he maintains that the reason why Sacred Scripture

---

[5] Strictly speaking, the colloquial German word for "Assumption", *Himmelfahrt* [trip to heaven], is incorrect; only Jesus could travel to heaven by his own power!

is silent on the subject is "because of the overwhelming wonder [of what happened when Mary went home to the Father], not to throw men's minds into consternation. For I dare not say—though I have my suspicions, I keep silent." Later on, he again refrains from making a definite statement: "I cannot decide for certain, and am not saying that she remained immortal. But neither am I affirming that she died."

Mary's Assumption into heaven in the oldest depiction: sarcophagus from Saragossa, Spain, Santa Engracia, *4th c.*

We can be sure, at any rate, that the legend of the *Transitus*, for all its fantastic embellishments, has a kernel of truth. A plethora of images was used, after all, in attempts to grasp a deeper truth that is indescribable. A sarcophagus in the Church of Santa Engracia in Saragossa, where our Lady is said to have been depicted for the first time on a pillar, perhaps comes closest to the truth. It comes from the fourth century and shows how God's hand grasps Mary's arm so as to draw her from the midst of the apostles to himself in heaven. When I see this image, I have to think of the wise words of the Ukrainian Greek Catholic exarch in Germany, Bishop Petro Kryk:[6] With her love, Mary brought God into the world, because she herself had received the Love of God previously. In this Love she remained until her death, and that is also why her death is called a "dormition", a "falling asleep": because love cannot die. Christ, who is love, must draw up to himself everyone who lives entirely in love.

---

[6] At the Twelfth Theological Summer Academy of the Initiative of Laymen and Priests in the Diocese of Augsburg, 2004, in Diessen.

Mary was too pure, too holy, too completely transformed into love itself, to suffer the fate of mortals and sinners. She simply had to become the *Assumpta* and hastened onward before us all!

For Mary's Assumption into heaven, body and soul, is also a promise of her Son to us. He took her to himself, as someday he will take us to himself. Until then, however, she is our patroness, our intercessor in this dark valley of tears, our hope, and our light.

~

EPILOGUE

We Fly to Your Protection . . .

There is a widespread misconception that Marian devotion started
with the Council of Ephesus in 431, when Mary was defined as the
Theotokos, the "Mother of God", an article of faith that is binding for
all believers. Generally dogmas are not innovations of creative theologians or popes but, rather, the magisterial endorsement of truths of
the faith that are hundreds of years old. As we have seen, the last two
Marian dogmas also go back to theological considerations and traditions of the first centuries.

In fact, Marian devotion is as old as the Church. Thus Joseph
Ratzinger, too, in his book on Mary, *Daughter Zion*, recalls "that the
gospel itself prophesies and requires veneration for Mary: 'Behold,
from henceforth all generations will call me blessed' (Lk 1:48)—this
is a commission to the Church. In recording it, Luke presupposes that
there was already praise of Mary in the Church of his time and that he
considers it a commission of the Church for all generations."[1] Furthermore, Elizabeth is depicted by Luke as the first to honor Mary, when
in Ein Karem—filled with the Holy Spirit, as the evangelist expressly
notes!—she exclaimed: "Blessed are you among women" and called
her virginal niece "the mother of my Lord" (Lk 1:42–43). If we know
that for a believing Jew there was only one Lord, namely, God, then
the first Marian title, "God-bearer" or "Mother of God" actually has
its origin here. In another passage, too, Luke alludes to an early form of
devotion to Mary, when he quotes "a woman in the crowd" as saying:
"Blessed is the womb that bore you, and the breasts that you sucked."
Jesus did not react unfavorably to her words but, rather, contrasted
the everyday biological fact with what really made Mary unique: her

[1] Joseph Cardinal Ratzinger, *Daughter Zion: Meditations on the Church's Marian Belief*,
trans. John M. McDermott, S.J. (San Francisco: Ignatius Press, 1983), 74–75.

obedience, her unconditional willingness to say *Fiat*: "Blessed rather
are those who hear the word of God and keep it!" (Lk 11:27–28).

Another New Testament writer who can be included among the
early devotees of Mary is Paul, who perhaps even witnessed the Dormition of the Mother of God when he participated in the council of
the apostles in the year 48. Soon afterward, probably in the following
year, he composed the Letter to the Galatians, which is considered
by theologians to be the oldest written Christian testimony. In it he
assigned to her a decisive place in his short summary of salvation history: "When the time had fully come, God sent forth his Son, born
of woman, born under the law" (Gal 4:4).

In the last book of the New Testament, John's Revelation, Mary
undergoes her apotheosis. Now she is no longer only the maiden from
Nazareth and Mother of the Lord but is the embodiment of the true
Israel, in which the people of God of the Old and the New Covenant
(that is, Israel and the Church) are one. As such she becomes the apocalyptic "sign in heaven": "A woman clothed with the sun, with the
moon under her feet, and on her head a crown of twelve stars; she was
with child and she cried out in her pangs of birth" (Rev 12:1–2). So
she confronted the dragon that threatened to devour her Child. "Then
the dragon was angry with the woman, and went off to make war on
the rest of her offspring, on those who keep the commandments of
God and bear testimony to Jesus" (12:17).

John, who wrote down his visions around the year 95 on the Island
of Patmos, refers in them directly to the Book of the Prophet Daniel,
whose images he adopts. After all, Jerusalem had been destroyed by
Titus twenty-five years before that, when in fact "the saints" had been
"given into [the] hand" of an eleventh king for three and a half years,
as Daniel says. But at that time no court sat in judgment, nor was "his
dominion . . . taken away, to be consumed and destroyed to the end",
as chapter 7 of the prophetic book went on to promise. The *parousia*,
the Second Coming of the Lord that Christians so yearningly awaited,
was delayed. Had Daniel then been wrong? Was "the kingdom and the
dominion and the greatness of the kingdoms under the whole heaven"
not given "to the people of the saints of the Most High" after all? John
succeeded in interpreting the prophet's images correctly. Still ringing
in his ears were Jesus' words: "My kingship is not of this world" (Jn
18:36). Even though the old Israel was prostrate and Herod's Temple
destroyed, the New Israel, the Church, despite all her afflictions, ap-

peared as radiant and unconquered as the Woman in his vision. The end of Jerusalem had only emancipated her from her parental home and accelerated her globalization. The gospel was already being proclaimed from Spain to India, from Germany to Ethiopia, in other words, in all three continents of the world as it was known then. No bloody persecution, no raging of an emperor, however diabolical he might be, could stop that. What the prophet had foretold for the New Israel, the Church, would ultimately come true: "Their kingdom shall be an everlasting kingdom, and all dominions shall serve and obey them" (Dan 7:27). With the Revelation of John, the beloved disciple of Jesus and the foster son of the Mother of God, Mariology definitively became ecclesiology, doctrine about the nature of the Church. From now on the faithful, especially in times of persecution, placed themselves under the protective mantel of the Mother of God, who was their Mother, too.

Anyone who wants to get an idea of how deeply rooted Marian devotion was among the first Christians just has to travel to Rome. There, in the northern part of the Eternal City, right on the Via Salaria, he will find one of the oldest catacombs. It bears the name of its foundress, Priscilla, who is described in a tomb inscription as the wife of Manlius Acilius Verus and *clarissima femina* ("most illustrious lady"), an honorific title that in ancient Rome singled out only the members of senatorial families for distinction. In Suetonius, a Roman chronicler, we read that during the rule of Emperor Domitian, her husband's family was accused of "trying to introduce novelties", whereby in all likelihood Christianity was meant. Around the middle of the second century, this same Priscilla donated a property belonging to her family on the Via Salaria to the Roman Church, which established a *coemeterium* there, an underground burial place, that same catacomb. It was used until well into the sixth century; in it seven popes and numerous martyrs from the years of the Christian persecutions found their final resting place.

But what makes the Catacomb of Priscilla even more interesting are its frescos, which are among the oldest examples of Christian art. One of the most beautiful shows Mary with the Child Jesus on her lap; it comes from the early years of the third century. In front of her stands Balaam, the seer and oracular priest from the time of the Exodus, who is pointing with his right hand to a star. It is the star of the Messiah, which he foretold, the Star of Bethlehem, the supernova from the year 5 B.C. Mary is sitting on a chair and is wearing a *stola* with short sleeves and a *palla*, which covers her head; her head is inclined toward her Child with maternal tenderness. It is a familiar picture, which since then has been copied tens of thousands of times by artists; indeed, it is an archetype of Christendom. Yet it is not the oldest depiction of Mary in this catacomb. A few chambers farther on the visitor finds what may be the most beautiful room in the complex, the Cappella Greca, which owes its name to two Greek inscriptions. It is decorated profusely with biblical motifs that are significant in salvation history, among them, depictions of the sacrifice of Abraham, of the prophets Moses and Daniel, but also of Christ at the Eucharistic banquet. But the central motif, painted on the middle arch of the vault, is the most familiar scene. It again shows Mary with the Child Jesus on her arm, but now being adored by the three magi, who can be recognized by their Phrygian caps. Even though its colors are somewhat faded today and the details can no longer be made out, it nevertheless has the greatest possible significance. For there is no doubt that the fresco dates back to the second half of the second century and is therefore the oldest unequivocally dated depiction of Mary in the world. The fact that today, around 1,830 years later, almost everyone recognizes the motif at first glance tells us a lot about the continuity of Christian art. Yet the early Christians depicted Mary in the catacombs not only in her role as Mother but even more often at prayer, in the *orans* posture that was conventional then, with her hands raised up to heaven, as she appears on the *Advocata* icon. Even then, therefore, the faithful knew about the power of her intercession. So it is hardly surprising that the walls with graffiti near the tomb of Saint Peter, over which Constantine the Great constructed the predecessor of today's Saint Peter's Basilica in the year 324, bear invocations to the Mother of God, which were scratched there by third-century Christians. At that time she was already invoked and honored together with Christ in the same breath with the Greek exclamation *nica* (actually *nika*) or the Latin *vince*; both mean "conquer".

Altogether different evidence of early Christian Marian devotion was discovered in 1917 in Egypt. It is a short prayer in Greek, written on papyrus, which was placed in a tomb with a dead person. As Papyrus 470, it was included in a famous collection, the John Rylands Library in Manchester, England, and in 1938 it was published for the first time. Papyrologists date it to the first half of the third century, which is a minor sensation. For the prayer is still in use today as an antiphon both in the Greek Orthodox and in the Roman Catholic Church; in the latter case, it is known by the first few words of it in Latin, *Sub tuum praesidium*. In modern prayer books, we find it with the following wording:

> We fly to your protection, O holy Mother of God; despise not our petitions in our necessities, but ever deliver us from all dangers, O glorious and blessed Virgin.

Here is a translation of the original text on the papyrus:

> We fly to thy mercy, O Mother of God.
> Reject not our pleading in our need,
> but save us in danger,
> O thou who alone art pure and blessed.

Previously scholars had thought that the title "God-bearer", which was declared a dogma at the Council of Ephesus, originated with the Cappadocian Fathers in the fourth century or at the Synod of Antioch in 324–325. And so overzealous theologians quickly tried to assign another date to the papyrus; it could only come from the second half of the fourth century, they said, or from an even later period. But the papyrologists would have nothing of it; their dating is unequivocal. So today it is generally believed that the prayer originated during the persecution of Christians under Septimus Severus (after 202) or under Decius (250). But it may also be even older.

This oldest of all Marian prayers is at the same time one of the most beautiful. It testifies to the profound trust that Christians of all times placed in the intercession of the Mother of God. This was the faith that carried them through times of need and persecution, and in this faith they were confirmed again and again by so many prayers that were answered. Mary never left them alone. She has always been our Mother, and she will be so eternally.

∼

Chronology

17:		Augustus calls for celebrations of the start of the tenth *saeculum* [age]
16:	Nov:	Mary is presented to the Temple
9:		Augustus dedicates the peace altar
7:	Sept:	Mary's service in the Temple ends
	Nov:	Announcement of John the Baptist
6:	April:	Mary is betrothed to Joseph
	May:	The Annunciation to Mary
	Sept:	Birth of John the Baptist
5:	March:	The Birth of Christ
	May:	Visit of the magi, massacre of the children in Bethlehem
	June:	Flight into Egypt
4:	March:	Herod's death
	May:	Archelaus becomes Ethnarch of Judea, return of the Holy Family

A.D.

6:		Judea becomes a Roman province
8:		Jesus' first pilgrimage to the Temple
28:		Wedding feast of Cana; Mary follows Jesus to Capernaum
30:	April:	Death and Resurrection of Jesus; Mary beneath the Cross and with the apostles in the Cenacle
	May:	Ascension, Pentecost; Mary lives with John on Zion
42:	Jan:	Dormition of the Mother of God?
	April:	Execution of James, the son of Zebedee, flight of Peter, beginning of the apostles' mission to the world; John goes (with Mary?) to Ephesus
48:		Council of the apostles in Jerusalem. Dormition of the Mother of God?

62:     Stoning of James the "brother of the Lord"

66:     Outbreak of the Jewish Revolt

70:     Destruction of the Temple by Titus

73:     Return of the original Christian community to Jeru-
        salem

95:     John on Patmos has visions of the Secret Revelation
        (Apocalypse)

Bibliography

The Holy Bible, Revised Standard Version, Second Catholic Edition. San Francisco: Ignatius Press, 2006.

Albani, Matthias. *Jesus von Nazareth, zu Bethlehem geboren*. Freiburg, 2003.

Alfieri, Nereo, with Edmondo Forlani and Floriano Grimaldi. *Contributi Archeologici per la Storia della Santa Casa di Loreto*. Loreto, 1967.

"Antonini Placentini". *Itinerarium*. Translated into German by J. Gildemeister. Berlin, 1889.

Badde, Paul. *Heiliges Land*. Gütersloh, 2008.

———. *Maria of Guadalupe: Shaper of History, Shaper of Hearts*. San Francisco: Ignatius Press, 2008.

Bagatti, Father Bellarmino, O.F.M. *The Church from the Circumcision: History and Archaeology of the Judaeo-Christians*. Jerusalem: Franciscan Printing Press, 1984.

———. *Excavations in Nazareth*. Jerusalem: Franciscan Printing Press, 1969.

———, with Michele Piccirillo and A. Prodomo. *New Discoveries at the Tomb of the Virgin Mary in Gethsemane*. Jerusalem: Franciscan Printing Press, 1975.

Bar-Am, Aviva. *Beyond the Walls: Churches of Jerusalem*. Jerusalem, 1998.

Baroni, Cesare. *Gli Annali Ecclesiastici*. Venice, 1593.

Bastero, Juan Luis. *Mary, Mother of the Redeemer: A Mariology Textbook*. Dublin: Four Courts Press, 2006.

Bauckham, Richard. *Jude and the Relatives of Jesus in the Early Church*. London: T&T Clark International, 1990.

Becker-Huberti, Manfred. *Die Heiligen Drei Könige.* Cologne, 2005.

Beckett, Wendy. *Encounters with God: In Quest of the Ancient Icons of Mary.* London: Continuum, 2009.

Ben-Chorin, Schalom. *Mutter Mirjam.* Munich, 1982.

Benedict XVI (Joseph Ratzinger). *Jesus of Nazareth: The Infancy Narratives.* Translated by Philip J. Whitmore. New York: Image, 2012.

———. *Maria: Benedikt XVI. Über die Gottesmutter.* Augsburg, 2009.

———. *Maria voll der Gnade.* Freiburg, 2008.

Berger, Klaus. *Die Urchristen.* Munich, 2008.

———, with Christiane Nord. *Das Neue Testament und frühchristliche Schriften.* Frankfurt, 2005.

Betz, Otto, with Rainer Riesner. *Verschwörung um Qumran?* Rastatt, 1999.

Blasone, Pino. *Our Lady, the "Pensive One": Marian Icons in Rome and Italy.* Internet (www.scribd.com), 2008.

Bongenberg, Salesia. *Allheilige Jungfrau—Gottesgebärerin: Die Urikone Marias in apostolischer Zeit.* Fulda, 1997.

Böttrich, Christfried, with Beate Ego and Friedmann Eißler. *Jesus und Maria.* Göttingen, 2009.

Brandmüller, Walter, ed. *Light and Shadows: Church History amid Faith, Fact and Legend.* Translated by Michael J. Miller. San Francisco: Ignatius Press, 2009.

———. *Qumran und die Evangelien.* Aachen, 1994.

Brown, Raymond. *The Virginal Conception and Bodily Resurrection of Jesus.* New York: Paulist Press, 1972.

———, with Paul J. Achtemeier, United States Lutheran-Roman Catholic Dialogue. *Mary in the New Testament.* New York: Fortress Press, 1978.

Bruce, Frederick F. *New Testament History.* Garden City, N.Y.: Doubleday, 1969.

Buchowiecki, Walther. *Handbuch der Kirchen Roms*, vols. 1–4. Vienna, 1967.

Büyükkolanci, Mustafa. *The Life and Monument of Saint John*. Selçuk: Efes Müzesi, 2001.

Cantalamessa, Raniero. *Mary, Mirror of the Church*. Translated by Frances Lonergan Villa. Collegeville, Minn.: Liturgical Press, 1992.

Carletti, Sandro. *Führer durch die Priscilla-Katakombe*. Vatican City, 1980.

Carmel, Alex, with Ejal Jakob Eisler. *Der Kaiser reist ins Heilige Land*. Stuttgart, 1999.

Carroll, Donald. *Mary's House*. London: Ave Maria Press, 2000.

Ceming, Katharina, with Jürgen Werlitz. *Die verbotenen Evangelien*. Wiesbaden, 2004.

Charlesworth, James H., ed. *Jesus and Archaeology*. Grand Rapids, Mich.: William B. Eerdmans, 2006.

———. *Jesus and the Dead Sea Scrolls*. New York: Bantam, 1992.

Climak, Fatih. *Reise zu den Sieben Gemeinden*. Istanbul, 1999.

Clark, Peter. *Zoroastrianism*. Eastbourne: Sussex Academic Press, 1998.

Claußen, Carsten with Jörg Frey, eds. *Jesus und die Archäologie Galiläas*. Neukirchen-Vlyun, 2008.

Comastri, Angelo. *L'angelo mi disse*. Cinisello Balsamo, 2007.

Congregation for the Doctrine of the Faith, ed. *The Message of Fatima*. Vatican City, 2000.

Connolly, Peter. *Living in the Time of Jesus of Nazareth*. Oxford: Oxford University Press, 1983.

Crossan, John Dominic, with Jonathan Reed. *Excavating Jesus*. San Francisco: HarperCollins, 2001.

Cruz, Joan Carroll. *Miraculous Images of Our Lady*. Rockford, Ill.: TAN Books, 1993.

Cunneen, Sally. *In Search of Mary: The Woman and the Symbol*. New York: Random House, 1996.

Demetrius, Bishop. *The Visit of the Holy Family to Mallawi.* Mallawi, 2001.

D'Occhieppo, K. Ferrari. *Der Stern von Bethlehem.* Gießen, 1994.

Edersheim, Alfred. *Der Tempel.* Wuppertal, 1997.

Egeria. *Itinerarium.* Translated into German by Georg Röwekamp. Freiburg, 1995.

Egyptian Ministry of Tourism. *The Holy Family in Egypt.* Cairo, 1999.

Ehrmann, Bart D. *Lost Scriptures: Books That Did Not Make It into the New Testament.* Oxford: Oxford University Press, 2003.

Eisenman, Robert H. *James, the Brother of Jesus.* New York: Viking, 1997.

Emmerich, Anne Catherine. *Leben der heil. Jungfrau Maria.* Munich, 1852.

———. *The Life of the Blessed Virgin Mary.* Springfield, Ill.: Templegate, 1954.

Eusebius of Caesarea. *Ecclesiastical History.* Translated by Roy J. Deferrari. 2 vols. New York: Fathers of the Church, 1953, 1956.

Finegan, Jack. *The Archaeology of the New Testament.* Princeton: Princeton University Press, 1992.

Flusser, David. *Das essenische Abenteuer.* Winterthur, 1994.

Förster, Hans. *Transitus Mariae.* Berlin, 2006.

———. *Weihnachten—eine Spurensuche.* Berlin, 2003.

Freeman-Grenville, G. S. P. *The Basilica of the Annunciation at Nazareth.* Jerusalem, 1994.

———. *The Basilica of the Nativity in Bethlehem.* Jerusalem, 1993.

———. *The Land of Jesus Then and Now.* Jerusalem, 1998.

———, with Rupert L. Chapman and Joan E. Taylor. *The Onomasticon by Eusebius of Caesarea.* Jerusalem: Carta, 2003.

Fürst, Heinrich. *Im Land des Herrn: Pilgerführer für das Heilige Land.* Paderborn, 2009.

Gabra, Gawdat, ed. *Be Thou There: The Holy Family's Journey in Egypt.* Cairo and New York, 2001.

Geoffrey-Schneiter, Berenice. *Fayum Portraits.* New York, 2004.

Gibson, Shimon. *The Cave of John the Baptist.* New York: Random House, 2005.

Gilbert, Adrian G. *Magi.* London: Bloomsbury, 1996.

Gilbert, J. P. *Das Leben Mariä, der jungfräulichen Mutter Gottes.* Leipzig, 1843.

Goodman, Martin. *Rome and Jerusalem: The Clash of Ancient Civilizations.* New York: Penguin Books, 2007.

Graff, Michael, with Heinz-Jürgen Förg and Hermann Scharnagl. *Maria: Erscheinungen, Wunder und Visionen.* Augsburg, 1999.

Grimaldi, Floriano. *La Basilica della Santa Casa di Loreto.* Ancona, 1986.

Guarducci, Margherita. *La più antica icone di Maria.* Rome, 1989.

Guastella, Salvatore. *La prodigiosa Madonna di San Luca.* Rome, 2008.

Guitton, Jean. *The Virgin Mary.* New York: P. J. Kenedy & Sons, 1952.

Haffner, Paul. *The Mystery of Mary.* Leominster: Gracewing; Chicago: Hillenbrand Books, 2004.

Hartmann, Stefan. *Die Magd des Herrn.* Regensburg, 2009.

Heiser, Lothar. *Maria in der Christusverkündigung des orthodoxen Kirchenjahres.* Trier, 1981.

Herodotus. *The Histories.* New York: Barnes & Noble Classics, 2004.

Hesemann, Michael. *Das Bluttuch Christi.* Munich, 2010.

———. *Die Dunkelmänner.* Augsburg, 2007.

———. *Der erste Papst.* Munich, 2003.

———. *The Fatima Secret.* New York: Dell, 2000.

———. *Der Jesus-Tafel.* Freiburg, 1998.

———. *Jesus von Nazareth.* Augsburg, 2009.

———. *Der Papst, der Hitler trotzte.* Augsburg, 2008.

————. *Paulus von Tarsus*. Augsburg, 2008.

————. *Stigmata: Sie trugen die Wundmale Christi*. Güllesheim, 2006.

————. *Die stummen Zeugen von Golgotha*. Munich, 2000.

Hirschfeld, Yizhar. *The Judean Desert Monasteries in the Byzantine Period*. New Haven: Yale University Press, 1992.

Houlden, Leslie, ed. *Decoding Early Christianity*. Oxford: Oxford University Press, 2007.

Iacobone, Pasquale. *Maria a Roma*. Todi, 2009.

Janssens, Laurentius, O.S.B. *Das Heiligtum Mariä Heimgang auf dem Berge Zion*. Prague, 1910.

John Paul II. Encyclical *Redemptoris Mater*. Boston: Pauline Books & Media, 1987.

Josephus, Flavius. *Jewish Antiquities*. Cambridge, Mass.: Harvard University Press, 1965.

————. *The Jewish War*. Translated by H. St. J. Thackeray. Cambridge, Mass.: Harvard University Press, 1997.

Jung-Inglessis, Eva-Maria. *Maria: Ihr Bild in Rom von den Katakomben bis heute*. Sankt Ottilien, 1999.

————. *Römische Madonnen*. Sankt Ottilien, 1989.

Kauffmann, Joel. *The Nazareth Jesus Knew*. Nazareth, 2005.

Khalil, Marcos Aziz. *The Principal Ancient Coptic Churches of Old Cairo*. Cairo, 1985.

Kidger, Mark. *The Star of Bethlehem*. Princeton, N.J.: Princeton University Press, 1999.

Kienast, Dietmar. *Augustus, Prinzeps und Monarch*. Darmstadt, 2009.

Kimball, Glenn. *Hidden Stories of the Childhood of Jesus*. Houston, Tex.: BF Publications, 1999.

Klauck, Hans-Josef. *Apokryphe Apostelakten*. Stuttgart, 2005.

Kluckert, Ehrenfried. *Die Heiligen Drei Könige und ihr Weg nach Köln*. Augsburg, 2010.

Kopp, Clemens. *Die heiligen Stätten der Evangelien*. Regensburg, 1959.

———. *Das Mariengrab*. Paderborn, 1955.

Kresser, Gebhard. *Nazareth, ein Zeuge für Loreto*. Graz, 1908.

Kriwaczek, Paul. *In Search of Zarathustra*. New York: Vintage, 2003.

Kroll, Gerhard. *Auf den Spuren Jesu*. Leipzig, 1988.

Küchler, Max. *Jerusalem*. Göttingen, 2007.

Kummer, Regina. *Siehe, deine Mutter*. Augsburg, 2006.

Lambelet, Edouard. *The Escape to Egypt according to Coptic Tradition*. Cairo, 1993.

Landau, Brent. *Revelation of the Magi*. New York: HarperCollins, 2010.

Levi, Emanuele. *Da San Sisto sull'Appia al SS. Rosario a Monte Mario*. Rome [undated].

Lietzmann, Hans. *Geschichte der Alten Kirche*. Berlin, 1999.

Loffreda, Stanislao. *Holy Land Pottery at the Time of Jesus*. Jerusalem, 2003.

Lohfink, Gerhard, with Ludwig Weimer. *Maria: nicht ohne Israel*. Freiburg, 2008.

Lucentini, Mauro et al. *The Rome Guide*. Northampton, Mass.: Interlink Books, 2012.

Ludwig, Gumpert, O.F.M. *Die Basilika in Nazaret*. Munich [undated].

Makarian, Christian. *Maria aus Nazareth*. Hildesheim, 1997.

Malaty, Tadros Y. *Die Gottesmutter bei den Vätern und in der Koptischen Kirche*. Regensburg, 1989.

Mancini, Ignazio. *Archaeological Discoveries Relative to the Judeo-Christians*. Jerusalem, 1984.

Mandeville, John. *Mandeville's Travels*. Oxford: Oxford University Press, 1960.

Manetti, Diego, with Stefano Zuffi, eds. *Vita di Maria*. Milan, 2010.

Mathewes-Green, Frederica. *The Lost Gospel of Mary*. Brewster, Mass.: Paraclete Press, 2007.

Mazar, Eilat. *The Complete Guide to the Temple Mount Excavations*. Jerusalem, 2002.

McDonald, Alexander. *The Holy House of Loreto: A Critical Study of Documents and Traditions*. New York: Christian Press Association, 1913.

McNamer, Elizabeth, with Bargil Pixner, O.S.B.: *Jesus and First-Century Christianity in Jerusalem*. Mahwah, N.J.: Paulist Press, 2008.

McRay, John. *Archaeology and the New Testament*. Grand Rapids, Mich.: W. B. Eerdmans, 1991.

Meinardus, Otto F. A. *Coptic Saints and Pilgrimages*. Cairo: American University in Cairo Press, 2002.

——. *Das Heilige Land: Auf den Spuren Marias von Nazaret*. Frankfurt, 1998.

——. *In the Steps of the Holy Family from Bethlehem to Upper Egypt*. Dar Al-Maaref, 1963.

Melzer, Gottfried. *Loreto*. Lauerz, 1998.

Messori, Vittorio. *Ipotesi su Maria*. Milan, 2005.

Mina, Ermia Ava. *The Holy Family in Egypt*. Marriout, 2000.

Monelli, Nanni. *La Santa Casa a Loreto, la Santa Casa a Nazareth*. Loreto, 1997.

——. with Giuseppe Santarelli. *L'Altare degli Apostoli nella Santa Casa di Loreto*. Loreto, 2005.

Müller, Beda, O.S.B. *Maria und die Ôúkumene*. Kisslegg, 2004.

Murphy-O'Connor, Jerome. *The Holy Land*. Oxford: Oxford University Press, 2008.

——. *St. Paul's Ephesus*. Collegeville, Minn.: Liturgical Press, 2008.

Newman, John Henry. *Discourses Addressed to Mixed Congregations*. London: Longman, Brown, Green, and Longmans, 1849.

————. *Maria im Heilsplan* [anthology of his writings on Mary, translated into German]. Freiburg, 1953.

Nicolai, Vincenzo, with Fabrizio Bisconti and Danilo Mazzoleni. *Roms christliche Katakomben*. Regensburg, 1998.

Nicolini, Giorgio. *La Veridicità Storica della Miracolosa Traslazione della Santa Casa di Nazareth a Loreto*. Ancona, 2004.

Niessen, Johannes. *Panagia Kapuli*. Dülmen, 1906.

Nigosian, S. A. *The Zoroastrian Faith*. Montreal: McGill-Queen's University Press, 1993.

N. N. *St. Mark's Church and Monastery in Jerusalem*. Jerusalem [undated].

Perry, Paul. *Jesus in Egypt*. New York: Random House, 2003.

Petrozzi, Maria Teresa. *Bethlehem*. Jerusalem, 2000.

Pixner, Bargil, O.S.B. *Paths of the Messiah: Messianic Sites in Galilee and Jerusalem*. San Francisco: Ignatius Press, 2010.

Polo, Marco. *The Book of Ser Marco Polo, the Venetian, concerning the Kingdoms and Marvels of the East*. Translated by Colonel Henry Yule, C.B. 2 vols. London: John Murray, 1871.

Pontifical International Marian Academy. *The Mother of the Lord*. Staten Island, N.Y., 2007.

Posener, Alan. *Maria*. Reinbek, 1999.

Prause, Gerhard. *Herodes der Grosse*. Hamburg, 1977.

Pritz, Ray A. *Nazarene Jewish Christianity*. Jerusalem, 1992.

Ratzinger, Joseph, *Daughter Zion*. Translated by John M. McDermott, S.J. San Francisco: Ignatius Press, 1983.

————. with Hans Urs von Balthasar. *Mary: The Church at the Source*. San Francisco: Ignatius Press, 2005.

Riesner, Rainer. *Essener und Urgemeinde in Jerusalem*. Gießen, 1998.

Roberts, Courtney. *The Star of the Magi*. Franklin Lakes, N.J.: Career Press, 2007.

Roberts, Paul William. *Journey of the Magi*. London: Raincoast Book Distribution, 2007.

Rohner, Beat, O.S.B. *Maria und Joseph*. Einsiedeln, 1878.

Ronci, P. *Basilica di Santa Maria Nova/Santa Francesca Romana*. Rome [undated].

Rossini, Orietta. *Ara Pacis*. Rome, 2009.

Russo, Laura. *Santa Maria in Aracoeli*. Rome, 2007.

Sacchi, Maurilio. *Terra Santa sulle orme di Gesu*. Jerusalem, 1999.

Saller, Father Sylvester, O.F.M. *Discoveries at St. John's Ein Karim*. Jerusalem, 1982.

Santarelli, Giuseppe, O.F.M. Cap. *I Graffiti nella Santa Casa di Loreto*. Loreto, 2010.

———. *Loreto*. Bologna, 1988.

———. *La Santa Casa di Loreto*. Loreto, 1996.

Scheffczyk, Cardinal Leo. *Maria, Mutter und Gefährtin Christi*. Augsburg, 2003.

Schindler, Alfred. *Apokryphen zum Alten und Neuen Testament*. Zurich, 1988.

Schnabel, Eckhard. *Urchristliche Mission*. Wuppertal, 2002.

Schreiner, Klaus. *Maria*. Cologne, 2006.

Seewald, Peter. *Jesus Christus: Die Biographie*. Munich, 2009.

Seymour, P. A. H. *The Birth of Christ*. London: Virgin Books, 1999.

Shoemaker, Stephen J. *Ancient Traditions of the Virgin Mary's Dormition and Assumption*. Oxford: Oxford University Press, 2002.

Silas, Musholt P., ed. *Nazareth*. Jerusalem, 1995.

Stegemann, Hartmut. *Die Essener, Qumran, Johannes der Täufer und Jesus*. Freiburg, 1993.

Steinwede, Dietrich. *Nun soll es werden Frieden auf Erden*. Düsseldorf, 2010.

Stemberger, Günter. *Jewish Contemporaries of Jesus*. Minneapolis: Fortress Press, 1995.

Stern, Ephraim et al., eds. *The New Encyclopedia of Archaeological Excavations in the Holy Land*, vols. 1–5. Jerusalem and New York: Israel Exploration Society & Carta, 1993–2009.

Stock, Klemens, S.J. *Maria, die Mutter des Herrn im Neuen Testament*. Vienna [undated].

Stumpf, Gerhard, ed. *Maria, Mutter der Kirche*. Augsburg, 2004.

Tabor, James D. *The Jesus Dynasty*. New York: Simon & Schuster, 2006.

Tamanti, Giulia, with Claudia Tempesta. *Icona della "Madonna Advocata"*. Rome, 2009.

Thiede, Carsten Peter. *The Cosmopolitan World of Jesus*. London: SPCK, 2004.

———. *Ein Fisch für den römischen Kaiser*. Munich, 1998.

———. *Jesus: Der Glaube, die Fakten*. Augsburg, 2003.

———. *Jesus und Tiberius: Zwei Söhne Gottes*. Munich, 2004.

———. *Die Messias-Sucher*. Stuttgart, 2002.

———. *Der unbequeme Messias*. Basel, 2006.

———, with Matthew D'Ancona. *The Jesus Papyrus*. London: Weidenfeld and Nicolson, 1996.

Thierry, Elie Remy. *Das Mysterium des Hauses der Heiligen Jungfrau in Ephesus*. Izmir, 1990.

Trebilco, Paul. *The Early Christians in Ephesus from Paul to Ignatius*. Grand Rapids, Mich.: W. B. Eerdmans, 2004.

Vermes, Geza. *Die Geburt Jesu*. Darmstadt, 2007.

Wilkinson, John. *Jerusalem Pilgrims before the Crusades*. 2nd ed. Guildford: Aris & Philips, 2002.

Wise, Michael, with Martin Abegg and Edward Cook. *The Dead Sea Scrolls: A New Translation*. New York: HarperCollins, 1996, 2005.

Wrembek, Christoph, S.J. *Quirinius, die Steuer und der Stern*. Kevelaer, 2006.

Yavetz, Zvi. *Kaiser Augustus*. Reinbek, 2010.

Zaloscer, Hilde. *Porträts aus dem Wüstensand*. Vienna, 1961.

Ziebertz, Günter Johannes. *Du bist voll der Gnade*. Leutesdorf, 2000.

Ziegenaus, Anton, ed. *Totus Tuus*. Regensburg, 2004.

Photo Credits

Color photographs (insert) are numbered left to right, top to bottom:

Michael Hesemann: 2–3, 6–7, 14–15, 18–26, 34–35, 38–39, 43.

Yuliya Tkachova: 1, 5, 13, 16, 27–33

Archive of Michael Hesemann: 4, 7, 17, 36, 40–42

Michael Hesemann with kind permission of the Delegazione Pontificia per il Santuario della Santa Casa di Loreto: 8–12

L'Osservatore Romano: 37